The Authentic

C000179346

The Authentic Leader

Neil Thompson

First published 2016 by
PALGRAVE

Palgrave in the UK is an imprint of Macmillan Publishers Limited, registered in England, company number 785998, of 4 Crinan Street, London, N1 9XW.

Palgrave Macmillan in the US is a division of St Martin's Press LLC, 175 Fifth Avenue, New York, NY 10010.

Palgrave is a global imprint of the above companies and is represented throughout the world.

Palgrave® and Macmillan® are registered trademarks in the United States, the United Kingdom, Europe and other countries.

ISBN 978–1–137–47267–0

This book is printed on paper suitable for recycling and made from fully managed and sustained forest sources. Logging, pulping and manufacturing processes are expected to conform to the environmental regulations of the country of origin.

A catalogue record for this book is available from the British Library.

A catalog record for this book is available from the Library of Congress.

Library of Congress Cataloging-in-Publication Data
Thompson, Neil, 1955- author.
  The authentic leader / Neil Thompson.
    pages cm
  Includes bibliographical references and index.
  ISBN 978–1–137–47267–0 (pbk.)
  1. Leadership.   2. Existentialism.   I. Title.
  HM1261.T465 2015
  303.3'4—dc23   2015027818

Printed in China

Contents

CONTENTS

The author

Neil Thompson is an independent writer, educator and adviser. He has held full or honorary professorships at four UK universities and has over 38 years' experience in the people professions as a practitioner, manager, educator and consultant.

He has 34 books to his name (16 with Palgrave Macmillan). These include:

People Skills (Palgrave Macmillan, 4th edn, 2015)
People Management (Palgrave Macmillan, 2013)
The People Solutions Sourcebook (Palgrave Macmillan, 2nd edn, 2012)
Effective Communication (Palgrave Macmillan, 2nd edn, 2011)
Promoting Equality: Working with Diversity and Difference (Palgrave Macmillan, 3rd edn, 2011)
The Critically Reflective Practitioner (with Sue Thompson, Palgrave Macmillan, 2008)
Power and Empowerment (Russell House Publishing, 2007)

He has also been involved in developing a range of other learning resources, including e-books, training manuals, DVDs, e-learning modules (www.avenuelearningcentre.co.uk) and the innovative online learning community, the *Avenue Professional Development Programme*, geared towards promoting continuous professional development, based on supported self-directed learning principles (www.apdp.org.uk).

His training manuals include one on leadership (Gilbert and Thompson, 2010) and another on supervision (Thompson and Gilbert, 2011).

He has qualifications in: social work; management (MBA); training and development; mediation and dispute resolution; as well as a first-class honours degree in social sciences, a doctorate (PhD) and a higher doctorate (DLitt). His PhD and DLitt focused on existentialism. Neil is a Fellow of the Chartered Institute of Personnel and Development and the Royal Society of Arts, elected to the latter on the basis of his contribution to workplace learning. He was the founding editor of the *British Journal of Occupational Learning* and was also previously the editor of the US-based international journal, *Illness, Crisis & Loss*. He currently edits the free e-zines, **THE** *humansolutions* **BULLETIN** and *Learning IMPACT* (www.neilthompson.info/connect). His personal website and blog are at www.neilthompson.info.

List of figures

For Mark Drakeford

Preface

Dominant approaches to leadership have much to offer, but are far from adequate because they tend to pay too little attention to the complexities of what it means to be human. Existentialism is a philosophy that can cast light on many aspects of leadership, particularly in terms of the key value of authenticity, which involves taking ownership – individually and collectively – of our choices and our actions and making sure that those we lead do so too.

From an existentialist perspective, leadership is in large part about maximizing human potential, individually and collectively. This is why authenticity is presented as a key value underpinning effective leadership. Without authenticity, there will be a tendency for individuals and groups to deny responsibility for their actions; to fail to recognize what they have control over; and thus underestimate how much of a difference they are capable of making. A lack of authenticity is also likely to lead to a lack of trust, with little or no sense of shared endeavour, as there is insufficient sense of the power to bring about positive change. In this sense, a lack of authenticity is a form of (personal and collective) self-disempowerment.

By contrast, when authenticity is to the fore, there is a clear focus on what can realistically be achieved, what needs to happen to achieve it and what may get in the way of doing so. Authenticity involves avoiding the trap of self-deception in which we give ourselves the message that there is little or nothing we can do – a common feature of workplace cultures characterized by low morale (and thus a lack of leadership). Authenticity is an important basis for setting and pursuing goals, rooted in a strong sense of agency and empowerment. It is for this reason that this book argues that, without authenticity (on the part of leaders and their followers), leadership is doomed to failure or partial success at best. However, it is important to note that the understanding of authenticity put forward here (what might be called existential authenticity) is quite different from the oversimplified notion of authenticity that is used by a wide range of leadership writers and trainers.

Existentialism addresses complex issues, and the esoteric language favoured by so many existentialist writers can make the ideas seem impenetrable. An important feature of this book, therefore, is that it succeeds in 'getting past the jargon'. Existentialism is a complex philosophy, but it can be explained clearly, with helpful links to real-life practice situations made. Indeed, an important feature of existentialism is the linking of theory and practice, the appreciation of the important connections between philosophical ideas and 'lived experience' (*le vécu*, as Sartre called it). This is a key part of what makes existentialism an important theoretical foundation for leadership practice: it casts light on important ideas, but also relates these to the actual grassroots challenges that leaders face.

This ground-breaking book not only explains key existentialist concepts as they relate to leadership, but also maps out their implications for practice. It will therefore be of value to students, educators and practitioners in the leadership field. It has the potential to act as a foundation for developing more sophisticated theoretical understandings of leadership, while also providing important foundations for improving practice – nicely reflecting existentialism's commitment to a philosophy of lived experience.

The focus of this book is on the human dimensions of leadership, recognizing that attempts to bring people together in a sense of shared endeavour are likely to be far less effective if the complexities underpinning the nature of human existence are not appreciated or understood. This introduction to existentialist thought in relation to leadership will explain in more detail how existing approaches generally do not do justice to the complexities involved, and therefore tend to rely on an oversimplified conception of individual and group identity, social interactions, motivation and morale, cultural influences and organizational dynamics. Existentialism is presented as a much more sophisticated theory of human behaviour and interaction that gives us a much firmer platform of understanding on which to base our leadership practice.

The book focuses primarily on organizational or workplace leadership across the public, private and voluntary sectors, as that reflects my professional and intellectual background. However, the book will no doubt offer important insights to people interested in other forms of leadership: military, political, sporting, academic, community or whatever, as the broad themes and much of the specific detail will apply across all forms of leadership. It is also worth emphasizing that, while there are strong links between leadership and management, it is not only managers who can be called upon to provide leadership. Indeed, providing a contribution to leadership can be seen as an element of all professional roles (Thompson, 2015).

The overall aim of this book is to provide an introduction to an existentialist approach to leadership which can both enhance theoretical understandings and provide a firm foundation for practice. More specifically, it seeks to establish the importance of authenticity as a central value underpinning effective leadership; to introduce key existentialist concepts and demonstrate their relevance to leadership theory and practice; and to critique models of leadership that neglect existential concerns and oversimplify the nature of human existence (and of leadership).

Discussions of the relevant concepts are woven in with reference to key leadership themes so that you can see the connections between the new ideas being introduced and the established ideas about leadership that you are likely to be familiar with. If you are not familiar with philosophical approaches, you may find the ideas challenging at first, but a little perseverance should enable you to make sense of the important messages the book is putting across. Numerous examples are given throughout the book and these should help to enable you to develop a clear understanding of these complex issues.

Existentialism is a well-established philosophy which was highly fashionable at one time, a fact that brought considerable problems because of the tendency for very important complex ideas to be oversimplified and thus distorted. At the other extreme, existentialism has been largely forgotten by many thinkers. For example, many ideas that are presented as 'postmodernist' have their roots in existentialism (Howells, 1992a; Thompson, 2010). But, whether in fashion or out, existentialism is a school of thought that offers immense explanatory power in relation to life in general and, as I shall be arguing here, in relation to leadership in particular. Part of what this book will do is to critique existing models of leadership and how such conceptions are put into practice and show, from an existentialist perspective, why they are lacking in particular ways. It will also show how a good understanding of some key elements of existentialist thought can cast significant light on leadership, not only from a theoretical, intellectual point of view, but also in relation to actual practice. This book should therefore provide the foundations for a genuinely authentic – and effective – leadership.

Acknowledgements

I am grateful to a wide range of people who have contributed to my understanding of both leadership and existentialism and to the development of this particular text. They are too numerous to mention all by name, and so my acknowledgements will be limited to those who have played a particularly important role. First of all, I want to acknowledge the key role of the late Kathleen Ambrose, my former French teacher from more years ago than I care to remember. She was the person who first got me interested in existentialism. Recognizing that I was bored with what I saw as the superficiality of the French literature I was supposed to be studying as part of my A-level syllabus, Miss Ambrose pointed me in the direction of Sartre and Camus and encouraged me to read their work, as she was wise and insightful enough to recognize that the depth of their work was what I needed. That was where a lifetime of study of existentialist thought began.

The next major step in my philosophical education was under the guidance and support of Colin Richardson of Keele University, who was my supervisor for my PhD. His wisdom, enthusiasm, encouragement and critical insights, not to mention his great warmth and support, were invaluable elements in taking my learning forward. He has acted as a role model to me in so many different ways.

Charlotte Williams of RMIT in Australia, formerly of Keele University, was the supervisor for my higher doctorate which focused on existentialism and well-being. Much of what was covered in that project has been brought to bear in this current work. Charlotte's commitment to the project and recognition of its value were very helpful indeed and much appreciated.

Another important person in my existentialist journey has been Dr Jan Pascal of Bishop Grosseteste University. Jan's expertise in, and enthusiasm for, existentialist thought have been a very welcome part of my life for some years now and her friendship and colleagueship have been very important to me, both in general and specifically in relation to my work in developing existentialist thought.

When it comes to leadership, the list of people I have learned from in terms of how not to do it would be a very long one indeed. However, on a more positive note, I want to acknowledge the positive role played by Andy Whitgreave and Clive Curtis, formerly of the then Cheshire County Council, the late and much-missed Jo Campling, independent publishing adviser, Catherine Gray, formerly of the publishers, Bernard Moss of Staffordshire University, Ian Hume, formerly of the Open University, Gerald Pillay of Liverpool Hope University and Gerry Rice of the University of the West of England. I also want to acknowledge the role of the late Peter Gilbert, formerly of Staffordshire University, whose work on leadership and spirituality encapsulated beautifully the strong message of this book about the need to understand leadership as a profoundly *human* endeavour.

Catherine Gray also deserves mention and thanks for the important role she played in the commissioning of this book. She played a key part in shaping its focus, and her recognition of its value and potential was a key factor in making the project a reality in what is already a very crowded market and intellectual space, with so much being published on the subject of leadership. I am very grateful to her for spotting what was distinctive and valuable about this text that would help it to stand out from the wide range of publications on this important topic.

I am also grateful to Peter Hooper and his team at the publishers who picked up where Catherine left off in the editorial role. They succeeded in being very helpful, despite having such a hard act to follow.

Thanks are due to Clive Curtis, formerly of Cheshire County Council, Graham Thompson, formerly of Bangor University and Dr John Rae, formerly of Salford University, for their helpful comments on an earlier draft of this book.

And, of course, no acknowledgements page in any of my books would be complete without highlighting the support I have received in so many different ways from Dr Sue Thompson. What a fantastic leader she could have been, and has been in her own way.

Introduction

This book proposes what is in many ways a new approach to leadership. But why would we want a new approach when the bookshop shelves are already straining under the weight of so many books on leadership, with a bewildering array of ideas and approaches? It is my contention that certain assumptions commonly found in the leadership literature and the associated education and training activity, are, as I shall show, deeply flawed. I therefore believe that the time is right to look at leadership in new ways, ways that avoid the common pitfalls of (i) oversimplifying very complex issues; and (ii) failing to do justice to the specifically *human* aspects of the workplace in general and leadership in particular. A key feature of the book is that it is based on the recognition that attempts to bring people together in a sense of shared endeavour are likely to be far less effective if the complexities underpinning the nature of human existence are not appreciated or understood.

This introduction will explain in more detail how existing approaches to leadership generally do not do justice to the complexities involved and therefore tend to rely on an oversimplified conception of individual and group identity, social interactions, motivation and morale, cultural influences and organizational dynamics. Existentialism will be presented as a much more sophisticated theory of human behaviour and interaction that gives us a much firmer platform of understanding on which to base our leadership practice.

The main aims of the book are to:

(i) provide an introduction to an approach to leadership grounded in existentialist thought which can both enhance theoretical understandings and provide a firm foundation for practice;

(ii) establish the significance of authenticity as a vitally important value underpinning effective leadership;

(iii) introduce key existentialist concepts and demonstrate their relevance to leadership theory and practice. Discussion of these concepts will be woven in with reference to key leadership themes so that readers can see the links between the new ideas being introduced and the established ideas about leadership that they will be familiar with.

(iv) provide a critique of models of leadership that neglect existential concerns and oversimplify the nature of human existence in general and of leadership in particular.

To set the scene for the chapters that follow this introduction will now address the key questions of: What is leadership? What is authenticity? What is an authentic leader? and, significantly: Is this a book about theory?

WHAT IS LEADERSHIP?

The term 'leadership' is one that is used in a wide variety of settings, often with subtly different meanings. It has become such a well-used term that it is now almost a cliché. But, for the purposes of this book it is important to be clear what is meant by leadership. We need to recognize that it is a *unifying concept* – that is, something which connects different aspects of a phenomenon or set of circumstances. It is not a simple or direct concept that relates to a single issue in a straightforward way, but rather one that brings together different aspects. This echoes Wittgenstein's (2009) conception of games. He argued that there are no singly definitive aspects of a game, nothing that uniquely constitutes a game. For example, many games will be competitive, but not all. So, competitiveness is a common feature, but not an essential or defining one. Many games will involve a set of rules, but not all, and so this is again a common feature but not a defining one. Therefore, while there may not be a single defining feature, there are various elements that can combine to produce meaningful understandings.

One of the main features of leadership that is important to focus on is the idea that it should provide some guidance on where a group of people are going and how they are going to get there – and, in the process, creating a sense of shared endeavour as captured in the idea that 'we are in this together' (Thompson, 2012a). This element of leadership is often referred to as path-goal analysis (House, 1971). It involves establishing the goal to be achieved and the path or avenue for achieving that goal. As Gill (2011) puts it: 'Leadership is showing the way and helping or inducing others to pursue it. This entails envisioning a desirable future, promoting a clear purpose or mission, supportive values and intelligent strategies, and empowering and engaging all those concerned' (p. 9). Northouse (2010) echoes this point in arguing that: '*Leadership* is a process whereby an individual influences a group of individuals to achieve a common goal' (p. 3).

From my own point of view, an aspect of leadership that needs to be emphasized, but which sadly rarely is, is the key role of shaping culture. Organizations develop sets of habits, taken-for-granted assumptions and unwritten rules that become a very powerful influence on individuals and groups of staff within an organization (or, indeed, the organization as a whole), so a leader is someone who is able to shape that culture, at a collective level, in a positive direction. Individuals develop their own mindset or what Bourdieu called 'habitus' (Grenfell, 2012). This refers to a set of characteristic ways of thinking, behaving and feeling which have such a powerful influence on how we perceive the world and how we interact with it. 'Habitus' needs to be understood in the context of what Bourdieu called a 'field' — that is, a particular 'social arena' or area of activity and relationships. As Grenfell (2012) explains, habitus is the subjective element of practice. It refers to the ways of understanding and relating to the world developed in the course of individual life trajectories.

A field is the objective network of relations, the context in which each person's habitus operates. This fits well with the existentialist concept of the dialectic of subjectivity and objectivity which we will discuss in more detail later.

Cultures can be seen as a form of a collective version of a mindset or habitus shared by a group of people. It can relate to a relatively small group of people, perhaps just a handful as part of a team, or across a whole organisation employing thousands of people. But the defining feature of a culture is that it becomes taken for granted; it becomes 'the way we do things round here', and therefore emerges as a very powerful influence, because, for the most part, we are not aware of how it is shaping our actions, attitudes and assumptions. It is this lack of awareness, its insidious influence that makes it so powerful as a shaper of thoughts, feelings and actions.

One key aspect of this challenge of shaping a culture is the importance of creating a sense of security and confidence, so that employees feel safe, secure and valued. If they feel that the culture is one that is unsafe, where levels of trust are at a low ebb, then their motivation will be limited and their wariness at a high level. Their commitment similarly will be limited, and this can then make achieving the goals and clarifying the path towards achieving those goals all the harder. This is not simply a matter of physical security (for example, in terms of freedom from aggression or violence), nor of emotional security (for example, in terms of feeling free form bullying and harassment). Rather, it is more fundamental than this, a sense of security that comes from feeling part an enterprise where you feel that you belong, where you will be valued and validated, affirmed and appreciated — in short, where you will feel 'at home' and therefore able to commit yourself to achieving your best. The technical term for this is 'ontological security', and this will be an important concept that we will draw upon more fully later.

Leadership can be understood, then, as a means of clarifying where a group of people need to get to, what steps they need to take to get there and then creating and sustaining a culture that is conducive to motivating people to achieve those goals and follow that path. One common mistake over the years has been to assume that it is the leader's role to *decide* where the group needs to get to. In most settings, the overall 'mission' of the organization may well be predefined (to earn profit, to provide public services and so on), but within those broad parameters there is usually plenty of scope for identifying specific goals to achieve. If maximum commitment and engagement are to be achieved, then a culture that not only allows, but actually expects, people to be involved in setting goals and deciding on what steps need to be taken to meet them. Reverting to a command and control approach of telling people what to achieve and how to achieve it may be effective at times, but it certainly will not be conducive to achieving optimal results. Authentic leadership needs to be seen as far more than just another variation on the theme of the leader as the 'boss' telling their underlings what to do.

It is now generally recognized that leadership is something that is required of managers in organizations across all sectors, but what is often not so clearly recognized is that leadership is not simply something that applies to managers alone (Thompson, 2015). Arguably, everyone within an organization should have a degree of leadership, in the sense that they should be helping to create and sustain a positive culture and should be helping to move in the direction that they and their colleagues need to go in. This is what is often referred to as shared or distributive leadership (Carson *et al.*, 2007). The idea behind it is that you do not need to be a manager to play a key role in enabling people to move forward constructively by helping to shape and sustain a positive and empowering culture. Indeed, in some workplace settings, the people who are paid to be leaders may be having little impact on the culture, while other members of the staff group may prove very influential. Where such people are using their influence in a positive direction, they provide an example of this broader notion of distributed leadership. Where they are using their influence in a negative direction – for example, by contributing to low morale, negativity and cynicism, then they represent both a challenge to leadership and an indication that the current leadership arrangements are not working.

WHAT IS AUTHENTICITY?

In its everyday meaning authenticity refers to being genuine and sincere and therefore not being false or fake. In its technical sense and in the way it will be used in this book, there are elements of this definition that will apply, but it can also be quite different in some respects. The way the term authentic has been used in the leadership literature has tended to rely on a fixed notion of selfhood. Therefore, in relation to authentic leadership, there is a tendency for this to be defined in terms of leaders being urged to be 'true to yourself' , as if we all have a fixed personality or 'real' self that we can reach if we delve down deeply enough. For example, Irvine and Reger (2006) claim that: 'We have also learned that certain *authentic moments* occur when one is connected to one's "true" self, to one's "own truth"' (p. 5 – see also George, 2003; and Goffee and Jones, 2006).

However, this is highly problematic because of the premise that human beings have a fixed or 'essential' self. This is a highly dubious assumption to make (Ford and Harding, 2011; Golomb, 1995), as it rests on a simplistic understanding of selfhood or identity that does not do justice to the complexities involved. We will explore this issue in more depth in Part II of the book, but for now I want to point out that the way authenticity is being used in this book is diametrically opposed to the way it is used in the general literature about 'authentic leadership'. When used in the usual leadership sense, once again this relates back to a fixed or essential self, the notion that there is a 'real' me underneath the surface of how I relate to other people and engage in the social world more broadly.

As we shall see, the version of authenticity which underpins this book (what might be called *existential* authenticity) is not so simplistic as to assume that individuals have a fixed self. Rather, selfhood is seen as a much more complex process of how we interact with other people, with wider circumstances and our own hopes, wishes and fears.

It is also important to emphasize that authenticity as it is used here is not to be equated with the way it is often used in marketing these days, the sort of false romanticism about finding 'authentic' products and services (see Boyle, 2004, for a critique of this). The significance of authenticity is far greater than this sort of superficial consumerism would have us believe.

In existentialist terms, it is important to distinguish between authenticity and bad faith. Authenticity is the opposite of bad faith. Sartre used the term 'bad faith' to refer to the tendency for individuals to, in effect, lie to themselves, to deny (and seek to avoid) their own freedom and their own ability to choose. The existentialist idea of authenticity encompasses the need to acknowledge that, while we are surrounded by all sorts of constraints and limitations, we are none the less free to make choices. Sartre (1995) uses the example of a prisoner in a cell who is presented with a meal and, although the prisoner is clearly within highly straitened circumstances, that person still has the ability and indeed the necessity to choose whether to accept the meal, to eat it, to throw it or whatever. So, the point being made here is that, however restricted our circumstances may be, the need to choose remains. This means that we cannot choose not to choose. For example, if we see a job advertised and we are considering applying for it and we know when the closing date is, if we do not apply before that closing date (because we may say to ourselves that we have not been able to decide), in effect we *have* decided. That is, knowing when the closing date was and knowingly not putting in an application before then means that we chose not to apply. So this sense of radical freedom, this sense that, at root, we cannot avoid choice means that we must take responsibility for our actions and their consequences. We must be aware that selfhood, for example, is a process largely governed by the choices that we make.

This is where bad faith comes in, because to deny that we have those choices, to create a deterministic picture of ourselves, is to act in inauthentic ways. It means that we are not taking ownership of our actions, the choices that underpin them and the direction that we are therefore taking in making those choices. It is as if we are disowning the control we have over the choices we make and thereby disempowering ourselves in the process, denying ourselves the opportunity to make a positive difference.

An example of bad faith would be someone who claims that they cannot undertake a particular activity because it is not 'in their nature' or 'they are not that sort of person', whereas in reality, this is an oversimplification of complex issues about how individuals and indeed groups react to the options that they are faced with on a day-to-day basis.

Two important terms in the (existentially) authentic leadership vocabulary are agency and ownership. Agency refers to the recognition that we can act, we can be 'agents', that we are not just passive victims of circumstance. Whatever adversity life may throw at us, we are still in a position where we can, and indeed have to, make choices about how we respond to that situation. This brings in the idea of ownership — that is, the recognition that we have to take responsibility for our actions, for the choices we make, and therefore their consequences. These two terms, agency and ownership, are fundamental to the idea of empowerment (Thompson, 2007a). Part of the existentialist conception of authentic leadership is the necessity to recognize empowerment as a fundamental factor. Empowerment is about helping people gain greater control over their lives (and this clashes significantly with the idea of bad faith, which involves denying ownership of our actions). As I have already noted, if people indulge in bad faith, they are in a sense disempowering themselves; they are denying themselves control (that is, agency and ownership) of their actions.

What is also important in this regard is the significance of self-awareness, and Sartre (2003) writes of the importance of understanding this in terms of two key concepts, facticity and transcendence. Facticity relates to the limitations placed upon us, those things that we cannot change, that we have no control over. For example, if I am cut I will bleed, I cannot choose not to bleed. So, facticity refers to many aspects of the context we as human beings find ourselves in, in terms of having certain doors closed off to us. However, transcendence is another key term because what this refers to is our capabilities, our ability to go beyond the limitations of facticity. So, while there may be aspects of a situation we cannot control, there will none the less be many aspects we can act upon, and we will have the opportunity to influence those circumstances and, indeed, to learn from them. This is what transcendence is about. To transcend literally means to go beyond, so we are in a position where we are limited by certain circumstances (facticity), but we are able to react as we see fit to those circumstances (transcendence).

This book is rooted in existentialist philosophy. I have been studying existentialism for over 40 years now, and from the very beginning to this present moment I have found it a fascinating subject and a very rich source of insight and understanding. It is not intended as some sort of explanatory panacea, with all the answers, but it certainly does have the potential to understand many aspects of leadership and the workplace in which it operates.

One of the key aspects of existentialism is that it is holistic. That is, it tries to paint a picture of human beings in a way that does justice to the complexities and the wide range of aspects involved in human existence. It looks at 'the big picture', rather than settling for just one aspect in isolation (for example, in the way a number of texts have a strong psychological focus and pay relatively little attention to the wider social context). This is contrary to the positivistic approach to human understanding which tries to pin people down in terms of laws of science. As Ladkin (2010) explains:

The great majority of Western-based leadership theories are derived from research methods based in positivistic ways of knowing. In particular, the assumption that the approach used in the physical sciences can apply to examining leadership is witnessed by the large number of studies aimed at identifying particular leadership characteristics, traits or competencies. In this way, leadership is 'broken down' into its component parts and then, taking this method to its logical conclusion, those traits, characteristics or competencies are measured using a variety of psychometric or ideographic indicators. (p. 4)

The positivistic way can be seen as beginning with some notion of the truth and trying to fit our world into it. This can be seen as 'squaring the circle', as it were. Existentialism, by contrast, begins with the world and tries to find truths about it (following in the tradition of Nietzsche – see Kaufmann, 2013).

Another key part of this is the recognition that human experience is *dynamic* – that is, it is constantly changing (Foley, 2013). Sartre in particular emphasized the dialectical nature of human experience, recognizing that there is constant change as the basis of human experience, and that much of this comes from the interaction of conflicting forces. So, it is not simply a matter that things are constantly changing as if they are following some sort of predetermined path, but, rather, recognizing what happens in terms of those changes will owe much to the significance of how various conflicting forces interact and constantly produce new realities.

A commonly used term in the existentialist vocabulary is 'flux', and this refers directly to this tendency for things to change constantly, whether at a rapid or slow pace. This is parallel with the Buddhist notion of 'samsara' which refers to: 'incessant motion' (Foley, 2013, p. 15). Everything in the universe is fluid, dynamic, constantly changing.

To do justice to the complexities of the workplace in particular and human existence in general we therefore need to have this holistic and dynamic approach to leadership and associated issues.

Existentialism offers just such a set of concepts. It is attuned to human complexity, particularly those aspects of the workplace that are distinctively human and not amenable to technical or mechanistic approaches. As Allcorn (2005) acknowledges, the workplace is full of the complexity of humanity. If we are dealing with people, then by definition we are dealing with complexity.

What this means is that existentialism offers us a framework of understanding which goes beyond the simplistic and superficial rigid notions associated with positivistic approaches to science. People are far too complex to be fitted into a set of scientific laws that hope to be able to explain human experience in its totality.

Existentialism is prone to a number of common misunderstandings, one of which is the idea that it presents life as meaningless. It is therefore often (wrongly) assumed that existentialism is a negative philosophy of despair or, to use the technical term, nihilism. The reality is more complex. Existentialism is based on the idea that there is no ultimate or absolute meaning to life, no predefined 'Truth' about life or pre-established purpose. However, this does not mean that life is meaningless. On the contrary, existentialism emphasizes that human existence is necessarily a meaningful experience because we are constantly creating meaning (individually and collectively). We develop frameworks of meaning that give shape to our lives and our relationships.

The important point is that these meanings evolve as we act and interact with one another. To use the technical term, they are 'emergent', rather than predefined. Meanings, then, are not fixed; they are in a constant process of negotiation and renegotiation. Authenticity involves recognizing this and not relying on fixed ideas that unnecessarily limit us.

Existentialism focuses on what it means to be human and a central part of that is the recognition that, although we are constantly making choices, we have a tendency to try to explain our actions in ways that remove ownership for them from us – in other words, there is a tendency to act in bad faith. Existential authenticity is fundamentally about avoiding bad faith and recognizing the implications of the complexities of being human.

WHAT IS AN AUTHENTIC LEADER?

If we try and combine the issues of leadership, authenticity and existentialism, we should be able to produce a picture of what I am proposing as an authentic leader. First of all, it is important to recognize that this is not the essentialist popularized idea of an authentic leader that I mentioned and criticized earlier. Authentic leadership in the sense being used in this book is a matter of taking ownership of our own actions and encouraging others to take ownership of theirs (and supporting them in doing so). A key part of this is shaping a culture to create the foundations of empowerment, so that everybody involved is committed to moving forward, positively, taking ownership for the collective endeavour and not seeking refuge in bad faith. Indeed, a key part of leadership is being able to encourage the development of other leaders (Follett, 1924) and this is entirely consistent with existentialism.

In the sense I am using it here, authentic leadership encompasses traditional notions of honesty and integrity, but goes beyond these. A good example of this would be in the work of Tillich, an existentialist writer who wrote about the courage to be and this related in a sense to the courage not to be, that is, to face up to the fact that we are finite mortals, that we must all face death sooner or later (Tillich, 2000). His idea was that it is in facing up to the reality of our finite existence that we get the courage to engage with the challenges that we face. We can apply this logic as well to leadership, so that the courage to lead can be seen to encompass the courage to fail – that is, the willingness to risk failure. This means moving away from the common problem of being risk averse, of being unwilling to address the risk involved in all aspects of human existence.

In particular, what I will be emphasizing as a key element of authentic leadership is the importance of trust, respect and credibility. Without trust there is going to be very little movement in a positive direction. Without respect leaders will be in a very weak position when it comes to influencing culture in a positive direction, and, without credibility, they will struggle to be able to create the sense of security that is an important foundation of a positive working environment. The importance of trust, respect and credibility is therefore a point to which we will be returning from time to time.

We can understand trust, respect and credibility as important aspects of authenticity, in the sense that: (i) without them we will struggle to influence others in helping them to avoid bad faith; and (ii) without authenticity on our part, we will struggle to earn trust, respect and credibility. There is therefore an important two-way relationship between trust, respect and credibility on the one hand and authenticity on the other.

This links in to another important theme that will feature in the book, namely the importance of leaders being committed to getting the *best* out of their followers and not the *most*. What I mean by this is that, if leaders simply pile on the pressure to their staff, give them as much work as they possibly can, then they risk alienating the people they are trying to lead. But, if they focus on trying to get the *best* out of their followers – that is, if they help them to learn, help them to feel valued and supported and to achieve optimal job satisfaction, then the consequences are likely to be much more positive all round.

At times I will talk about authentic leadership being a matter of influencing the culture in a positive direction, and by this I mean in a way that benefits everyone involved, leaders, followers and their organization and all its stakeholders. Just as assertiveness entails seeking win–win outcomes (that is, positive results for all involved), authentic leadership involves developing mutually beneficial partnerships.

IS THIS A BOOK ABOUT THEORY?

Yes and no is the short answer. Because the ideas I am putting forward are largely rooted in existentialist philosophy, then clearly there are strong theoretical elements involved. I make no apology for that, as I am a firm believer, after over 38 years of working with people and their problems, that the complexity of the issues and challenges we face is such that we need a fairly well-developed and sophisticated understanding of what we are dealing with. That is where theory in general, and existentialism in particular, come into their own, as they offer a sound foundation for a helpful level of understanding to equip us to wrestle with the intellectual, practical and moral challenges involved.

But this is not a theoretical book in the sense of text that begins and ends with theoretical analysis and covers nothing else. The focus here, as is the case with my work in general, is on the integration of theory and practice – that is, not simply exploring theoretical ideas for their own sake, but, rather, examining how theoretical ideas can be of help in making sense of the often confusing, multifaceted, constantly changing world of people.

I will talk more about these issues in Chapter 7, but for now I wanted to make it crystal clear that this is not purely a book about theory. It is a book about how theoretical ideas, when used appropriately, have a great deal to offer in terms of casting important light on significant aspects of practice in ways that make us better equipped to rise to the challenges involved.

STRUCTURE AND CONTENT

The book is divided into three parts, with each part containing three chapters. The first part focuses on leadership in context. Chapter 1 concentrates on problems with leadership theory, while Chapter 2 complements this by focusing on problems associated with leadership practice. In the third and final chapter in Part I there is an emphasis on the social context in which leadership takes place, emphasizing the need to go beyond the common problem of looking at leaders in isolation, as if they are individuals without any wider social context to take into consideration.

Part II focuses on how existentialist thought can help to inform authentic leadership. Chapter 4 has as its title 'Authenticity and its importance', and looks in more detail at the specifically existentialist conception of authenticity, as opposed to the populist one currently widely used. Chapter 5 examines the topic of ontology, the study of being, and draws on a number of existentialist concepts to enable us to broaden and deepen our understanding of leadership. Chapter 6 concentrates on the role of meaning, and looks at how perception is significant in shaping the way we understand our work and the way we respond to it. As we have noted, one common misunderstanding of existentialism is that it is a philosophy that proclaims life to be without meaning. As we shall see in more detail in Chapter 6, this is actually very far from the truth. The concept of meaning is central to existentialist thought.

Part III focuses on how authentic leadership can take shape in practice. Chapter 7 looks at key aspects of what it means to be an authentic leader in real-life practice situations. Chapter 8 focuses on a set of scenarios involving the potential for authentic leadership and examines how existentialist ideas can be useful in each of these particular cases. Chapter 9 explores eight principles drawn from existentialist thought and maps out how each of these principles can have a bearing on authentic leadership in practice.

With the exception of Chapter 8, each chapter contains a small number of 'Practice focus' illustrations, short cameos intended to exemplify and bring to life some of the issues under consideration. They are not intended to be case studies in the educational sense, although, with suitable development, tutors or trainers could easily use them as the basis of case studies for teaching or training purposes.

Each chapter also contains a small number of 'Voice of experience' quotes. Again these are intended to bring some of the ideas to life by way of illustration. Both the Practice focus illustrations and the Voice of experience quotes are based on my experience over an extensive period. They relate to either specific instances I have come across or are typical of comments or examples I have encountered many times. I am aware that, like diagrams, many people find these illustrative 'add-ons' helpful, but not everybody does. So, if you are one of the people who does not find them helpful, simply read on and pass them by, as they are not essential to understanding the points that are being put across.

It is also important to note that this is a book that addresses a complex reality using a complex philosophy. It will therefore be inevitable that, at times, you may struggle to grasp some of the concepts being used. However, to facilitate your understanding, there is a short glossary at the end of the book which provides a reminder for some of the key concepts. So, if at any point in working your way through the book you come across a concept that was mentioned earlier in the book, but you have forgotten precisely what it means, rather than having to trace it back through what you have read, you can simply refer to the glossary at the end.

Finally, I feel it is important to reiterate that, in keeping with my earlier book, *People Management* (Thompson, 2013a), the focus of this book is on the *human* dimensions of leadership. An approach to leadership that fails to address the complexities and subtleties of what it means to be human beings trying to work effectively in tandem with other human beings can hardly justify being referred to as 'authentic'. It is also highly unlikely to be effective, or at least nowhere near as effective as an approach that recognizes, and fully appreciates, the significance of the workplace as a distinctively *human* social space. As Allcorn (2005) puts it: 'The workplace is saturated with our humanity' (p. 21).

Leadership in context

CHAPTERS

INTRODUCTION TO PART I

Part I is intended to highlight problems with existing approaches to leadership and thereby lay the foundations for making the case for a new, existentially based approach premised on authenticity. It contains three chapters. Chapter 1, 'Problems with leadership theory', argues that, despite the fact that so much has been written about leadership, there is much we still do not understand about it and much of the current theoretical base has significant flaws. This is not to say that current thinking needs to be abandoned, but I do make the case for rethinking significant aspects of it. I am not arguing that existentialist thought is in itself flawless as an explanatory framework, but by laying it out explicitly in this book (especially in Part II), I am both identifying its strong points and giving others the opportunity to identify any weak points so that it can be developed and improved over time.

A major part of the problem is that the dominant approach has been a 'positivistic one' – that is, one that adopts a largely natural science approach to human affairs, looking for fairly objective 'laws' of human behaviour and interaction. The approach taken here, by contrast, is based on the premise that a more humanistic approach rooted in existentialist philosophy has far more capacity to help us understand human experience. This is because positivism adopts a fairly rationalistic and mechanistic approach to human existence that does not actually fit with what life is really like. Existentialism, by contrast, recognizes that our lives are governed as much by emotion as by reason and that the depth, diversity and richness of human experience cannot be adequately captured by the confines of the 'scientific method'.

Chapter 2, 'Problems with leadership practice', complements Chapter 1 by exploring various aspects of how leadership is commonly put into practice and argues that it is not just the theory base that needs rethinking. While the theoretical flaws outlined in Chapter 1 will have a knock-on effect in terms of leadership practice, there are also concerns about how leadership is currently practised that do not relate directly to the theory base. A consideration of these makes up the main content of this chapter. These concerns include:

- *Vision* Although there is much talk about vision in a leadership context, my experience leads me to believe that such vision is often absent and, when present, is often superficial and oversimplified.
- *Communicating the vision* Even where there is a helpful and positive vision, the ability to communicate it effectively is often not clearly in evidence.
- *Tokenism* I have come across many instances of leaders using the language of leadership, but largely functioning within a traditional command and control framework, generally oblivious to the contradiction between what they are saying and what they are doing.
- *Fighting workplace cultures* Effective leaders need the skills and confidence to shape culture in a positive direction, but fighting a culture is doomed to failure, as cultures are more powerful than individuals.

Existentialism has something to say about each of these, and the concept of authenticity is particularly applicable. This chapter will therefore lay the foundations for exploring, in Part III, how practice capabilities can be greatly enhanced by the insights offered by existentialist thought.

Chapter 3 is entitled 'Leadership in social context'. Like so many other aspects of human experience, dominant approaches to leadership can be criticized for being 'atomistic', as mentioned in the Introduction – that is, they focus very narrowly on the individual and pay little or no attention to wider social factors, despite the fact that these are likely to be major influences on how individuals (and groups) experience their reality. This chapter therefore seeks to establish the need to understand leadership in its social context by taking account of how sociological considerations cast further light on these important issues. The aim is not to replace psychological considerations with sociological ones, but rather to show that a holistic approach requires us to consider both individual and wider factors – and, indeed, the complex interactions between the two.

Early existentialist writings were criticized for lacking a sociological dimension to their work and for therefore being too individualistic. They did not take enough account of social and political constraints on choices and actions or the ways in which choices made could be influenced by social and political considerations. However, later texts – especially in the work of Sartre – explicitly addressed wider sociopolitical concerns, and these too are very relevant to authentic leadership.

Issues to be explored include:

- *Group development, seriality and the group-in-fusion* How groups form and how they can go awry;
- *The social construction of meaning (and the role of organizational cultures as frameworks of meaning)* How individual meanings reflect, and are influenced (but not determined) by, wider sociopolitical factors;
- *Power, authority and oppression* How authenticity relates to these important social and organizational factors;
- *Social structures and processes* How individual and group choices reflect, and are reflected in, these powerful contextual factors; and
- *The inevitability of conflict as a feature of human interaction* An exploration of how authenticity involves recognizing, and responding positively to, workplace conflicts.

The overall focus of Part I is laying a foundation of understanding of what, from my perspective, needs to change in relation to leadership in terms of certain aspects of its theory base, some elements of common practice and the dominant tendency to individualize leadership and thereby fail to develop a holistic understanding that incorporates key features of the wider social context. This sets the scene for Part II where we will look in more detail at alternative theoretical approaches informed by existentialist understandings of authenticity and related concepts. Part II will then be counterbalanced by a focus on what the ideas developed in Part II mean in terms of actual leadership practice.

Part I is by no means comprehensive or exhaustive in its coverage, but it should provide a sufficiently robust platform of understanding on which to build a fuller appreciation of the complex range of issues involved. In particular, I hope that it will begin to stimulate an interest in how existential authenticity, when properly differentiated from the populist essentialist understandings of authenticity, can provide a helpful basis for shaping leadership theory and practice.

chapter 1   Problems with leadership theory

INTRODUCTION

In this chapter I outline a number of what I see as fundamental flaws in the type of theoretical thinking that is generally applied to leadership. I will in each case relate those flaws to how an approach to authentic leadership premised on existentialism offers a sounder foundation for understanding and future practice. The reason for doing this is to counter any complacency about the extent of our understanding of leadership. Although it is a topic that has spawned a huge number of publications, training programmes and media coverage, there remains much that we do not understand about it, and, as this chapter will illustrate, there are certain widely used aspects of leadership theory that are problematic in their ability to capture the human complexities associated with it.

PROBLEMS IN THEORY

Perhaps one of the most significant problems in leadership theory is the reliance for the most part on positivistic and naturalistic approaches – that is, on approaches that wish to define and identify fundamental laws of human behaviour, as if what happens in a social science context can be understood as being directly parallel to what happens in the natural sciences. Positivism is based on the idea that only science can offer truth (Armstrong, 2011). It is premised on the view that human existence can be understood through natural science methods – that is, by the discovery of underlying 'laws' that govern human behaviour, thought and feeling.

This is inconsistent with existentialism, which argues the case for theoretical approaches which are holistic and humanistic – that is, approaches that do not artificially break things down into component parts, but seek to understand the complex whole of what it means to be human. It involves recognizing that it does violence to the nature of being human to try and find mechanistic ways of understanding what happens in people's lives, whether that is in the workplace or beyond. This tendency to reduce complex multi-level phenomena to a single level of 'scientific laws' is often referred to as 'reductionism'. As Sibeon (2004) points out, this is not an adequate way of addressing the complexities of social life. Ladkin (2010) reinforces this point in stating that:

> In 1935 [Husserl] gave a key lecture, 'Philosophy in the Crisis of European Humanity', in Vienna which argued that the tools of modern science are not equipped to address questions of meaning and significance central to human lives. For instance, positivist science might be able to establish certainty about the chemical components of bread but it could not lead us to any conclusion about the ethics of wealth and what we might do about the fact that some human beings have more than their needs for bread, while others starve. (pp. 16–17)

Hames (2007) is similarly critical of positivistic approaches to leadership:

> Reductionism was the powerful driving force behind much of the twentieth-century's scientific research, the assumption being that if we could only understand the parts we would be sure to comprehend the whole. Unfortunately we didn't allow for the dynamic nature of complex systems: knowing the details, even intimately, doesn't guarantee the whole system will function as you would like or expect. (p. 90)

Leadership is about *people* – recognizing their strengths and areas for development; helping them achieve their best and addressing any problems that may be getting in the way of their doing so. People, from an existentialist point of view, need to be understood not in static terms, but, rather, as constantly 'in process' – becoming rather than simply being. There is therefore a need to focus on what is often referred to as 'emergence' – that is, the idea that we are not fixed entities that stay stable. Sprintzen (2009) explains:

> Nothing is fixed, nothing is permanent, nothing lasts in spite of our continual need to attach ourselves to that which is infinite, everlasting, and eternal. Energy is ceaselessly at work, only stopping for brief periods when confronted by equal and opposite energy in a state of temporary equilibrium; everything undergoes continual transformations in complex transactions with its ever-changing environs. (p. 191)

This relates closely to the existentialist concept of 'flux', which involves the recognition that, as human beings, we are constantly changing and evolving within wider circumstances that are also constantly changing and evolving. Kierkegaard captured this somewhat poetically when he used the phrase 'the cosmic dance of life' (Henry, 1997). Flux does not mean that there is no stability, just that any stability is temporary and the result of efforts to maintain it. What we perceive as the stable nature of human existence is either:

(i)   changing at a slow pace so that it appears not to be changing (for example, our bodies appear to be stable, but are none the less changing all the time – but just at a rate that is not immediately perceptible to us); or

(iii) we are reconstructing something on a daily basis (for example, personality characteristics that we 'renew' each time we behave in accordance with them). The technical term for this is 'autopoiesis', a concept borrowed from biology to refer to the way in which biological organisms can renew themselves (for example, the way our skin regenerates as old cells die off and new ones form). This process of stability through renewal (that is, stability as a by-product of – autopoietic – renewal and change, rather than as the opposite of change) is a concept that we will return to in Part II when we explore the significance of organizational cultures and their implications for leadership.

I am not arguing that science has no role to play. My concern is the over-extension of scientific theory from the natural world, with its laws and regularities, to the world of human experience, which has certain

7

regularities, but also much more that does not fit into a narrow perspective based on laws. The problem, then, is not science, but, rather, 'scientism' – the tendency to fit the round phenomenon of human experience into the square peg of scientific reductionism.

We will continue to place artificial and unnecessary barriers in the way of the development of our understanding of leadership if we do not take on board the fact that it is fundamentally a *human* phenomenon, and not just a set of technical skills or characteristics. To capture the full meaning of leadership involves capturing the full meaning of human behaviour in a social context. It really is as complex as that. It is therefore highly unlikely that we will ever develop a comprehensive understanding of what is involved in leadership. However, we can take our understanding forward in significant ways if we replace the narrow positivism that has dominated leadership thinking with a more holistic approach that is more fully attuned to the specifically human elements – and, by human, I mean influenced as much by emotions as by reason (if not more so); biological and spiritual beings; each of us unique but in a social context; free to make our own choices, but within a context of constraints and powerful influencing forces; constantly changing ('becoming' rather than simply 'being'), but with a strong sense of continuity and biography (selfhood); with very many strengths, but also immense vulnerabilities and fragilities; and capable of doing considerable good, but also catastrophic harm.

I will now outline some common flaws in leadership theory, as I see them, and comment on each of these in turn from the perspective of what existentialist thought has to offer as an alternative.

Essentialism

I begin with what is probably the most significant weakness, the tendency to oversimplify by ascribing essential features to leaders, reducing the complex multi-level phenomenon of leadership to a set of characteristics, as in trait theory (Gilbert, 2005). This type of theory fails to capture the dynamic nature of human existence. As I have often had to point out to students and other learners, working with people can never be likened to painting by numbers; it is a much more subtle and involved process. Trait theory involves identifying a number of characteristics that can be associated with successful leadership and, while I would not deny that there are some common characteristics among groups of leaders, it can be seen that the whole approach is misguided, in the sense that it fails to do justice to the complexities involved in one human being trying to influence a number of other human beings in a particular direction. While clearly some forms of behaviour or characteristics can be seen as positive foundations of leadership, this sort of endeavour (trying to pin all our hopes on identifying and nurturing such characteristics) is to adopt a woefully simplistic view of what is involved.

The main drawback of essentialism is that it denies or minimizes the potential for change and therefore acts as an obstacle to progress. If, as essentialism implies, we have a 'true' self, an immutable set of personality characteristics that represent who we 'really' are, then the scope for personal growth, development and transformation is severely limited. This is doubly significant for leaders, as it means that:

(i) Leaders are limited in terms of their own potential for growth and learning. Essentialism places artificial limits on what individuals can achieve in terms of growth and change.

(ii) There are also significant limitations placed on what employees can achieve too. For example, an employee who is deemed to have a 'shy' nature will be deemed to be incapable of carrying out tasks that involve some degree of extraversion, such as public speaking, because they are seen as 'not that sort of person'. In reality, however, shyness can be understood as a set of behaviours and emotional responses that have been learned and which can be unlearned – for example, through intensive skills training.

Essentialism can therefore be seen to write people off, to disempower them and/or to contribute to their own self-disempowerment if essentialist ideas are internalized. That is, people can convince themselves that they are not capable of certain things. This can manifest itself as such self-defeating comments as: 'I'm no good at that; I'm not that sort of person' or 'It's not my nature' or 'That's not the way I was brought up'. Each of these reflects a set of unnecessary boundaries to progress.

Essentialism can also apply at a group or organizational level. That is, whole cultures can be characterized by self-defeating views about what can or cannot be achieved together. This can be very significant in relation to morale, an important factor that will feature a great deal in our later discussions.

PRACTICE FOCUS 1.1

Peter was a very experienced worker whose work was of a satisfactory nature, but he had not shown any sign of improvement, growth or development over the years. However, when Sylvia took over as his manager she would not accept that he was incapable of improving. To begin with Peter came up with various excuses as to why he was not able to perform to a higher standard, all of them based on the idea that he was who he was and that was the end of the story. It took some time for Sylvia to get past this, but she was eventually able to show him changes he could make to his practice that produced better results (for the organization and its stakeholders) and higher levels of job satisfaction for him. She was gradually able to break down his essentialist defences and help him become more confident and positive about what he could achieve. Not only was he then able to go from strength to strength, but it also gave a positive message to the other staff about Sylvia's competence as a leader and about the developments they could make.

Heroism

This involves romanticizing leadership and distracting attention from the important role of taking ownership of our actions. So often the leadership literature identifies key figures, such as Gandhi, Mother Teresa and often military personnel, who have had a highly significant impact on large numbers of other people. In some respects this makes them very good examples of leadership and what it can achieve. But, by focusing specifically on these unusual, highly charismatic, exceptional people, we get a distorted picture of what leadership is all about. This approach makes it appear as though leadership is something special and out of reach of most people in the workplace. This is both unfair and unhelpful, as it fails to acknowledge what are often excellent leadership practices in many of our workplaces. In some respects the heroic approach to leadership follows on from the trait approach, in so far as it concentrates on certain characteristics and, in doing so, it solidifies what is actually a very fluid process and phenomenon.

Gill (2011) is also critical of the 'heroism' approach to leadership:

> The 'heroic' model of solo leadership that attributes greatness, charisma and near-infallibility to a single leader is flawed … Totalitarian regimes 'led' by a single leader – whether in countries or companies – are testimony to this view. What CEOs who are effective leaders themselves do is to create a 'leadership culture' that is characterized by collective or distributed leadership and therefore a multitude of leaders throughout the organization. (p. 28)

The point about the role of leaders creating a leadership culture is a highly important one, and this topic will feature in our discussions in Part II. Leadership is not about being a shining star, a beacon of individual excellence, but rather someone who has the skills and aptitude to help others to become stars or at least to achieve their best. In effect, heroism paints a very misleading picture of what leadership is intended to achieve. It implies that leadership is exceptional, something out of the ordinary, and something carried out by people who are out of the ordinary. This creates an unnecessary (and unhelpful) distance between leaders and followers and therefore undermines any sense of shared endeavour or collective spirit – the exact opposite of what leadership should be achieving.

Because heroism implies that leadership is something that applies mainly to exceptional circumstances, it has little or nothing to say about ordinary working life and is therefore of little value in taking our understanding forward. It can also be counterproductive in at least four main ways:

(i)   It can demotivate leaders by lowering their confidence. If the message being given out is that to be a leader you need to compete with the likes of Winston Churchill and Florence Nightingale, then the

11

result can be that people who are capable of being excellent leaders may lose any aspiration to be involved in leadership activities because they believe the stakes to be too high. Even if it does not prevent such individuals from taking steps towards leadership positions, it may give them an unnecessarily low sense of what they can humbly achieve in comparison with such exalted figures (despite the fact that they may be capable of achieving excellent results within their own field and sphere of influence).

(ii) It can misdirect motivation. This relates to situations which are, in a sense, the polar opposite of (i) above. Instead of people being demotivated by what they see as an unattainable level of heroic leadership, they find themselves drawn to the appeal of being a hero, of achieving some sort of cult status. Hames (2007) exemplifies how this may appeal to some people:

> In conventional terms a leader is someone possessing preeminent status, power or charisma. It is the leader who forges the vision and issues clear directives, accepting as part of their leadership role, responsibility for the overall performance of the enterprise. The most frequently used metaphors for this 'white knight' style of leadership range from the general leading his troops into battle to the orchestral conductor, the situational leader – even the servant-leader concept of Robert Greenleaf, on which so much contemporary leadership theory is based. (pp. 240–1)

The net result, however, is that the focus of attention is then on the individual and their personal ambitions. This puts the needs of the individual leader at the forefront, thereby placing the needs of the employees and the organization in a secondary role. But, more than this, it becomes self-defeating. This is because a leader who settles for personal achievement and does not encourage a collective approach, is far less likely to be a successful leader and therefore far less likely to achieve the kudos and personal advancement they achieve. The irony, then, is that success in leadership comes from not putting your own needs first. A heroic approach to leadership can discourage some people from doing this in a misguided attempt to achieve hero status.

(iii) It can give unrealistic expectations of what can be achieved and thereby set people up to fail. For example, Grint (2005) warns of the dangers of putting leaders on pedestals from which they may fall. He argues that talking of saints and sinners, saviour and scapegoat:

> hoists leaders onto pedestals that cannot support them and then ensures those same leaders are hoist by their own petard. What this also reveals is the consequence of attributing omnipotence to leaders – we, the followers, are rendered irresponsible by our own action, for when the gods of leadership fail their impossible task – as fail they must eventually – we followers have a scapegoat to take all the blame for what is, in reality, our own failure to accept responsibility. (pp. 43–4)

Pedestals do not encourage a sense of shared endeavour. They create a sense that total responsibility lies with the leader, and this discourages followers from taking ownership of their part in the situation. Again this goes against the spirit of leadership as a process of encouraging shared responsibility. I have long had reservations about the term 'followers', as it implies a passive role (the leader is the active party and the followers are the ones who take his or her lead), and that is not compatible with my view of leadership or indeed of what existentialism teaches us about leadership. Ashman and Lawler (2008) also express concern about an uncritical use of the notion of followers:

> Frequently there is a strong temptation to objectify other people in the workplace in the same way that a piece of equipment is objectified – they become something 'for me to use to meet my own ends' and such a perception is often found in the treatment of 'followers' by leaders. Across all existentialist philosophy, however, there is a recognition that despite every individual's desire to objectify other human beings, they cannot, because the *Other* is quite unlike a tool or piece of technology, another person possesses a consciousness like their own. In other words, the *Other* has his or her own free will that encroaches on the freedom of the individual. The leader may

desire or demand that subordinates follow, but ultimately, whether they follow or not is *always* dependent on the personal choice of each worker, regardless of coercion or their apparent inferior position. (p. 259)

The notion of the heroic leader on a pedestal reinforces a message of passivity and thereby promotes an unhelpful model of leadership that is not consistent with the notion of existential authenticity.

(iv) It can distract attention from the key role of empowerment. Heroes stand out from the crowd through their courageous exploits – for example, military leaders whose personal bravery in battle saved the day. Heroic leaders can play a role in empowering others, as Gandhi indeed did through his promotion of non-violent protest, but the glamour associated with heroism is not always compatible with a commitment to empowerment. As I mentioned above, heroic leadership gives the impression that leaders operate in exceptional circumstances and this takes attention away from leadership in the workplace. It therefore plays down the importance of empowerment as a feature of successful organizational practices. Helping people gain greater control over their lives (which is, after all, what empowerment is all about) across our workplace settings is not a good fit with a focus on individual achievement as a hero.

These four problem areas clearly show that we have to be very wary of notions of heroic leadership, but this is not to say that there is no role for heroes or heroism. History shows us that there have been some significant advances brought about by such key figures at certain times, and I have no intention of disrespecting that. However, it would be a significant mistake to confuse this type of exceptional leadership with the everyday leadership that is needed across all sectors. In a nutshell, leaders can be heroes and heroes can be leaders, but it is perfectly possible – in fact, it is happening every day – for leaders to do an excellent job without even the slightest hint of heroism. So, it is vitally important that we do not allow ourselves to be seduced by dramatic tales of heroic leaders and make the mistake that their adventures are what leadership is really all about.

Voice of experience 1.1

I felt quite uncomfortable about the whole notion of leadership at first. I suppose I associated it with the idea of legendary figures who have hit the headlines or made history at some point. That wasn't why I came into management; I had no heroic aspirations. I just wanted to make a positive difference to people's lives by helping them to do the best they could in their work. But I was lucky to have a manager who was able to put me right on that and show me that leadership isn't really like that and that my idea of wanting to help people achieve their best is entirely consistent with leadership.

Kate, a section manager in a local authority

A consensus model

The term 'consensus model' is one used in sociology to refer to attempts to understand society which fail to take account of the significance of conflict, attempts which assume that everybody within a society is perceiving what is good or bad, what is helpful or unhelpful, in broadly the same way. The early sociologists (Comte, Durkheim and Weber, for example) helped us in significant ways to develop a better understanding of society. However, implicit in their theoretical developments was an assumption that societies are based on shared interests. This original view came to be referred to as a 'consensus' model as it is based on the idea that there is a fundamental consensus across all social groups, an assumption that we are all 'on the same side', with shared interests. The reality is very different, of course, with there being significant differences of need, interest and perspective across different social groups and cohorts.

The alternative view, what came to be referred to as a 'conflict' model, is represented in the work of Marx, who pointed out that there are significant class structures in operation that are rooted in the fact that different class groups (the owners of the means of production and those who have to sell their labour to make a living – capitalists and the proletariat, to use the technical terminology) have different and opposing interests (McLellan, 2000). What is in the interests of labour (increased wages, for example) is likely to be contrary to the interests of capital (a concomitant reduction in profit). The feminist movement pointed out similar disparities between the interests of men and women in patriarchal societies, with women's interests for the most part subordinated to those of men (Richardson and Robinson, 2007). Since then, other groups and their advocates have added weight to the need to take account of differences of interest (and associated power imbalances) across groups (for example, Back and Solomos, 2009, in relation to race/ethnicity; Oliver and Barnes, 2012, in relation to disability; and Powell, 2005, in relation to age). Some commentators have grossly oversimplified this distinction between consensus and conflict models and made it much more rigid than it needs to be, but the basic idea (that a consensus model neglects to take into consideration conflict and opposing interests) remains a helpful and important one.

A consensus model therefore presents a distorted and oversimplified understanding of society. Applying such a model to leadership and what is involved in it can equally be seen as a mistake. It fully fails to address the need for leaders to have well-developed conflict management skills and the ability to recognize the significance of conflict and not attempt to brush conflictual issues under the metaphorical carpet. The need to adopt a conflict model raises a number of important issues:

(i) It cannot be assumed that everyone with a team, section or organization (whatever domain of leadership may apply in the particular circumstances) will have the same goals, interests, values or intentions. While this may superficially be the case, we need to be aware that there may be (in fact, probably are) all sorts of actual or potential conflicts beneath the surface. If these are not identified and articulated, the result can be people pulling in different directions and undermining any sense of collective approach or solidarity – often without even realizing that it is happening, creating confusion and tension and thereby standing as an obstacle to optimal working.

In rejecting a consensus model, then, we are making a commitment to recognizing that conflicts of interest are not aberrations from the norm of consensus and harmony, but, rather, a reflection of the fact that conflict is part and parcel of everyday life, the workplace being no exception (Coleman and Ferguson, 2014). What can often disguise this fact is the tendency to equate conflict with hostility. It is commonly assumed that, if there is no hostility, there is no conflict. It needs to be recognized that hostility represents a conflict that has gone from bad to worse, but many conflicts do not reach the stage of hostility – either because they are resolved before reaching that point or because they remain at a low level without escalating (which can often do more damage than hostility – see my comments below). Leaders who naively assume that conflict is not an issue because they see no signs of hostility can be lulling themselves into a false sense of security. What is much wiser is to be attuned to conflict, to be able to recognize the subtle tell-tale signs and respond accordingly.

Part of existentialism is the acknowledgement that conflict is part and parcel of human experience. Where there are people, sooner or later there will be conflict (although not necessarily hostility). We shall return to this point, and its implications for authenticity in Part II.

(ii) A failure to deal effectively with conflict situations can have very detrimental consequences. Not only is it wise to be attuned to conflict issues, but also it can be very unwise not to respond appropriately to conflict situations when they do arise. Sadly, some managers have a tendency to shy away from conflict, to adopt an ostrich approach to it, in the hope that it will just go away so that they do not have to deal with it. This involves (at least) three main sets of risks:

- *Smouldering* This relates to situations in which there are one or more underlying conflicts that can remain beneath the surface for a certain amount of time, but which can then burst into flames at any moment. This means that they can have a negative effect over time, which then gets significantly worse when matters come to a head. Both of these elements (the slow burn and the bursting into flames) can do a lot of harm in terms of morale and a sense of solidarity, generating considerable tension, ill feeling and mistrust – all of which can present major challenges for leaders to deal with and do untold harm in the process.
- *Festering* This is similar to smouldering, except without the bursting into flames element. This can be worse because, with smouldering, the situation can come to a head and give the opportunity

to clear the air and move on positively. However, festering can do long-term damage, as the insidious effects of unresolved conflict can go on for days, weeks, months, even years, all the time creating problems and standing in the way of people achieving their best. Conflict can lower morale and thereby present a significant obstacle to effective leadership by standing in the way of the development of a strong sense of shared endeavour. At the same time conflict can distract people to the extent that they are unable to focus fully on achieving optimal results, maximizing learning and promoting creative approaches. The price to pay for allowing conflicts to fester is therefore a very high one.

- *Undermining credibility* Where it is known to employees that a leader is aware of a conflict situation, but is not doing anything about it, the net result can be an undermining (if not total destruction) of that leader's credibility. The message given to staff by this failure to rise to the challenge is that the leader cannot be trusted to take the necessary steps to ensure smooth running and create a positive working environment. Later in this chapter I will comment on the significance of the leader's role in promoting a sense of security. Not dealing with conflicts that staff are aware of will undermine not only faith in that leader, but also any sense of security. So, once again, we are talking about a high price to pay for not addressing conflict issues, in this case a price that denies us the core leadership qualities of trust, respect and credibility.

(iii) Leaders need to be aware of the significance of power and be well equipped to respond appropriately to the challenges involved. Leadership involves exercising power, but effective, authentic leadership also involves being attuned to the various subtle ways power operates, incorporating their own use of power and that of others. Power can be positive and productive or negative and destructive. Which is to the fore can depend a great deal on how power is handled. Therefore a leader who adopts a consensus model and thereby fails to appreciate the significance of power is ignoring a significant element of organizational life. We will be returning to the theme of power, but for now I want to emphasize that any approach to leadership which neglects conflict also neglects power, and that is likely to prove a costly error.

(iv) The potential for sabotage is ever-present. Conflict, whether open or hidden, can be a basis for sabotage. Unfortunately, some people will have their own agenda that runs counter to the interests of their colleagues and/or their organization. This can lead to throwing a clog in the works (the original literal meaning of sabotage) to cause harm or disadvantage – directly or indirectly – to colleagues and/or the organization. Furnham and Taylor (2004) explore the significance of destructive workplace behaviours. It is important to realize that, even in the best-run organizations, sabotage is a potential problem.

PRACTICE FOCUS 1.2

> Karel was a manager of the repairs department in a large engineering company. He was aware that there was long-standing ill feeling between two of his staff, but he just put this down to a mild form of rivalry between the two men. He paid it little attention and felt no need to do anything about it. However, he changed his attitude when his most valued employee informed him that he was leaving. Sorry to be losing such a key member of the team, he wanted to find out more about why he had decided to leave. What came as a complete surprise to him was his colleague telling him that it was the constant bickering, the bad feeling and the tension that had made him look for a job elsewhere. Karel had had no idea that the conflict was having such a negative effect. He could see now that he had made a mistake in not taking the conflict seriously and had not appreciated what an effect on morale such conflict could produce. This had been a difficult lesson for him to learn, but he realized that this was a mistake he should be very careful not to make again in future.

Atomism

This is a philosophical term that refers to the tendency to see individuals in isolation and therefore to neglect the wider cultural and structural factors that have a significant bearing on the behaviour and reactions of individuals. For example, consider this definition of leadership from

Northouse (2010) quoted earlier: '*Leadership* is a process whereby an individual influences a group of individuals to achieve a common goal' (p. 3). The Chartered Institute of Personnel and Development (CIPD) offers a similar view: 'Leadership may be defined as the capacity to influence people, by means of personal attributes and/or behaviours, to achieve a common goal' (CIPD Leadership Factsheet). While there is much truth in this approach to defining leadership it remains totally at an individualistic level and pays no attention whatsoever to the wider social factors that are likely to have a significant bearing. As I will be emphasizing throughout this book, leadership is not simply about influencing individuals; it is a much bigger endeavour than that. We will focus on these particular issues in Chapter 3 in greater detail.

Early existentialist thought focused heavily on individual factors. For example, Kierkegaard (Watts, 2003) placed great stress on subjectivity and the need for the person not to be lost in wider concerns. Nietzsche wrote about what he called 'self-overcoming' and the potential for individuals to be free spirits, rather than simply conformists who follow the herd (see Kaufmann, 2000). This individual focus has continued throughout the development of existentialist thought and remains a key element. However, some elements of Heidegger's work recognized wider social factors (Heidegger, 1962), and Sartre's later works placed them at centre stage (Sartre, 1973; 1982). So, while individual factors are important, they need to be understood in their wider context, otherwise we get a distorted picture that fails to take account of the key role of wider cultural and structural factors.

In my own work around these issues I have used the idea of PCS analysis as conceptual tool to make sense of the complexities involved (Thompson, 2011a). PCS refers to personal, cultural and structural factors. While Personal factors are important and an essential part of understanding human experience, we have to understand that such personal elements do not operate in isolation; they will be influenced by wider Cultural factors (shared meanings, for example). These cultural factors need, in turn, to be understood as part of a wider whole in terms of the Structural level – the ways in which social structures centred around class, race, gender and so on have a strong influence in shaping ideas and assumptions at the Cultural level. We will revisit PCS analysis in Part II, but for now the point I want to emphasize is that to focus

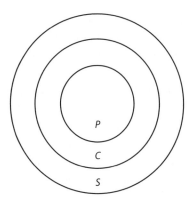

FIGURE 1.1 **PCS analysis (from Thompson, 2012b)**

narrowly on individual factors without taking account of cultural and structural issues is to adopt a very partial and misleading view.

Atomism can be seen to be the opposite of holism. The adoption of a holistic approach takes account of the overall context and not just the individual in isolation. As Goffee and Jones (2006) put it: 'The exercise of leadership is contextual. Always' (p. 83). They go on to argue that:

> human actions – whether involving leadership or not – do not take place in a vacuum. They are conditioned by the social realities in which individuals act. These social realities form an important part of the context. They can be no more wished away than can gravity. Effective leadership involves recognizing the limitations of context as well as the potential opportunities. Skillful leaders are realists. They have a well-developed sense of what can be changed – and what cannot. They understand the real conditions in which they must operate, and work within those constraints. (p. 84)

Those 'social realities' can be understood as cultural (relating to shared meanings) and structural (relating to the structure of society).

One of the dangers of atomism is that its narrow focus can lead to individuals being pathologized – that is, being seen as responsible for matters that are better understood from a wider, social or organizational viewpoint. One example of this is stress. An atomistic view of stress can lead to the assumption that stress is a sign of a weak individual, thereby preventing its nature as a complex, multi-level phenomenon from being explored and addressed (Thompson, 2009a). This can lead to a vicious circle in which someone who is experiencing stress through no fault or flaw of their own is being blamed for their problems, a process which adds extra pressure, while also making it less likely that the person concerned will ask for help or support when they need it.

Such pathologizing can also provide fertile soil for bullying, in so far as it creates an atmosphere in which a vulnerable person can be open to exploitation from unscrupulous others who want to capitalize on what they see as weakness.

Despite the predominance of atomistic thinking, we need to be cognizant of the fact that such narrow thinking is unhelpful and not supportive of the collective ethos needed for effective leadership.

Voice of experience 1.2

There were only seven of us doing the work of what should be a team of 12. We were really struggling to cope and we were worried that the situation was going to make us ill. Our manager was off sick, which was part of the problem. The manager who was filling in for her had no sympathy whatsoever and just kept telling us that we were paid to cope. If our manager hadn't come back from sick leave and given us proper support who knows what would have happened. It was a really worrying situation.

Ian, a probation officer

No recognition of emotions

Considering the positivistic approach to leadership that has been so common over the decades, it is not surprising that the dominant way of looking at leadership has been a rationalistic one. While there are clearly strongly rational factors involved in leadership, it would be a significant mistake not to recognize that – because we are dealing with *human* phenomena – there will inevitably be emotional factors to consider as well (Bolton, 2005). Some of these will have specific existential connotations (for example, anguish and anxiety, as we shall see in Part II), but there is also the wider field of emotions in the workplace that needs to be given greater attention – for example the significance of stress, as we can draw close links between poor or non-existent leadership on the one hand and high levels of stress on the other (Kelloway and Barling, 2010).

Of course, emotion is not something entirely new to the leadership field. As Hall and Janman (2010) point out, charismatic leadership can be understood as a form of highly effective approach to communicating around emotions. Concepts like 'emotional intelligence' (Murphy, 2006) and 'emotional competence' (Thompson, 2013b) are receiving increasing attention, placing greater weight on the need to go beyond a purely rational approach to organizational life in general and leadership in particular. Similarly, the current emphasis on workplace well-being as an important basis for organizational success (Kinder *et al.,* 2008; Thompson and Bates, 2009) introduces a need for emotional issues to be taken into consideration as a central part of promoting well-being.

The role of emotion is an important element of existentialist thought. As Gill (2011) explains:

> Martha Nussbaum suggests that emotions are ways in which human beings direct their attention to objects and that they cannot be separated from perception or cognition. Mary Warnock argues likewise:
>
> [Jean-Paul] Sartre ... was convinced ... that one cannot separate the emotions from the intellect, that the emotions have objects (they are intentional) and that loving or hating or feeling disgust for an object is a way of perceiving that is bound up in all our understanding and knowledge of the world, giving intelligibility to that world. (p. 317)

From a Sartrean perspective emotions are not just personal inner feelings (that would take us back to atomism); they are reflections of how we engage with other people and indeed with the wider world more broadly. This fits well the development of a sociological approach to emotion which complements and, in some ways, challenges the dominant psychological approach to this aspect of human life. The idea that emotions are sociological as well as psychological is evidenced by the fact that emotions are expressed differently in different cultures (Parkinson *et al.*, 2005). For example, how grief is expressed and understood varies across cultures (Parkes *et al.*, 1997) and over time (Kellehear, 2007).

The emotional demands on leaders should not be underestimated. It can be a very challenging undertaking that can, at times, leave leaders feeling anxious, fearful, unconfident, isolated and under immense pressure. Leaders can be seen to have a responsibility for promoting workplace well-being, but it would be naïve not to recognize that they can often need the benefits of it themselves.

Trying to adopt a wholly rational approach to the workplace and leaving no room for emotions can be seen as a form of bad faith, and therefore a failure of authenticity. Humans are indeed rational creatures, but we are also emotional creatures – it is a case of 'both and' rather than 'either or'. Authentic leadership needs to take account of this, rather than settle for the one-sided rationalistic approach that is so commonly adopted and which omits consideration of a major element of what it means to be human.

No recognition of loss and grief

This continues and extends the theme of the neglect of emotional factors. Grief can be seen as a reaction to any significant loss and not just to death, and so it is likely that there will be significant numbers of people experiencing some sort of grief reaction in the workplace at any given time. The tendency for these factors to be given little or no attention is something that is recognized as a flaw in our thinking about such matters. In an earlier work (Thompson, 2009b) I have commented in detail about the dangers associated with not recognizing the significance of loss and grief issues in the workplace. Grief that is unrecognized and not given full support is known technically as 'disenfranchised grief' (Doka, 2002), and it has long been recognized that this type of grief can be particularly difficult to deal with because of the lack of social support associated with grief reactions that are not being recognized or validated.

As we shall see in Part II, a fundamental part of authentic leadership is the ability to influence meanings (for example, through shaping culture). Grief involves a process of disruption of meaning (Neimeyer and Sands, 2011). Marris (1996) talks of grief as a reaction to the disintegration of the whole structure of meaning associated with the person (or thing) we have lost:

> The intense anxiety and hopelessness of the bereaved arises from their sense that no claims of reality can any longer mean anything to them. The evidence of grief suggests that the emotional structure which sustains our purposes is too closely integrated for purposes even unrelated to a loss to survive intact. (p. 47)

Significant losses in our lives can, in effect, turn our lives upside down. Our frameworks of meaning can be affected so profoundly that we become totally confused and disorientated. With some losses, particularly traumatic ones, we can even experience 'biographical disruption', a reaction which involves temporarily losing our sense of who we are. We feel so confused, so profoundly different from how we felt before the loss that we have a significantly altered sense of who we are and how we fit into the world (Thompson, 2012c). Marris (1996) again offers apt comment:

> When someone is bereft of a crucial relationship, nothing seems to make sense any longer: the world has become meaningless instead of a generalizable structure of beliefs sustaining the bereaved through the particular loss, interpreting it and setting it in a larger context of meaning, the beliefs themselves may be invalidated, compounding the sense of loss so, for instance, C. S. Lewis describes how, on his wife's death, he underwent a bitter crisis of faith; and widows I interviewed in a London study described the same rejection of religious consolations in which they had believed. (p. 47)

This biographical disruption, or the general disruption of meaning associated with a major loss, can have significant effects on us. Individuals so affected may not be able to operate machinery safely or be relied upon to make balanced professional judgements. The common tendency to try and brush grief-related issues under the carpet and simply make supportive and reassuring noises is therefore a dangerous strategy to adopt. When we also take into consideration that grief arises in response to any major loss and not just to death (Thompson, 2012c), then we should begin to realize that grief is a much more common feature of working life than is generally realized. If we take seriously the idea that authentic leadership is premised on being attuned to what it means to be human, then clearly a neglect of matters related to loss and grief is not consistent with the concept of existential authenticity. If our aim, as leaders, is to get the best out of people, then failing to pay attention to their often intense needs when they are at their most vulnerable is clearly not a wise course of action.

| PRACTICE FOCUS 1.3 | Patrick and Alan were very experienced and highly qualified engineers who worked together in the same organization, a medium-sized manufacturing company. They both had 10-year-old daughters who were members of the same dancing troupe. Tragically, both girls were killed in an automobile accident while en route home from one of the dancing displays they had been involved in at a charity event. On returning to work after the funerals both men were struggling to come to terms with their major loss. In some respects it was helpful that they had each other to rely on, but in other respects, knowing that both girls had died made it an even harder burden to bear, as it made a more emphatic impression that the world is such a cruel and unfair place. What did not help was that their line manager took a very unsympathetic approach to their situation. He expressed his condolences and acknowledged their major losses, but then went on to say that they should leave their problems and worries at the workshop entrance. He made it clear that he did not expect to make any allowances for them and that the best thing would be for them to get back to normal and work as usual. They were both taken aback by this approach and said so. The response they got was for the |

> initial message to be reaffirmed: 'back to normal'. They found this hard to stomach and, after a few weeks of what they experienced as a heartless response from their line manager, they both decided to leave. Within their particular industry, their skills were much in demand so they knew they would have little problem finding work in a more supportive and human environment. When their line manager realized he was losing two highly valued engineers who would be very difficult to replace, he appreciated how badly he had handled the situation, but by now it was too late – the damage was already done.
>
> From Thompson (2009b)

In keeping with my earlier comments about the emotional demands on leaders, we should also note that leaders too will face their own grief challenges from time to time, a fact which reinforces the dangers of allowing cultures to develop which have a tendency to brush loss and grief issues under the carpet.

Neglect of security

The dominant thinking in the leadership literature pays little or no attention to the significant role of security. This is a particularly significant flaw from an existentialist point of view, as a key concept in existentialism is the notion of 'ontological security'. I will explore this in more detail in Chapter 5, but for present purposes I simply want to propose that it is necessary to have a better understanding of how feelings of security in the workplace play a major role in developing a sense of well-being. By the same token, if there is little sense of security, then this can significantly undermine well-being, with all the problems associated with a low level of morale. Without a sense of security, teams and whole organizations can descend into a vicious circle involving lower levels of confidence leading to lower morale, less learning, less creativity, more defensiveness and more risk-averse behaviour, and this sort of vicious spiral can present some major challenges to leadership.

Existentialism is premised on the key concepts of flux and contingency. Flux, as we have seen, means that everything is changing or 'emergent', constantly evolving. Contingency can be summarized as the idea that there are few if any guarantees. In other words, uncertainty is part of what it means to be human. As Marris (1996) comments:

> Uncertainty is a fundamental condition of human life. We try to master it by discovering the regularities in events which enable us to predict and control them. When they do not turn out as we expected, we look for ways to revise our understanding, our purposes and means of control. When we cannot foretell what will happen, we try to keep our choices of action open; and when none of those choices seems hopeful, we try to withdraw into familiar certainties or fall into despair. (p. 1)

This reflects the existentialist understanding of security as basically our ability to cope with insecurity. That is, no one can be fully secure in the everyday sense of the word (free from risk and threat). Existential security (or ontological security, as we shall be calling it in Part II) comes from being able to manage the uncertainties and insecurities we encounter, as described by Marris above. Leaders can have a crucial role to play in this, in so far as their actions and attitudes can either undermine people's ability to cope with the challenges of insecurity (contingency) to reinforce and support them. Ironically, failing to reinforce a sense of security can feed anxiety and anguish and therefore make a reliance on bad faith all the more likely, while also encouraging defensive and risk-averse behaviour. The result, then, is not greater authenticity (and the benefits it brings), but, rather, significant obstacles to authenticity.

A key issue when it comes to security is confidence. An employee struggling to achieve a sense of security is far less likely to feel confident (and therefore far less likely to achieve their best). In contrast, someone whose sense of security is boosted by effective leadership is likely not only to have more self-confidence, but also to have more confidence in their leader (taking us back to the key theme of the central role of trust, respect and credibility).

Without some degree of security, staff will understandably be less likely to embrace culture change, to be creative and to learn. The result is an inherently conservative culture that blocks progress.

Voice of experience 1.3

One of the best managers I have ever worked with had this uncanny knack of making people feel secure and confident. Just her very presence gave us a sense that, whatever arose, we would be able to deal with it. You just can't imagine what a positive impact that had. It made us all feel more confident. I suppose what it came down to was that she just came across as so human, such a genuine person.

Alan, a human resources manager in a financial services company

CONCLUSION

This is not a comprehensive account of flaws in leadership theory, but it should be sufficient to establish that there is much that needs to be done to make sure that leadership theory is adequate to the challenge of appreciating and responding to the complexities of human existence. What needs to be understood, therefore, is that, for authentic leadership to be more than an empty phrase, leaders need to go beyond the populist understandings of selfhood that fail to do justice to the complexities of human experience and develop more sophisticated understandings that give us a clearer, fuller picture of what is involved in leadership and, indeed, in authenticity. Existential authenticity does not involve being true to an essentialist self, but rather, to a conception of human existence – our own and other people's – as fluid and dynamic, with each of us challenged with taking ownership of our actions.

This book will explore leadership from a more theoretically well-developed approach by drawing on a range of existentialist themes and concepts. Part II of the book will focus in particular on these but, before we get to that point, I have more to say about flaws in current leadership. Having reviewed some flaws in leadership theory, I will now move on, in Chapter 2, to explore some common flaws in leadership practice.

chapter 2 | Problems with leadership practice

INTRODUCTION

The flaws in theory that were identified in Chapter 1 will, of course, have implications for practice, but there are also problems that can be identified that relate to how leadership is carried out in practice, irrespective of the theoretical underpinnings that have been drawn upon. Indeed, much of the difficulty in practice arises not from practices based on flawed theory, but, rather, on flawed 'practice wisdom' that has grown up over time (in large part due to the influence of the training and consultancy industry that has adopted a number of assumptions not to be found in the textbooks, but which have none the less proven influential in shaping actual practice at the ground level – see Furnham, 2004 and Furnham, 2006 for a discussion of this).

Sartre made the important point that existentialism is about 'lived experience' (*le vécu*) (Sartre, 2003). That is, it is not simply a matter of focusing on abstract theoretical principles, but, rather on concrete, real-world issues – how those principles 'pan out' in reality. This is important as a general point about existentialist philosophy and its role as an explanatory framework, but it is particularly relevant in relation to leadership. Authentic leadership is not about positivistic laws of human behaviour; it is about appreciating the complexities of human existence. That appreciation needs to be at not only a theoretical level (frameworks of understanding), but also a practical level (the consequences for real people in real situations) – and, importantly, in terms of the relationship between theory and practice (a very significant topic that we will discuss in more detail in Chapter 7).

The remainder of this chapter will take the form of a discussion of various aspects of leadership practice that are in one or more ways problematic when it comes to authenticity. I shall outline each of these in turn and comment on their significance.

VISION

Vision, understood as a clear picture of what leadership is intended to achieve (a matter of being able to envisage the desired future state, the destination that the team or group of staff or organization are trying to arrive at) and the importance of communicating that vision, are strong themes in the history of leadership theory and practice (Gilbert, 2005). Although these ideas continue to feature in the leadership literature and have much to commend them in some ways, they are not without their difficulties. For example, I can identify at least four different problems with the idea of vision.

The first of these problems is that the vision is often absent. In many settings there is no real sense of vision, no real feeling of striving towards a set of future goals. In many organizations the focus is on surviving, not thriving – that is, on simply getting through the working day without undue difficulties, with little or no sense of a high level of commitment geared towards a motivating, or even inspiring, vision put forward by a leader. The basis of this is the notion of 'satisficing' which involves making compromises just to get the job done, just enough to meet minimum standards. The main problem with this approach is that it locks people into their problems. What I mean by that is this narrow focus on current pressures and demands results in losing sight of any sense of vision and, with it, significant sources of motivation. The reduced level of motivation can add to the pressures and thereby reinforce a sense that what is important is just getting through the day, dealing with the immediate problems and concerns. This encourages short-term thinking, a loss of focus and a tendency to drift. In such cases leadership as a force for positive influence can get lost in the push to deliver on current short-term challenges.

Where there is no vision at all there is likely to be little or no motivation to do more than the bare minimum; there will be little or nothing that encourages people to move beyond this. Consequently there will be little or no enticement to engage with organizational goals, to identify with them and get a sense of shared endeavour. In short, there will be little scope for commitment or, the other side of the coin, job satisfaction and a desire to achieve one's best.

This comes back to the key theme of organizational culture. Where a culture is not informed by clarity about goals and the plans for achieving them, sheer force of habit can become the predominant driving force – that is, instead of present actions being informed mainly by future aspirations, they come to rely on past action, the habits that have grown up over time. This means that relatively little control is being exercised, and there is a very real danger that staff (and managers) can become passive victims of their culture – driven by the dead weight of habit, rather than by their goals and values.

It could even be argued that, where there is no vision, there is no leadership. If there is no clarity about what is to be achieved or the possible pathways for achieving it, there is little to guide us in moving forward. This will generally mean that either (i) there is no movement – the workforce stagnates, creating a whole range of problems as a result (low morale being a primary one); or (ii) movement is random and haphazard – people are not sure where they are going; they are stumbling forward in an uncontrolled way, rather than following an agreed plan of action. This can have potentially catastrophic results (imagine a team of staff involved in child protection work stumbling forward haphazardly, with no real strategy to guide them, no sense of shared goals or how best to achieve them).

Having a vision will not automatically avoid these problems developing or offer any sort of magic solution, but it can be seen as a step in the right direction. It gives us a firmer foundation to build on.

The second problem is that visions are often not shared, in the sense that there may be no accepted consensus about what the vision means or how it should be put into practice. What can happen in such circumstances is that there may well be an assumed vision that is intended to be applicable, but does not actually make much impact on what happens, because there are unrecognized conflicts that are not being addressed.

Problems will arise where there are such complicating factors or other important issues that are not being recognized or addressed. Examples of this type of situation could include:

- *Professional differences* In some work contexts there will be people from different professional backgrounds working together. This can mean different priorities, different values and different aspirations across these groups. If the vision does not take account of these differences, the result can be different groups of people pulling in different directions, thereby totally going against the idea of the sense of shared endeavour that leadership seeks to develop and sustain. This can lead to in-fighting, particularly if the groups of professionals concerned do not realize what is happening and simply blame other groups for 'being awkward' or standing in their way. In some circumstances success may depend on professionals working collaboratively together (that is, they are not simply carrying out their duties separately from other professional groups or in isolation from one another – for example, community nurses and occupational therapists working with older people). Even where those professionals are keen to work effectively together and committed to making it work, if the vision does not take account of different professional standpoints, there is a high risk of failure, a risk that a vision that should be bringing people together with a shared sense of purpose is actually driving them apart.
- *Group rivalries* It is not only professional differences that can be problematic if not taken into consideration. There can also be rivalries – for example, between departments – that can get in the way of having a shared sense of what is to be achieved. For example, a vision may make life easier for people in the production department, but cause additional pressures for people in sales and marketing, or vice versa. It is unlikely that a vision across the board will be of equal appeal to all groups.
- *Different understandings* At times a vision can be expressed so vaguely that it leaves considerable scope for different people to interpret it in different ways. Such differing interpretations can, of course, prove highly problematic.
- *Paying lip service* Some people will have problems with a vision, but will not voice them; they will not articulate their concerns. They will

therefore just go through the motions to make it look as though they are 'on board', but have no real commitment to it.

- *Sabotage* Others who have concerns but are not prepared to articulate them may even go so far as to find subtle ways of sabotaging the successful implementation of the vision. If there is no real sense of shared endeavour, just a vision imposed from above, sabotage becomes a real possibility.

These examples illustrate that simply to announce a vision and expect everyone to share it and embrace it is based on a forlorn hope. For a vision to work effectively it needs to be one that is shared by all concerned and not one that is imposed from without. As Lawler and Ashman (2012) explain:

> To recognize others as having their own subjective and objective freedom would involve organizational leaders relying less on traditional modes of control exercised by management and developing a true 'empowerment' where all those involved in an inter-subjective, sense-making dialogue. This requires an inter-personal engagement, not ignoring but acknowledging and negotiating power asymmetries. Over-reliance of the 'vision' created and handed down by leaders is in these terms inauthentic and is itself limited and limiting as it prevents the enrichments described by Sartre [the inter-subjective development of reciprocal meaning]. (p. 340)

This passage raises some important issues:

- Vision should not be based on simply issuing instructions. Unfortunately, many managers do not recognize that organizational success comes through people (Thompson, 2013a), and they therefore totally miss the point of leadership and the power of developing a motivating vision to move people forward constructively. Sadly, many people fall back on a traditional command and control approach where they rely on issuing instructions, rather than encouraging and supporting their followers to help them use and develop their abilities to the full. They do not appreciate that this is more likely to alienate them than to motivate them.

- There needs to be a focus on empowerment. Instructions from above give people less power. Helping people to achieve their best helps them to gain greater, not lesser, control over their lives. Empowerment relies upon 'interpersonal engagement' geared towards negotiating positive ways forward.
- The vision needs to be meaningful if it is to have any impact on motivation (we will return to this point below).

PRACTICE FOCUS 2.1	Liam was a manager in a high-tech manufacturing company. The company was at the cutting edge of their field and prided themselves on having a proactive and dynamic management team. They had developed a clear vision for the company and had developed a well-deserved reputation for high-quality leadership. However, Liam was from a more traditional background and was used to giving instructions rather than facilitating empowerment. The mismatch between the vision and the reality for the staff under his leadership created a lot of tensions and dissatisfactions, resulting in a low level of morale. What started to develop then was a vicious circle in which the low morale produced lower levels of work (quality and quantity), which then made Liam become even more directive and issue stronger instructions. It got to the point where one of the senior managers had to step in as they could see that Liam's section was struggling while others were doing well. The senior manager then faced the challenge of helping Liam adjust his management style without alienating him or undermining his confidence.

A third problem with vision is that it is often superficial and oversimplified and therefore fails to engage people. Where there is what people tend to see as an insubstantial vision, this can cause resentment and provoke a cynical response, which, of course, is highly counterproductive in terms of what leadership is intended to achieve. If people feel that the vision that is being spouted is all rhetoric and no reality and lacks any real depth or meaning, then they are highly unlikely to embrace it, and, in fact, this may do more harm than good. This is because it can lower morale and make people disengaged, rather than encourage a constructive engagement with the organization and its goals. A vision that is not meaningful to the people who are intended to embrace it will do nothing to challenge bad faith and could well go some way towards encouraging it as a way of trying to cope with a workplace that is not helpful in creating a sense of engagement or commitment. At times even the leader can become cynical about the vision and thereby add fuel to the flames of resentment and disillusionment. It would be fair to say that an empty vision will often do more harm than having no vision at all.

Fourthly, if targets are the only vision for an organization or a team, then this means that leadership has been swallowed whole by managerialism – an approach to organizational life that relies on a top-down, target-driven style of management that treats people just as resources, and not as primarily *human* resources. Going back to our earlier discussions, it is an approach that focuses on getting the most out of people, rather than the best.

The tendency to focus on targets as a source of motivation runs counter to the idea of authentic leadership. For some time now much management practice has been based on the false premise that setting relatively meaningless targets for people will motivate them to achieve their best. In reality, it is far more likely that this will produce at best a minimal compliance with what is required to get the job done and, at worst, considerable alienation (Thompson, 2013a). Ballat and Campling (2011) comment on the significant problems associated with a focus on targets:

> There is evidence that, as well as supporting improvement, target- or indicator-driven activities can have, in themselves, a range of unhelpful unintended consequences. Researchers from the University of York and the University of St Andrews report a range of such consequences (Goddard *et al.*, 2000). They have found consistent evidence of:
>
> - *tunnel vision* – concentration on areas that are included in the performance indicator scheme, to the exclusion of other important areas;
> - *suboptimisation* – the pursuit of narrow local objectives by managers, at the expense of the objectives of the organisation as a whole;

- *myopia* – concentration on short-term issues, to the exclusion of long-term criteria that may show up in performance measures only in many years' time;
- *measure fixation* – focusing on what is measured rather than the outcomes intended;
- *complacency* – a lack of motivation for improvement when comparative performance is deemed adequate;
- *ossification* – referring to the organisational paralysis that can arise from an excessively rigid system of measurement;
- *misrepresentation* – the deliberate manipulation of data, including 'creative' accounting and fraud, so that reported behaviour differs from actual behaviour;
- *gaming* – altering behaviour so as to obtain strategic advantage.

Steve Iliffe covers similar ground, describing the risks of a system where economic factors outweigh professional imperatives in shaping GPs' behaviour. He describes three main risks: poor performance in domains where performance is not measured; hitting the target but missing the point; and discrepancies in data recording (Iliffe, 2008, p. 112). Even Chris Ham, health policy academic and head of the King's Fund, and a proponent of performance targets, acknowledges the dangers of disempowering front-line staff, stifling innovation and overloading the organisations providing care to patients (Ham, 2009). To this list we might add cynicism, disengagement and low morale in staff, and anxiety and mistrust in patients. (p. 166)

It should be clear, then, that a vision based simply on targets is highly problematic. It fails to take account of the complexities of human life and is therefore far removed from the idea of authentic leadership.

COMMUNICATING THE VISION

Even where a clear and helpful vision exists, it is often not communicated to the people who need to be able to embrace it. Often what are described as visions end up as simply paper documents gathering dust on a shelf. They are often couched in managerialist jargon that can alienate people (for example the notorious 'Mission Statement' that is often a source of considerable amusement among ground-floor staff). For a vision to be meaningful, it needs to be communicated in the language of shared endeavour ('we are in this together'). If it is seen as something that is pie in the sky or something that is just intended to make annual reports look impressive, then it is highly unlikely that people will connect with what it is all about, and there will be once again a failure of leadership.

It is therefore important to be clear about what is meant by 'communicate'. It is not simply a matter of notifying staff in a one-directional way. For communication to take place, the 'message' has to be received as well as transmitted (Thompson, 2011b). There therefore has to be a good understanding established of the 'message' the vision is intended to convey. Without this there will be little or no engagement and therefore little or no ownership – thereby making authentic leadership an unattainable goal. Of course, a key part of establishing this understanding can be involving staff in developing the vision in the first place.

For a vision to be meaningful it needs to clarify why the organization exists (what goals it is intended to achieve) and what each person's role is in that. Consider this example from Gilbert (2005):

> When Kennedy visited NASA Base during his presidency, he asked a janitor what he did. The janitor did not say 'I'm sweeping the floor', though he had a broom in hand, but he told the President, 'I'm helping to get men into space'! (p. 14)

This is a good example of an inclusive approach in which everyone can be made to feel welcome, valued and supported. This is not to be idealistic and deny that there will never be conflicts of interest in organizational life or there will never be any disruptive elements, but a vision that helps people feel part of an important shared endeavour will go a long way towards preventing or minimizing such challenges. As Fevre *et al.* (2013) comment, based on their research into workplace problems: 'the key predictor of the troubled workplace is that individuals feel that they do not matter' (p. 61).

What can also occur where the vision is not communicated effectively is that 'bubble thinking' can arise. This is a term I use to describe situations where people become so engrossed within their own circum-stances, with their own deadlines, their own workload, their own computer, their own narrow sphere (hence the term 'bubble thinking') that they have lost sight of the wider picture, they have lost sight of what the organization is all about (or their profession as well). They are focus-ing narrowly on those issues that demand their attention in the short term, and there is no holistic vision that is driving them forward. This, then, brings us back to the notion that people will tend to focus on surviving, not thriving, just getting through the day effectively, rather than achieving the best results possible. This then has a knock-on effect in terms of motivation and morale, because, if people are focusing on simply surviving, this sort of minimalist outlook can create a vicious circle in which people get little or no job satisfaction, which then leads to an even lower level of motivation and a form of semi-burnout or even, in some cases, full-scale burnout (Maslach and Leiter, 2000). By contrast, if an authentic leader can engage people in understanding and supporting the overall vision for the team and/or organization, then it can create a virtuous circle whereby increased effort produces better results, which in turn produce a higher level of job satisfaction and a stronger sense of belonging and engagement. This sort of positive dynamic is one that it is important for leaders to aim for, but failing to communicate a clear, helpful and meaningful vision is likely to undermine any such efforts.

A further central aspect of communicating the vision is having the interpersonal skills to be able to base leadership on human-to-human connection – that is, to recognize the human dimensions of the work-place and have the skills and the commitment to engage with people in a truly human fashion and not in a purely technical or administrative way simply to get the job done. Staff are unlikely to be receptive to messages from above that are delivered in an impersonal way or a way that lacks human warmth and empathy.

Buber (2013) introduced an important distinction between what he called I-Thou and I-it ways of relating to one another. He used these terms to refer to very different types of interaction that produce very different types of consequences. I-Thou refers to those interactions which are based on mutual respect where each party listens and pays attention to the other and is concerned for the well-being of the other party in and through that interaction. Buber points out that this has the effect of humanizing both parties in the interaction. I-it interactions, by contrast, are where there is simply a focus on getting the job done, on achieving the results. It is mechanistic and simply functional, losing sight of the importance of human-to-human interactions in terms of personal effectiveness. An I-it interaction, says Buber, is one that dehumanizes both parties. This is important to emphasize. It is not simply a matter of one person dehumanizing another through a purely instrumental approach, but, more significantly, that person dehumanizing him- or herself in the process. Unfortunately, managerialist approaches rooted in the idea of focusing on motivating people through target setting tend to encourage I-it interactions. They tend to focus attention on ticking the box and not considering the wider implications of this type of behaviour or approach to people management. Similarly, visions that are perceived as meaningless, as rhetoric with no reality, can encourage I-it relations and interactions.

Indeed, an important consideration from a leadership point of view is that I-it cultures can develop – that is, workplaces characterized by a norm of people relating to one another (and particularly to management) in I-it ways. This is often a reflection of (and contributor to) low morale and thus a lack of leadership effectiveness. Effective interpersonal relationship skills, centred around an I-Thou approach, can prevent this from happening and provide an important basis for promoting high levels of motivation and engagement.

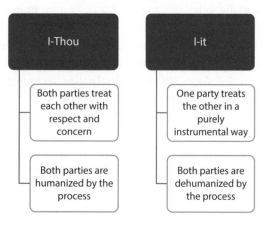

FIGURE 2.1 **Buber's I-Thou and I-it**

> ### *Voice of experience 2.1*
>
> I was unemployed for a while because I left my old job before I had got a new one. But I just had to get out of there; the atmosphere was so stifling. Morale was rock bottom, there was no sense of camaraderie and people looked upon the management with contempt. It was awful. People were barely civil towards each other. It was all just about surviving the onslaught of all the referrals that kept flooding in, and the more people focused on just getting by, the worse the atmosphere got.
>
> *Cheryl, a social worker in an adult services team*

A research report by the Chartered Institute of Personnel and Development (CIPD, 2013) on leadership makes for sorry (and worrying) reading when it shows that: 'only 8% of junior managers and supervisors thought that being good at motivating the team made them effective' (p. 5). Balance this against the important point made in the same report:

> Research shows that 80% of the variation in the employee engagement levels is down to the line manager (MacLeod and Clarke 2009). Equally the degree of employee discretionary effort depends on the quality of their relationship with the line manager (Corporate Leadership Council 2004). (p. 7)

While an attitude to leadership that excludes a focus on motivation persists, there will be little scope for empowering visions to be communicated effectively. We will return to the important topic of motivation in Part II.

Finally, in terms of communicating a vision, it is worth noting that existentialist thought helps us to move beyond a simplistic instrumentalist approach to communication. As Ashman and Lawler (2008) comment:

> Taking account of the intimate connection between leadership and communication it is remarkable that the concept of communication is

taken so much for granted in the literature on leadership. The conventional view appears to be that communication is a process that involves no more than the transmission and reception of information or that such transmission in itself results in positive outcomes such as experiencing involvement or commitment or becoming 'enlisted' (Kouzes & Posner, 1987). Thus, problems of leadership that are often seen as occurring as a consequence of faulty communication can be corrected by simply opening up channels and reiterating or clarifying the content of the message (Fisher, 1974). Communicating, therefore, becomes a competence or skill to be acquired by the leader as a means of overcoming the followers' inability to comprehend their role in the organizational scheme of things. (p. 254)

From an existentialist point of view, communication is a far more complex and holistic phenomenon of human connection and, as such, a key element of leadership (Thompson, 2011b). If we reduce communic-ation to simply a technical process of conveying information (rather than a shared process of creating meaning), then the task of effectively communicating a vision is highly likely to remain unachieved.

TOKENISM

It is unfortunately the case that I have often come across situations where the language of leadership is being used, but what is actually hap-pening is that the management practices associated with it fall into the traditional command and control manner. Returning to the CIPD report that refers to the sobering fact that so few managers recognized their role in motivating staff, we need to be aware that, even where the lan-guage of leadership is being used extensively, this does not necessarily mean that there is a genuine commitment to effective leadership or an adequate understanding of what leadership is all about. Without such a commitment what we have is tokenism – people making it look or sound as though leadership is being practised when it is not. This can, of course, alienate staff by destroying the all-important trust, respect and credibility that leaders need. It can also prevent the manager(s) con-cerned from progressing in their work by deepening and extending their knowledge, skills and confidence. The problems associated with tokenism can therefore be quite significant in their impact.

PRACTICE FOCUS 2.2 | Karen was a training manager in a large company in the petroleum industry. Part of her role was to deliver leadership development programmes for senior managers and executives. She had been doing this for years and really enjoyed it. One of the things she had learned, though, was that she had to watch out for people who were happy to talk the talk but who showed no signs of being able or willing to walk the walk. Over time she developed quite an expertise in spotting the people who made all the right noises but showed little or no evidence of being able to put the ideas into practice in a genuine or meaningful way. Thankfully such people were in a minority, but Karen was aware that even one manager engaging in this sort of tokenism was enough to do a lot of damage. Where she identified such individuals she would set up a mentoring arrangement with a more experienced (and committed) manager to try and move the situation forward positively. She was aware that some managers were tokenistic because they lacked the confidence and/or capability to lead authentically, while, for others, the problem seemed to be related to cynicism which often came about because the manager concerned had had limited experience of receiving positive leadership.

What can also come under the heading of tokenism is what I refer to as 'backseat driving'. This is where managers interfere unnecessarily in the working practices of their followers, issuing instructions and micromanaging instead of encouraging staff to make their own decisions and supporting them in doing so. The effect is likely to be one that disempowers people, as opposed to the much more positive and constructive approach of being an enabling manager who empowers employees to achieve their best. I once ran a course on leadership which I began by asking participants what they hoped to gain from our two days together. The first person to speak was a man who said that he was hoping to learn some strategies for getting his staff to do as he told them without his having to spend so much time constantly checking up on them. He was then challenged (gently and tactfully) by members of the group that this was not leadership. He did not really respond to their comments, but later in the course he spoke about how he was committed to empowering his staff and appeared totally oblivious to how this was not at all consistent with his initial comment (or some of the other things he had said during the course).

I have also run courses on professional decision making where significant numbers of participants have expressed concern about how they are not allowed, let alone empowered, to make their own decisions, as the culture they work in is premised on the unwritten rule that it is the manager who makes the decisions. Of course, this sort of backseat driving deskills staff, reinforces a command and control mentality and overloads managers who are then faced with a lot of decisions to make that are not actually their remit. In my experience, this situation can arise from two sets of factors (or a combination of them both):

- *Work pressures* I am aware that what can easily happen is that busy managers faced with staff constantly coming to them with concerns about a decision they need to make can easily fall into a habit of just telling the member of staff what to do rather than support them in making a well-balanced decision. In terms of time pressures, this means achieving short-term gains at the expense of longer-term developments. Where this way of working becomes established staff soon learn that the quickest (but certainly not safest) thing to do is to take their questions to their managers and allow them to make the decisions for them. The net result is that managers become even more overloaded and thus less likely to take the longer-term view and more likely to give quick responses to decisions. In the meantime staff who should be developing their decision-making skills and confidence over time are becoming deskilled and disempowered. It can even reach the point where staff are promoted to a management role and fall into this culture of 'backseat driving' with little or no experience of having made their own decisions – clearly a very dangerous situation to be in. Sadly, the whole process of backseat driving encourages bad faith. It provides a spur for staff to delegate their decision making upwards to their manager instead of taking ownership for their own areas of responsibility. It also encourages bad faith in managers who do not take ownership of shaping the culture in a more positive and empowering direction and resort instead to acting in a paternalistic way by making staff's decisions for them in a way that, in effect contributes to infantilizing them.

- *Anxiety and defensiveness* Cultures that are risk averse and driven by anxiety and defensiveness can provide a major impetus towards not taking ownership of decisions by putting them on someone else's desk. Managers who collude with, or even encourage, this behaviour are not taking ownership of their leadership role in shaping an empowering and secure workplace culture. Bad faith begets bad faith and authenticity is nowhere to be seen. To compound this it is sometimes the leader who is anxious and defensive and will fuel a backseat driving culture because they are not prepared to take the risk of allowing their staff to make (potentially flawed) decisions – their anxiety drives them to hold on to decision making and retain close control over what they should be trusting their staff to undertake (and supporting them in doing so).

What tokenism boils down to is not addressing the profoundly *human* nature of leadership, not recognizing that effective leadership is a matter of being able to interact with other people in a way that recognizes and affirms the fully human nature of both parties (I-Thou). One particular consequence of this is that issues around ownership are not addressed. This allows individuals (both leaders and followers) to indulge in bad faith and therefore behave in inauthentic ways which are counterproductive.

Voice of experience 2.2

I was amazed when I moved from the ENT department to the Orthopaedic Unit at how different the cultures were when it came to decision making. In ENT I was expected to make my own decisions, in consultation with all the key people, of course, and it felt good to have my professionalism respected and trusted. But when I moved over to orthopaedics it was like a different world. It soon became really clear that I was expected to report to the charge nurse and let him make the decisions. It think his heart was in the right place, but he didn't seem to appreciate that the message he was giving me was that I was not trusted and not valued. As you can imagine, I didn't stay there long.

Sheila, a nurse in a general hospital

FIGHTING THE CULTURE

I argued earlier that a key part of leadership is having – and using – the ability to shape a culture in a positive direction. Unfortunately, some leaders or would-be leaders fail to appreciate that there is a significant difference between shaping a culture and fighting a culture. Basically, cultures are far more powerful than individuals (Thompson, 2013a) and can therefore easily have more sway over the actions and attitudes of employees. Where leaders try to fight a culture, to hit it head-on, as it were, then this is doomed to failure. Such leaders are not recognizing the complexities of group formation and organizational dynamics (which we will discuss in more detail in Part II). They are oversimplifying a complex situation if they feel that they can simply overrule a culture and in doing so, demonstrating a lack of understanding of how organizational cultures work (Schein, 2010). They are not acknowledging the significance of engagement and a sense of shared ownership that are necessary to bring about a positive culture.

PRACTICE FOCUS 2.3 | Brian was an experienced probation officer who had been fortunate to work in a strong team with an excellent leader. However, when he was promoted he was transferred to another district and given charge of a very different team. He was surprised by the low level of morale and the degree of negativity and cynicism. Very quickly he could sense that he was being dragged down by the negativity and defeatism and he felt very uncomfortable about that. So, he decided he would have to change the culture. Every time he heard a negative or cynical comment he would challenge it and say that people needed to be more positive. At a team meeting he also said that he wanted to see a more balanced attitude towards work and less negativity. What he got to his face was a superficial commitment to try harder to be more positive, but what he got behind his back was a negative and cynical rejection of him as a leader, with a lot of gallows humour at his expense, portraying him as a sort of Walter Mitty character disconnected from the realities of working life. His decision to simply fight the culture, rather than use his skills to work with team members to change it, had simply reinforced the sense of negativity and therefore made his job a great deal harder, especially as he had lost trust, respect and credibility in the process.

As well as the example given in Practice focus 2.3 I have come across many instances of attempts to fight cultures head-on, rather than adopt a more sophisticated and skilful approach to shaping the culture, not least the following:

- The manager of a residential care home in which staff display dismissive ageist attitudes towards residents bans the staff from using patronizing language towards the people in their care. However, no attempt is made to explain why such language is inappropriate, and so the staff comply with the instruction by not using patronizing terms (like 'old dear'), but continue to convey patronizing attitudes through their tone of voice and nonverbal communication.
- The owner of a small chain of retail outlets is concerned about a culture of poor customer care, and so decides to arrange training on customer care for the staff group. However, no explanation is given for this and no other measures are put in place to change the culture, and so staff interpret the training initiative as a criticism, which serves only to create bad feeling and leave staff even less motivated to provide good customer care.

Of course, influencing a culture is not a simple or straightforward matter, and involves a number of skills – especially people skills (Thompson, 2015) – but there is much to be gained from investing time and effort in developing those skills (and the confidence that goes with them), as they can make a very positive difference when it comes to leadership effectiveness and the avoidance of cultural problems. It also needs to be recognized that bringing about culture change is something that needs to be done *with* the staff group, not *to* them. Simply trying to fight the influence of a culture is therefore not a wise move, but sadly it is a (doomed) strategy that I have encountered many times in many organizations.

CONCLUSION

This is not, of course, an exhaustive account of problems in leadership practice, but what I have presented should be sufficient to provide a meaningful picture of various ways in which leadership practice can be anything but authentic, anything but tuned into the complex reality of human beings who are faced with radical freedom and the need to choose. Much of the time the problems come from the managers concerned having either a limited understanding of leadership (for example, failing to appreciate how different it is from a traditional 'I am the boss' command and control model) or not being able to put leadership into practice (perhaps through a lack of confidence and/or the lack of suitable role model from their own experience of having been managed (sadly, a significant proportion of the people I have worked with in a training or consultancy capacity have told me, after we have explored what leadership is all about, that they have never experienced it). But it is also important to note that much of the time the problem comes from certain managers and others not appreciating leadership as a *human* phenomenon, something that, in many ways, relates to the very heart of what it means to be human. As we noted in Chapter 1, it is unfortunately the case that leadership is often approached from a positivistic perspective, which can give us many helpful insights, but which is too far removed (in its search for laws of behaviour and organizational function) from the complexities of human existence to do justice to them.

Voice of experience 2.3

I am close to retirement now and I have worked with a wide range of managers during my time. They have ranged from brilliant to appalling, superb to pathetic, but I have learned something from each of them. The ones I have learned most from are the ones who are real 'people persons', and I suppose that in itself is a lesson – that the real people persons are the ones who have proven to be the best leaders.

Kim, a community development manager for a voluntary organization

A recurring theme across the experiences I have encountered of poor or non-existent leadership practice has been the key role of trust, respect and credibility. The practice examples I have given here will do little to create a sense of trust, respect and credibility and, in fact, may do much to undermine these important features of effective and authentic leadership. The other side of the coin is that the problems of leadership in practice will also often have their roots in a lack of trust, respect and credibility – that is, these important elements of good leadership can be both contributory factors to, and consequences of, less than effective leadership practice. An important lesson to take away from this chapter, therefore, is the need to take seriously the importance of establishing and maintaining trust, respect and credibility.

My aim in this chapter has not been to paint a negative picture or to be defeatist about the potential for authentic leadership. On the contrary, my intention is to show the challenges that an existentially authentic leadership faces, so that, when we explore in Parts II and III how existentialist thought can cast light on leadership, we are well aware of the challenges involved and the pitfalls that need to be avoided.

One of the pitfalls emphasized in Chapter 1 was the danger of atomism – that is, the tendency to focus on individual issues and to neglect the wider social context. In Chapter 3 we return to that theme by exploring in some detail the need to make sure that our understanding of leadership is holistic, in the sense that it incorporates the lessons to be learned from taking account of the significant influence of the social contexts on working life in general and leadership in particular.

chapter 3   Leadership in social context

INTRODUCTION

Hames (2007), in an important study of leadership, argues that: 'Complexity teaches us that nothing happens in isolation and that most phenomena and events are interconnected in some form or other' (p. 90). This chapter explores the significance of that statement by exploring the key role of the wider social context in shaping workplace practices.

Authentic leadership involves being attuned to the complexities of the distinctively human elements of the workplace in terms of need for an approach that is, among other things:

- *Holistic* This means not making the mistake of focusing narrowly on individuals and failing to take account of the wider cultural and structural factors that can have a significant bearing on how the workplace is perceived and experienced by those operating within it. A holistic approach gives us a much more adequate understanding of what is involved, whereas an approach that relies on atomism is one that fails to go beyond the individual level.
- *Dynamic* This involves recognizing that leadership is a moving picture, a means of responding to the constant changes ('flux', to use the technical term) that are inevitable when groups of people come together on a regular basis. Although the leadership literature talks a great deal about change in organizations, it often fails to recognize the constantly evolving nature of the workplace and tends to focus instead on specific pre-planned changes – for example, as a result of a particular scheme or initiative.

- *Prepared for complexity* While there is much in life that is highly predictable, we need to be aware that there is also much that is unpredictable and uncertain – so many things that depend on so many other things. The technical term for this is 'contingency'. It is the other side of the coin from 'flux'. Because human existence is characterized by flux, then the uncertainty and unpredictability of contingency need to feature in our understanding.
- *Aware of the significance of conflict* In Chapter 1 we noted the danger associated with adopting a consensus model of society that fails to take account of the significant role of conflict in social relationships and in society more broadly. Turning our back on conflict amounts to another example of bad faith in action.

Authentic leadership therefore needs to be informed by at least a basic understanding of the social context in which leadership activities take place. As I have argued before (Thompson, 2011a), each one of us is a unique individual, but a unique individual in a social context. While atomistic thinking leads to an emphasis on the uniqueness of the individual, a holistic approach takes account of individual factors, but also takes into consideration the wider social factors that circumscribe individual experience, and – significantly – the complex interrelationships between the two sets of issues. If we ignore the significance of that context, then we get a partial, distorted and inadequate picture of the situations that we are called upon to deal with. This chapter therefore explores the significance of the wider social context and examines some key issues that emphasize the point that an atomistic approach focusing on individuals is far from adequate as a basis for effective leadership.

The holistic approach offered by existentialism (particularly Sartrean existentialism) is well equipped for addressing this wider social context by drawing on sociological insights, rather than simply relying on individualistic perspectives. For example, a sociological lens enables us to become more attuned to the significance of equality and diversity issues and sensitizes us to the detrimental role of discrimination. Atomism tends to reduce matters of discrimination to personal prejudices and, in so doing, fails to take account of institutionalized discrimination at cultural and structural levels (more about this below). As Bauman and May (2001) put it:

To think sociologically can render us more sensitive and tolerant of diversity. It can sharpen our senses and open our eyes to new horizons beyond our immediate experiences in order that we can explore human conditions which, hitherto, have remained relatively invisible. Once we understand better how the apparently natural, inevitable, immutable, eternal aspects of our lives have been brought into being through the exercise of human power and resources, we shall find it much harder to accept that they are immune and impenetrable to subsequent actions, including our own. (p. 11)

This passage is significant in terms of: (i) highlighting the need for a sociological approach to equality and diversity; and (ii) moving us away from essentialist ideas about what are presumed to be fixed and immutable aspects of our lives. Both of these issues are of importance in relation to leadership. (i) is important because leaders who do not tune into the subtleties of discrimination and therefore unwittingly allow it to feature within their workplace can pay a heavy price in terms of trust, respect and credibility and, of course, people will not be achieving their best if they are subject to discrimination. (ii) is important because there is a danger that essentialist ideas will unnecessarily limit the scope for positive change that leaders are capable of bringing about. Authenticity involves avoiding the bad faith involved in assuming that matters we can control and/or influence are beyond us – for example, by assuming that aspects of a workplace culture cannot be changed.

| PRACTICE FOCUS 3.1 | Barry had been an accounts manager in a predominantly male engineering company before he was appointed as head of finance in a voluntary organization in which the staff group was approximately 85% female. He had not given any thought to the change in gender make up of his work situation, and so he continued to behave very much like he had done before. He had been quite a popular figure in his earlier post, and so at first he found it hard to understand why people did not seem so fond of him in his new setting. It took him a long time to realize that there were different sensibilities in working with a predominantly female |

group. But, to his credit, he did appreciate the need to make the effort to adjust. He was aware that he needed to understand what differences wider social factors like gender could make to the atmosphere and unwritten rules in a workplace, but he was also aware that he had to avoid simply stereotyping women and men and thereby, in effect, digging himself into a deeper hole. He had already learned a lot about these issues, but realized he still had a lot more to learn.

Hall and Janman (2010), in their important text, emphasize the significance of context. They are, rightly in my view, critical of traditional approaches to leadership which pay little or no attention to the context in which leadership practices take place. They are, though, aware of the potential difficulties involved in adopting a holistic approach:

> To reconcile the person and the social is a real challenge for psychology and sociology generally, not just the field of leadership specifically. Some of the more experienced authors in this sector have said that 'to speak of personality and social structure in the same breath is as close as one can get to heresy'. (p. 78)

This reflects the common compartmentalization to be found in the academic world where researchers and theoreticians have their own disciplinary focus and often pay little heed to the lessons to be learned from other disciplines or, indeed, from the adoption of a more holistic model.

However, it is not just in academic circles that such problems persist. The atomistic approach associated with the widespread notion of 'common sense' also leaves little room for an appreciation of the significance of the social context. As Hall and Janman go on to say: 'What is true is that as human beings we do struggle hard to see our connectedness to the world around us and to each other. Whether leader or follower, we need to consciously recognize we are all no more and no less than the sum of our relationships with others, our total social capital' (p. 165).

This chapter can therefore be seen as a means of counterbalancing the type of traditional approach that Hall and Janman reject. First we look at the importance of group development and the ways in which groups influence individual and collective behaviour. For this we draw on Sartre's (1982) theory of groups formation from an existentialist perspective. We then focus on the foundational role of meaning and acknowledge the strong elements of 'social construction' of it – that is, the ways in which individual meanings have their roots in wider social frameworks of meaning. This leads into a discussion of power and empowerment, important aspects of leadership and the workplace more broadly. Power is linked to social processes and social structures and these are precisely our next focus of study. Finally, we revisit the inevitability of conflict, as conflict is an important part of not only the wider social context that this chapter is concerned with, but also of existentialist thought.

GROUP DEVELOPMENT

This is an aspect of leadership that is often neglected but one in which existentialism can be seen to have an important part to play in casting light on some of the subtle but very powerful processes that affect group development. Sartre (1982) describes four elements or stages in group development. He uses the term 'series' to refer to a group of people who have no particular connection or shared interests.

First, he uses the example of people waiting for a bus where they are together as a form of group, but there is no sense of connection across them. The only thing that brings them together is their shared desire to catch a bus. He goes on to argue that, if the bus arrives and there is not room for everybody, then this can create conflict within that series. But it remains the case that there is no sense of shared endeavour within a series.

They are, in a sense, simply isolated individuals who happen to have come together without any real sense of shared purpose. Where teams, or indeed whole staff groups, across an organization are not functioning well, they can amount to simply being a series, without any real group identity or sense of shared endeavour. For example, I have worked as a consultant with various organizations in which there have been groups of staff who nominally have the title of a team, but in no way function as a team, as a collective unit with a shared focus. They are simply a set of individuals who happen to share the same physical office space and have similarities in terms of the type of work they are undertaking. However, they do not necessarily have any sense that they are working together in a meaningful way. There is no feeling of collectivity.

Sartre goes on to describe what he refers to as a group-in-fusion, and this relates to how people can begin to get a sense of shared endeavour by having clarity about shared goals that they are trying to achieve, and perhaps also shared values that underpin their desire to achieve those goals. A group-in-fusion is therefore much more like a functioning team than a series. People recognize that they have much to gain by working together, supporting one another and working collectively towards achieving collective goals, rather than, as in a series, simply pursuing individual goals which may then end up conflicting (remember the example of the bus that does not have room for everyone).

A group-in-fusion can evolve into what Sartre calls a sworn or pledged group. This is where there is a firm commitment, a pledge as he calls it, to working together effectively. This could be, for example, a political organization where there is a strong sense of commitment to achieving certain political goals that are rooted in the sense of shared purpose and shared values. However, it is not only political groups that can adopt this sort of pledge and become a pledged group. This can apply in workplaces, too, where there is a very significant sense of being committed to a shared endeavour. This is teamwork at its best.

However, what can also happen, according to Sartre's analysis, is that a pledged group can, over time, become an 'institutionalized group'. This is where a culture develops in which certain powerful habits can stand in the way of achieving the goals. There is a certain irony here, in that people who have initially come together with such a strong sense of collectivity can then end up losing out because of that sense of collectivity. Abiding by the culture, not wanting to rock the boat, for example, can mean that the actions of the group are institutionalized – that is, they become fixed and even stereotypically clichéd in how they respond to the challenges as a group. This echoes the notion of 'groupthink' (Janis, 1982), the process whereby groups of people sacrifice wise and balanced decision making for the sake of 'not rocking the boat' or spoiling the sense of cooperation within the group.

Voice of experience 3.1

The office I used to work at was a dreadful place, everything was so rigid and driven by habit. I know it's good to have a strong culture, but it can get to be too strong and restrictive. I liked the real sense of teamwork we had, but as a staff team we were too set in our ways, with nobody wanting to try out any new ideas or, as the cliché goes, think outside the box. It felt nice and secure to work there at first, but after a while I started to feel that we were stuck in the mud. Vibrant we were not!

Chris, a sales director in a retail organization referring to previous experiences in a marketing department in another retail organization

This is a very shortened account of Sartre's work which is quite extensive in its detailed analysis, but it should be sufficient to make the point that Sartre's approach has significant implications for leadership. We can use his ideas to recognize that there is a need for leaders to make sure that the people they lead are not simply a series and are, at the very least, a group-in-fusion. But, what an authentic leader should be aiming for is a pledged group – that is, a group that shares a pledge to achieving the vision that is part of their organizational direction. However, a leader must also try to ensure that the pledged group remains a vibrant and dynamic group, continuing to evolve in response to changing circumstances, and does not become an institutionalized group which becomes solid and rigid ('sclerotized', to use Sartre's term).

This presents significant challenges for leaders, but the existentialist idea of authenticity is helpful, in so far as its emphasis on ownership of our actions (as opposed to bad faith which denies such ownership) means that we can begin to formulate plans that are rooted in a sense of a commitment to making a positive difference. That sense of making a positive difference has to begin with individuals, in a sense, as leaders cannot force people to adopt a particular attitude or approach. However, by influencing the culture in a positive direction and developing a pledged group, effective leaders can make a huge difference in terms of how they shape the attitudes and behaviour of individuals within that pledged group.

This takes us back to our discussion of vision in Chapter 2. If the vision is not meaningful or is not communicated effectively, it can at best be irrelevant and, at worst, a source of alienation and disaffection fuelling cynicism and a mistrust of management. Developing effective groups (more than a series but less than an institutionalized group) can be helped by having a positive vision to act as a guide. By the same token, an authentic leader who is able to develop a group that takes ownership of its actions and engages positively with its tasks and duties will also be in a strong position to develop a clear, helpful and positive vision that is meaningful for those who are part of it.

THE SOCIAL CONSTRUCTION OF MEANING

As we noted in the Introduction, the dominant academic approaches to leadership (and, therefore, indirectly, leadership development and practice) have their roots in a largely science-based paradigm. However, an important element of existentialist thought is the recognition that positivistic approaches that seek to measure, categorize and regularize human behaviour are woefully inadequate when it comes to understanding and appreciating the nuances and complexities of human experience. Existentialism adopts a phenomenological approach – that is, one which affirms the central role of meaning in people's lives. If we want to understand why people behave in a particular way or to influence that behaviour in a particular direction, then we need to be fully tuned in to the significance of meaning, because, without taking account of meaning, we will have a simplistic approach to human existence that completely fails to take account of key factors that drive people forward (or prevent them from moving forward).

In my earlier work (Thompson, 2011a) I have argued for the importance of recognizing that human experience can best be understood in terms of three interconnecting levels: the personal, the cultural and the structural (referred to as PCS analysis). Underpinning this theoretical perspective is the recognition that individuals (the Personal level) do not operate in a vacuum and are strongly influenced by frameworks of meaning that shape their perception of the world and their place within it (the Cultural level). It is also important to be aware that this cultural level itself does not operate in a vacuum and that it is embedded within the wider sphere of social structures (the **S**tructural level), reflecting the fact that society is not a level playing field, but, rather, operates in terms of social divisions (class, race/ethnicity, gender and so on). One of the flaws of an atomistic approach is that it concentrates on the personal level and pays little or no attention to the wider cultural and structural levels that have a significant bearing on what happens at an individual or personal level and how meanings are formed and acted upon at that level.

So, while each individual is indeed unique and will create her or her own understanding of the world, his or her own meanings, it would be naïve not to take account of the fact that these will be strongly shaped by the wider cultural level and the frameworks of meaning that go to make up that level. What we also need to appreciate is that language is a key part of this, in so far as language not only reflects reality, but also constructs it (Thompson, 2011b). This is because language is not only the means by which we relate to other people and to wider society, but also an important part of how we construct meanings in terms of our own understandings.

PRACTICE FOCUS 3.2

Lee was a manager in a software development company. His team were a very experienced set of software engineers. They were, understandably, very technically minded, and, largely because of this, spoke in a very technical jargon that meant very little to people outside that closed circle of engineers. Lee was starting to see that this use of language was causing problems, partly in terms of the non-technical staff who felt excluded from this 'club' (although most did not want to be part of this club as they saw it as 'nerdy' or 'geeky'), but partly also in terms of relationships with customers and other stakeholders. Lee realized that he couldn't blame the engineers for their use of language, as he recognized it was the norm they were used to, but he did realize that he would have to do something about the problem, as he could see how much damage it was already doing and how there was a considerable potential for it to get much worse.

In addition, it has to be acknowledged that frameworks of meaning are also linked to frameworks of power, in so far as the effect of a particular framework of meaning operating is not neutral in terms of power relations. As Illouz (2008) comments: 'meanings differ in their ability to constrain definitions of reality: some meanings are more powerful and binding than others' (p. 9). This takes us back to PCS analysis, with its recognition that meaning is not purely an individual, psychological matter, but also something that is closely associated with cultural formations and structural patterns that tend to serve as powerful influences (pushing us in a particular direction) and, at times, significant constraints (standing in our way of moving in a particular direction).

The work of writers such as Foucault illustrates the significance of what he terms 'discourses' – that is, structures of thought and action rooted in language that have major implications in terms of power (Faubion, 2002). Consider, for example, medical discourse, as illustrated by the notion of 'doctor's orders'. The idea that doctors have the power to give instructions to individuals is rooted in this framework of meaning, whereas, in reality, there are very few instances in which doctors have a legal right to give instructions. Medical discourse therefore constructs 'advice' as orders or instructions. This clearly has implications in terms of power relations. We therefore need to recognize that, when we are talking about meanings, we are also talking about power (Thompson, 2007a).

The structural level will also shape meanings. It is therefore important to recognize that, when we look at meaning, we are not simply addressing individual perspectives. While each individual will indeed have a unique perspective, their own 'habitus', to use Bourdieu's term, that unique perspective has to be understood in the context of wider cultural and structural influences. Grenfell (2012) explains the significance of Bourdieu's concept of habitus in the following terms:

> Habitus is, Bourdieu states, 'a socialized subjectivity' and 'the social embodied' (Bourdieu & Wacquant 1992a: 127, 128) – it is, in other words, internalized structure, the objective made subjective. It is also how the personal comes to play a role in the social – the dispositions of the habitus underlie our actions that in turn contribute to social structures. Habitus thereby brings together both objective social structure

and subjective personal experiences, expressing, as Bourdieu put it, 'the *dialectic of the internalization of externality and the externalization of internality'* (1977b: 72; original emphasis). (pp. 52–3)

It is worth looking at this passage a little more closely:

- *A socialized subjectivity and the social embodied* The subjective experiences captured by the term 'habitus' always needs to be understood in relation to a wider context, to one or more fields or social arenas.
- *The dialectic of the internalization of externality and the externalization of internality* 'Internalizing the external' refers to how external, objective factors influence us and become part of our world, features of our habitus. The 'externalization of internality' refers to how we act upon the world, how our inner thoughts and feelings shape the way we respond to the outside world.

We shall return to these important ideas in Part II when we explore the dialectic of subjectivity and objectivity, but, for present purposes, I want to point out that habitus helps us to understand meaning from a sociological perspective – re-emphasizing the point that there is much more to meaning than atomism allows us to see.

Meanings are also significant in relation to organizational cultures, in so far as a culture is a set of taken-for-granted assumptions, habits and unwritten rules and therefore, in a sense, a framework of meaning in its own right. A leader who is trying to shape a culture in a positive direction is therefore engaged in a process of 're-engineering' meanings, of developing new, more positive, empowering narratives. This has strong parallels with the concept of 'narrative therapy':

> Narratives can be helpful and empowering, but they can also be self-defeating and negative, a barrier to progress. The crux of narrative approaches to helping is working with people to assist them in 'rewriting' negative or problematic narratives and replacing them with positive, life-enhancing ones. (Thompson and Thompson, 2008a, p. 254)

I am not, of course, suggesting that leaders should see themselves as some sort of organizational therapist, but there is a real sense in which a leader is helping to develop a new narrative by shaping a culture in a direction that benefits everyone. As Gilbert (2005) puts it: 'A great deal of leadership is listening to people's stories and weaving these into a larger narrative tapestry' (p. 111).

A sociological approach helps us to understand that there are dangers associated with looking at individuals in isolation, whether we are talking about individual leaders or individual followers. There is much to be gained from taking account of the very powerful influences of wider factors. It is also important to recognize that these wider factors mesh together and are not simply isolated constructs. Sartre (2003) talked about the importance of understanding how individual and social factors intermesh by using the analogy of coffee and cream. Once coffee and cream are mixed together they become a new entity, rather than simply being two separate entities side by side. This can be contrasted with the idea associated with traditional approaches to human psychology which tend to see the social context as a passive backdrop to human action, rather than something that is intermeshed with that action. So the analogy switches from one of coffee and cream, in the existentialist

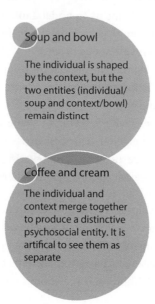

FIGURE 3.1 **Coffee and cream vs. soup and bowl**

sense, to one of soup and bowl where the soup reflects the individual who is contained (and constrained) within the bowl, but the soup and the bowl remain separate entities (Elkjaer, 2005). From an existentialist point of view, this latter conceptualization is an oversimplification of the realities of human existence in which aspects of our wider social situation become part of us, and we become part of that wider social situation (see the discussion below of dialectical reason). Sartre explained this by using the technical terminology of saying that we: 'interiorise the exterior and exteriorise the interior' (Sartre, 2003), echoing Bourdieu's comment quoted above. We will return to this point in Part II when we explore some key existentialist concepts in more detail, but for now it is important to understand that the key point being made here is that meaning needs to be understood in a wider sociological context. That context plays an active role, and is not just a passive backdrop when it comes to human thoughts, feelings and actions.

POWER AND EMPOWERMENT

I have already made the point that, when we are talking about meaning, we are also talking about power. This is important, because part of authentic leadership is to act in an empowering way and to support others in empowering themselves (as Mary Parker Follett put it as long ago as 1924). It is therefore worth considering some key issues relating to power and empowerment in order to develop a fuller understanding of leadership.

In an earlier work (Thompson, 2007a) I highlighted the four different types of power that have been identified by other thinkers in this field. It is worth exploring each of these in turn as they can be seen to have a significant impact in terms of leadership and particularly authentic leadership. The first type of power is 'power to'. This refers to having the capacity to behave in a particular way. As Coleman and Ferguson (2014) explain:

> Follett offered a view on power and authority in organizations that was a radical departure from the prevailing emphasis on power through control and coercion. She defined power simply as 'the ability to make things happen.' (p. 7)

The second type of power is 'power over'. This refers to the ability to make another person or persons behave or respond in particular ways. Power over can be used in a legitimate way, in which case it tends to go by the name of authority, or it can be used in illegitimate ways and is therefore a matter of the misuse or abuse of power. From a leadership point of view, this is particularly significant, as part of the ethos of shifting from traditional management practices towards ones based on leadership is a need to relinquish the traditional command and control approach which sees leaders as people who issue instructions and followers as people who carry out those instructions without having any opportunity or expectation to behave in innovative or more empowering ways. This is not to say that there will never be times when it is appropriate to issue instructions, but, from an authentic leadership point of view, power over needs to be seen as a last resort, to be used only when necessary, when there would be a significant price to pay if it is not used. However, if it becomes the first port of call, then it stands in the way of leadership.

The third type of power is 'power with', and this refers to solidarity. It is the power that is generated by people working together, being able to support one another towards shared goals. As Coleman and Ferguson (2014) once again helpfully explain:

> Follett suggested that one of the most effective ways of restricting the use of coercive power strategies at work was to develop the ideas, capacity, and conditions that foster *power with.* This presents employees and managers with an alternative approach to managing conflict. (p. 11)

This is clearly a key factor in terms of leadership. Part of the power dynamic that a leader will need to work on is in generating power with, of making sure that the whole is greater than the sum of the parts by bringing individuals together in ways in which they are able to get far more done (and get far more reward for getting things done) than would be the case in terms of individuals operating in isolation.

Voice of experience 3.2

When I took over the team there was no sense of team-work at all. I soon realized that my predecessor had been quite autocratic, so I had to set about changing all that. It took a little while to get the team members to take on board that my style was different and that I expected them to play a more active role in deciding how things would be run in the team. Most of them took to the idea straight away and enjoyed it once they had got past their initial reluctance. Even one person who seemed to panic if not given direct instructions to follow came round to the idea eventually.

Rob, the head of administration in a printing company

The fourth type of power is 'power from within', and this refers to the spiritual notion of certain circumstances having the effect of bringing out the best in people. For example, when somebody experiences a crisis or major loss in their life, they can, in certain circumstances, come out of that experience stronger, having benefited in some way from what they have been through. This is related to the idea of 'transformational grief' in which loss experiences can be devastating in terms of the pain, suffering and exhaustion that they bring about, but can none the less lead to people learning and growing as a result of the negative experiences they have encountered (Schneider, 2012). This, too, can be seen as an important part of leadership, in terms of the potential role for an authentic leader to help people to develop that power from within when such circumstances arise.

This brief overview of the four types of power should help to give a picture of how three of them are particularly significant in terms of how leaders need to operate if they are to achieve optimal outcomes. We have also seen that one of these powers (power over) is one that should be used only when necessary. There is a significant irony, then, that so many organizations rely heavily on that type of power and pay relatively little attention to the three forms of power that are much more suited to empowering (and effective) forms of management practice.

SOCIAL STRUCTURES AND SOCIAL PROCESSES

Earlier in this chapter, when I spoke about the benefits of PCS analysis in going beyond atomism to appreciate the powerful influences of cultural and structural factors, I made the point that the structural level is significant in terms of shaping meanings. It is now worth revisiting that idea to show how social location – that is, where people find themselves in society in terms of social divisions, such as class, race/ethnicity, gender and linguistic group – can have a significant bearing on their life experiences and, to use the technical term, their 'life chances' (the opportunities that will be brought to them or denied to them depending on where in these various hierarchies they are located). This reinforces the point I made earlier that society is not a level playing field. Where people are located will have major implications in terms of advantages and disadvantages. This will in turn shape how they experience the world, how they make sense of it, and therefore the meanings that they attach to it. So, being located in a particular setting has, from a structural point of view, implications for power in a direct sense (for example, the economic power associated with class position), but there is also the indirect issues of power that arise from the ways in which social structures influence the cultural level and the way people therefore make sense of the circumstances they find themselves in. For example, people from disadvantaged social groups can systematically receive 'messages' from the discourses at a cultural level that tell them it is not their place to achieve or to excel. This reflects Moss Kanter's (1977) view that, while powerlessness corrupts, absolute powerlessness corrupts absolutely.

It is important to be aware that PCS analysis is a dynamic approach. It is not simply a way of putting aspects of society into one of these three categories of personal, cultural or structural. The personal will constantly interact with the cultural. The cultural in turn will constantly interact with the structural. This is a development of Giddens's theory of structuration which emphasizes the importance of social processes and how they relate to the interaction of individual agency and wider social structures (Giddens, 1984).

PRACTICE FOCUS 3.3

Zafar was the newly appointed manager of a project team in the brewing industry. He was the only member of the team from a minority ethnic background and was younger than many of the team members. He was finding it difficult to get people to listen to him or take him seriously – it was as if they had no respect for him as a manager. At first, he thought it was just because they weren't used to him and the situation would improve steadily. However, if anything, it got worse over time. He sought the advice of his manager, Lynn, on the situation. She was annoyed when she heard what had been happening and began to suspect that this lack of respect was a reflection of racist attitudes towards Zafar. She therefore decided to meet with the team without Zafar being there so that she could make it clear that racist attitudes would not be tolerated. However, when she did meet with them she was amazed by their response. They were clearly very concerned that they were being perceived as racist, and seemed genuinely unaware that they had been disrespectful towards Zafar. Lynn began to wonder whether what was at issue here was not personal prejudice towards Zafar, but, rather, deeply ingrained cultural attitudes towards minority groups. She realized that there was clearly more to this situation than meets the eye.

In addition to social structures, we also need to consider social processes, as the latter are closely associated with the former, and these processes can be either positive or negative. Positive social processes would include empowerment (being able to help people gain greater control of their lives), partnership (being able to work with other people to achieve goals that would not be achievable if we worked on our own – power with) and emancipation (the process of being liberated from discriminatory and oppressive processes).

Negative social processes would include alienation (the ways in which certain people can be made to feel that they do not belong), that they are 'other', separate from the mainstream (Jaeggi, 2014). Another negative social process is 'anomie', which refers to a state of 'normlessness'.

This refers to situations in which people have no sense of how to behave in a particular set of circumstances. So, when somebody is put in a situation with cultural norms they have not encountered before, they will not know how to behave and can feel isolated and, in a sense, alienated by that process. Bourdieu also talks of 'hysteresis', which is a process involving a mismatch between habitus (what we feel comfortable with) and field (the particular context) – for example, spiritual needs in our lives being undermined by the emphasis on material factors in contemporary society (Hardy, 2012).

Although Bourdieu was not, strictly speaking, an existentialist, he was a near-contemporary of Sartre and de Beauvoir and his work fits well with theirs in a number of ways, particularly in relation to the sociological aspects of human existence. As Grenfell (2012) explains:

> Bourdieu argued that in order to understand interactions between people, or to explain an event or social phenomenon, it was insufficient to look at what was said, or what happened. It was necessary to examine the *social space* in which interactions, transactions and events occurred (Bourdieu 2005b [2000]: 148). (p. 65)

Social structures and processes are important parts of that social space. We will return to Bourdieu's ideas in Part II.

This brief overview of social structures and social processes should help to emphasize the significance of leadership in its wider social context. An approach to leadership that takes little or no account of these wider factors is clearly missing out in significant ways, and the resulting distorted and oversimplified picture can be very destructive in certain circumstances.

THE INEVITABILITY OF CONFLICT

A central concept in Sartre's existentialism is the idea that conflict is a necessary feature of human interaction. He argued, in his play, *No Exit*, that 'hell is other people', and what he meant by this is that other people can get in the way of what we are trying to achieve (Sartre, 1989). A simple, but important, example of this would be a traffic jam. If we are trying to get into, say, a city centre in the rush hour, we will be held up by the presence of hundreds or thousands of other people trying to get into that city centre at precisely that time. Other people block our efforts to achieve our goals. They stand in the way of our 'existential project' (an important concept that we will explore in more detail in Part II).

It is important to recognize that we should not confuse conflict with hostility. Sartre is not saying that fighting one another is at the heart of human experience, but what he is saying is tha there is the potential for our projects, the way we are living our lives, to get in the way of other people's projects (plans, ambitions, intentions), and, similarly, for their projects to get in our way (hostility is what can arise when conflict is not well managed). One of the implications of this is that an authentic leader needs to be tuned into the significance of conflict and have the skills and confidence to be able to address such issues constructively and effectively, rather than brush them under the carpet as a form of bad faith which attempts to deny that they exist.

Voice of experience 3.3

I always used to steer clear of conflict situations whenever I could and I wasn't really aware of what that was costing me in terms of respect from my staff. But when two staff started having a blazing row in front of everyone I had to intervene and assert my authority quite firmly. I didn't like doing it, but I was so glad I did because people started seeing me in a different light after that. I had clearly gone up in several people's estimation. Like I say, I didn't like doing it, but it made such a positive difference – I really learned a lot from that experience.

Rhodri, a deputy prison governor

A key part of conflict management is trust, respect and credibility. We return to this important theme because, where there is no trust, there is likely to be increased, rather than decreased, levels of conflict. Where there is little or no respect, again there is likely to be more, rather than less, conflict. And, if a leader lacks credibility, then their ability to address conflict issues effectively is likely to be severely undermined.

CONCLUSION

Each of the topics covered in this chapter could easily have formed the basis of a book in its own right. It therefore needs to be understood that this is by no means a comprehensive review of the significance of the social context for leadership. However, it should be sufficient to establish the key point that attempts to understand and practise leadership without a full awareness of the significance of the social context are potentially a recipe for disaster. Social aspects will, of course, also feature in later chapters as we seek to broaden and deepen our understanding of authentic leadership.

part II   Existential authenticity

CHAPTERS

INTRODUCTION TO PART II

We have already noted that existentialist theory is very complex, but it is also very powerful in explaining key aspects of leadership and the workplace context leadership is intended to address. The main focus of Part II will be to provide a good grounding in some of the relevant theoretical issues, but in a way that (i) does justice to the complexities involved; and (ii) none the less makes them clear and intelligible as a basis for practice. The various concepts introduced reinforce the importance of existential authenticity as a basis for high-quality leadership practice.

As with Part I, this part of the book has three chapters. Chapter 4, 'Authenticity and its importance', explores the key concept of 'bad faith', which refers to the common, but counterproductive, tendency to deny responsibility for our choices (and their consequences) by seeking explanations which lie outside our control. Authenticity is the opposite of bad faith; it refers to being clear about, and taking ownership of, our own actions. This is a vitally important concept for leadership, as leaders who indulge in bad faith will struggle to win the trust, respect and credibility of their followers. They will also struggle with the demands of self-leadership which can be seen to underpin high-quality leadership practice.

This chapter explains authenticity in more detail and demonstrates the problems associated with its absence and the benefits to be gained from developing it to the full.

Next comes Chapter 5, 'Understanding human existence: ontology'. It introduces a number of important existentialist concepts and explains them in ways that allow their applicability to leadership practice to be clear. The focus is on 'ontology', the study of being, which is a major underpinning of existentialism and therefore, indirectly, of leadership. The issues to be explored include:

- *The existential project* How we 'project' ourselves into the future through our choices, actions, plans and goals;
- *Being-for-others* The idea that all action is interaction; human actions do not occur in a social vacuum;
- *The dialectic of subjectivity and objectivity* How perceptions (subjectivity) interact with the outside world (objectivity) in mutually reinforcing ways;
- *The progressive-regressive method* How the present reflects influences from our past experiences (regressive) and our future hopes and ambitions (progressive); and
- *Self-creation, self-leadership and empowerment* Moving away from the essentialist notion that we each have a fixed personality; the fluid nature of identity has implications for self-leadership (and authenticity) and thus for leading others.

All terminology will be clarified, so that the philosophical jargon does not serve as an obstacle to understanding. The Glossary at the end of the book will also help you wrestle with some of the complex terminology.

Finally in Part II we have Chapter 6, which focuses on 'The role of meaning: phenomenology'. This chapter also introduces important existentialist concepts and seeks to explain them in ways that allow their applicability to leadership practice to be clear. The focus will be on 'phenomenology', the study of perception. This will include:

- *Meaning and spirituality* The inevitability of meaning-making processes and how these affect our sense of identity and how we fit into the wider world (hence the inclusion of a consideration of spirituality);
- *Identity and interaction* Explaining and exemplifying how we make choices in a context of constraints, and how those choices influence

our sense of who we are, how we relate to other people and how they relate to us (key elements of leadership practice);

- *Ontological security, trust and mistrust* Exploring how a lack of authenticity can feed a sense of insecurity and thereby replace trust with mistrust;
- *Leadership as culture management* Understanding cultures as frameworks of meaning, how powerful they are, but also how they can be changed through authentic practices; and
- *Realism: beyond optimism and pessimism* Reflecting existentialism's commitment to being holistic, seeing the whole picture, not just the positives (optimism) or just the negatives (pessimism).

Once again, all terminology will be clarified with a view to making sure that the philosophical jargon does not serve as an obstacle to understanding. This is because it is sadly the case that philosophical writings are generally based on obscure styles of writing that can distract attention from the theoretical and practical value of the ideas being (badly) expressed.

The overall 'message' of Part II is that there are important insights that can be gained from exploring existentialist thought and the light it can cast on authentic leadership. This paves the way for Part III where we shift the focus to the practice implications. Parts II and III can therefore be seen as two sides of the same coin. Both explore theory and practice issues, but in Part II theory takes centre stage, while practice hogs the limelight in Part III. The intention is that the deepening and broadening of understanding afforded by the discussions in Part II will help to equip you for getting the best results from the consideration of practice issues in Part III.

chapter 4 | Authenticity and its importance

INTRODUCTION

This chapter focuses on the key term of authenticity and tries to explain why it is of such significance in relation to leadership. In particular it seeks to differentiate the notion of existential authenticity from the essentialist authenticity that has been a feature of so many works on the subject of authentic leadership (for example, George, 2003; 2007). It will explore a number of key concepts which relate to how authenticity can be an important concept in making sense of the challenges of leadership with a view to casting light on existentialist ideas and can provide a sound foundation for developing leadership theory and practice.

We begin by clarifying what existentialism is and what distinguishes it from other schools of thought. We then examine the way in which the fluid nature of organizational culture tends not to be appreciated. This leads into a discussion of 'connectedness', a term drawn from the spirituality literature that fits well with both existentialism and leadership. Next comes an exploration of the 'dialectic of subjectivity and objectivity', a central feature of existentialist thought that has much to offer in making sense of authentic leadership. Following this is a discussion of the role of authenticity in relation to motivation. Finally, we revisit the theme of holism and argue the case for approaching authenticity from a holistic perspective.

EXISTENTIALISM

Existentialism is a philosophical approach that is generally associated with key thinkers in the early to mid-period of the twentieth century: such writers as Sartre, de Beauvoir, Merleau-Ponty and Heidegger, although in reality there are a wide range of thinkers and writers who could be included under the heading of existentialism (Camus, Fanon, Jaspers, Marcel, Merleau-Ponty, Tillich, de Unamuno and so on). In addition, although the term existentialism was not used in the nineteenth century, important contemporary thinkers, such as Kierkegaard and Nietzsche, were clearly strong influences on the development of existentialism, if not actually existentialist thinkers in their own right. There is also a significant literature relating to applied existentialist thought, especially in the counselling and psychotherapy world (van Deurzen, 2005).

In the Introduction I referred to Sartre's distinction between facticity and transcendence, and this is an important basis of existentialist thought. It acknowledges that there are things we can do nothing about (facticity) which constrain us in various ways, but it also takes account of the fact that there is always the option of transcendence, the ability to go beyond that which cannot be changed. We may not be able to do something about certain aspects of our lives, but how we respond, deal with or react to the things we cannot change are largely within our control, and that is what is meant by transcendence. For example, we may have no control over an event that happens (say, a member of staff having an accident), but we can have control over how we respond to it (Do we panic? Do we deal with the situation directly in a hands-on way? Do we get someone else to deal with it on our behalf?). Once we make a choice, we then find ourselves in a new situation, with new elements of facticity (aspects that we cannot change) and a new range of choices about how we respond to that situation (transcendence).

Authenticity, then, involves recognizing these two pillars of human experience: facticity and transcendence. Bad faith can involve a denial of either of these. It can involve not recognizing constraints and limitations and therefore becomes a form of idealism. On the other hand, it can involve not recognizing the scope for: (i) personal growth and change; and (ii) empowerment at individual and collective levels. In this regard, bad faith can be seen as a form of self-disempowerment – we deny ourselves opportunities to take greater control of our lives.

PRACTICE FOCUS 4.1	Lisa was the new manager of a planning department in a local authority. She had met most of the staff when she came for her interview and was impressed by how

friendly and welcoming they were. She could tell that there was a nice atmosphere there. On taking up her post that initial impression was strongly reinforced and she felt good about that. However, it was not all positive, as she soon started to realize that levels of confidence in the team were very low. There were lots of people telling themselves they couldn't do certain things and limiting themselves considerably in the process. It emerged that Lisa's predecessor had been quite an anxious and risk-averse manager and this had fuelled a culture of self-disempowerment, with staff members being reluctant to try anything new or go beyond just getting the basics done. Lisa recognized that she faced quite a challenge to undo all the harm that had been done, but she was none the less determined to create a more positive and confident culture that encouraged growth and development.

Existentialism, or at least some versions of it, particularly that associated with Sartre, recognize, and place firm emphasis upon, the wider social context, appreciating that this too is part of facticity – it is not just other people's actions that can get in the way of our projects, but also cultural and structural aspects of the social context that can obstruct us in various ways. However, there can also be transcendence at a social level – that is, the opportunity for groups of people, organizations or, indeed, whole societies, to bring about important political changes, even though certain aspects of our life and experience cannot be changed (at least not in the short term). Therefore, contrary to one common misperception of existentialism, it is a philosophy of hope and action, not of despair and resignation. This clearly makes it a potentially very worthwhile basis for leadership theory and practice.

Another important feature of existentialist thought that is very relevant to authenticity is the central role of flux and contingency. Flux, as we have noted, refers to the fact that human existence is dynamic – that is, constantly changing and evolving (we will return to this point below in relation to organizational culture). Contingency follows on from this and emphasizes uncertainty and unpredictability. Trying to act as if flux and contingency do not exist is a classic example of bad faith, as if to pretend that we have fixity (which is what essentialism is all about). Zimmerman (1993) relates this to eastern philosophical thought which emphasizes impermanence:

> According to Mahayana Buddhism, the truth is that all things – including humans – arise moment by moment without causation, hence from absolute 'nothingness' or emptiness, *sunyata*. Despite the apparent 'solidity' of the phenomena we encounter, they are impermanent and 'empty.' So long as humans conceive of themselves as permanent things (such as egos), suffering ensues from the craving, aversion, and delusion associated with trying to make the impermanent permanent. (p. 252)

Heidegger in particular was interested in links between eastern thought and his own ideas, but it is also fair to say that there are many parallels between aspects of eastern thought and existentialism in general (see, for example, Billington, 1990 and Froese, 2006). The aspect that is worth emphasizing here is that to be authentic involves recognizing the constantly shifting nature of the world we encounter each day and not delude ourselves into thinking that we have no scope for acting upon what appear to be fixed personalities, cultures or structures.

REIFICATION OF CULTURE

One of the important elements of leadership that has already been highlighted is the ability (and need) to shape culture in a positive direction. Authenticity is important here because, unless we take ownership for our actions individually and collectively, the ability to shape a culture in a positive direction is denied to us. As we have seen, a culture is a set of habits, taken-for-granted assumptions and unwritten rules, but this does not mean that it cannot be changed. Reification is a technical term which means taking a fluid, changing phenomenon and presenting it as if it were fixed and rigid (to reify literally means to 'treat as a thing').

A helpful concept that enables us to understand more fully how cultures work is that of autopoiesis. This is a term used in biology to refer to the self-regeneration of cells (for example, the way our skin is constantly losing cells but gaining new ones through this process of self-reproduction). The term is also used in sociology by analogy to refer to the way social systems reproduce themselves. This can be seen to apply very clearly to what happens in cultures in general and organizational cultures in particular. Habits and unwritten rules develop when a group of people come together and these become the norm, the expected actions, attitudes and expectations. As new members join the staff group they are quickly 'socialized' into the culture – that is, they quickly learn the ropes and, in their efforts to fit in and be accepted as one of the team, they then play a part in renewing the culture for a new generation of members.

What makes this a powerful and effective process is that most of the time we are not even aware that it is happening. Cultural autopoiesis happens at a very subtle level and the positive feeling of 'belonging' it generates helps to ensure that cultural norms persist over time. The culture, as a framework of meaning, thereby continues to be a strong influence. The process is generally effective even if the meanings that are being transmitted to the next generation of staff members are negative, destructive, counterproductive or dangerous. Cultures do not have a mind or will of their own – they are, in a sense, the powerful meanings that develop from the dead weight of habit, from so many people doing the same things so many times over such a long period of time. This is, of course, why leaders need to be able to tune in to the cultures they are working in and seek to shape them in a positive direction, as the culture itself could be (and often is) a major source of problems and obstacles to achieving optimal results.

Many people in organizations adopt a very deterministic approach to culture; they see it as 'just the way it is' and therefore beyond change or influence. But, given that culture comprises habits and unwritten rules that can be changed and frameworks of meaning that can be renegotiated and reshaped, this defeatist, pessimistic attitude towards culture change is unwarranted. The bad faith inherent in reifying culture denies the potential for leadership. Part of this process of reification is an effort to establish some sense of fixity. This can be a misguided approach to security. We will return to the issue of security in Part II, but for now I want to emphasize the point that trying to establish some sort of rigid, fixed, reified notion of culture is a barrier to authenticity, as it means that we are not prepared to work with the flux and contingency that are basic characteristics of human experience in general and the workplace in particular.

This notion of culture as not being fixed and immutable reflects the much wider understanding of human experience as something that is fluid and constantly changing, rather than the oversimplified notion of a fixed entity. Foley (2013) explains Bergson's (1934) view on this:

> Reality no longer appears essentially static, but affirms itself dynamically, as continuity and variation. What was immobile and frozen in our perception is warmed and set in motion. Everything comes to life around us, everything is revitalized within us. A great impulse sweeps forward beings and things. We feel ourselves uplifted, borne along, carried away. We are more fully alive and this increase of life brings with it the conviction that grave philosophical enigmas can be resolved and even perhaps that they may not be raised, since they arise from a frozen vision of the real and are only the translation, in terms of thought, of a certain artificial weakening of our vitality. (p. 12)

Bergson is not generally seen as an existentialist thinker, but in reality his philosophy chimes very well indeed with existentialist thought. Certainly when it comes to understanding flux and contingency, Bergson's work is extremely helpful. His work offers a positive approach to flux and contingency. Instead of seeing them as problems to be solved or threats to protect ourselves from, he acknowledges that flux and contingency offer the potential for channelling change in a positive direction – what should be familiar territory for an authentic leader.

Voice of experience 4.1

For ages I thought that organizational culture was something you just had to learn to live with and could do nothing about, but then I went on a two-day leadership course and a lot of the focus was on what you could do to influence a culture. It totally changed my mindset about culture. The trainer was quite clear that there are no short cuts or easy answers when it comes to culture change, but I suppose I had been at the other extreme of assuming there was nothing you could do.

Sean, a manager in a construction company

Cooper (2012) argues that: 'To be an authentic individual entails that one stands in appropriate relationships to other human beings' (p. 44), and so, from a leadership perspective, we can see that how we relate to other people is part of authenticity. This brings us to the important notion of 'connectedness' and it is to this that we now turn.

CONNECTEDNESS

The term 'connectedness' has its roots in the spirituality literature (Hyde, 2008) and refers to the importance given to how people relate to one another and how our sense of being part of something larger than ourselves is an essential part of our spirituality. This is often the role that religion plays for many people in terms of their spirituality, but, of course, we should not make the mistake of assuming that religion is the only form of spirituality. While not everybody is religious, everybody has spiritual needs (for a sense of meaning, purpose and direction, for example) and spiritual challenges. Existentialism has much to offer our understanding of spirituality in general (Thompson, 2007b) and in relation to connectedness in particular (for example, Sartre's work on the significance of group dynamics as discussed in Chapter 3). Schultz (2005) comments on how the use of existentialist ideas can increase the sense of connectedness:

> In concrete terms, applying existential concepts leads to the idea that employees, by virtue of their increased connectedness, will change their workplace fewer times. The company and the employee will feel genuine loyalty and motivation towards each other, and their competency will improve. The company will find it easier to attract new workers and capital from the outside, and can to a greater degree fulfill its employees', customers' and others' expectations. (p. 4)

In Chapter 3 we explored the role of meaning as a key factor underpinning leadership. Spirituality is, of course, also concerned with matters relating to, among other things, meaning. Writers such as Zohar and Marshall (2001) have made the case for leaders to incorporate spirituality into their approach to leadership. They use the term SQ as a parallel with IQ to refer to the 'intelligence quotient' associated with spiritual intelligence – that is, a leader's ability to help people find meaning in their work. As Gill (2011) explains:

> Spiritual leadership is about creating meaning and value for people, in their work life, family life or community life. Zohar and Marshall suggest that a high-SQ leader is likely to be a servant leader: 'bringing higher vision and values to others and showing them how to use it ... a person who inspires others' [Zohar and Marshall, 2001, p. 16]. Spiritual intelligence does not merely reflect existing values: it leads to new values. (p. 314)

While I have my doubts about the wisdom of trying to measure spiritual intelligence and give it some sort of meaningful score, I do recognize the value of leaders taking seriously the challenge of making working life meaningful. This fits well with the existentialist approach to authenticity and meaning. We shall return to this topic in Chapter 6.

Leadership is based on interaction with individuals and groups, and this makes it a highly complex phenomenon. It therefore needs to be recognized that a key element of leadership is the ability to manage complexity (Hames, 2007). People do not operate in a vacuum, as we have seen. There are the cultural and structural factors to be considered. Also, if, as Sartre says, existential authenticity involves recognizing the situation we are in and its implications (particularly our role in changing or sustaining that situation), then authentic leadership needs to be premised on a recognition of the key role of interaction, and thus of communication. In turn, we need to recognize the central role of communication in connectedness, in creating a sense of shared endeavour. It goes without saying, of course, that leaders need to be effective communicators. However, communicating in ways that create a sense of connectedness involves a set of skills above and beyond day-to-day communication and interaction (which takes us back to our discussion in Chapter 2 of the importance of being able to communicate a vision effectively).

Focusing on individuals in isolation can therefore be seen as a significant barrier to authentic leadership, as it fails to appreciate the central role of such factors as communication, interaction and connectedness. One existentialist concept that can be helpful in this regard is Buber's distinction between I-Thou and I-it (Buber, 2013) that we discussed in Chapter 2. As noted earlier, communication can be reduced to simply conveying information and doing so in ways that harm trust, respect and credibility and which can be disempowering for the person(s) on the receiving end of that communication (I-it). On the other hand, communication can be empowering and bring about a genuine human connection that strengthens trust, respect and credibility (I-Thou). It is this latter, of course, that contributes to connectedness, to helping people feel that they belong and that they are part of something bigger than themselves.

Another important implication of this is that authentic managers need to be able to manage their own pressures, concerns and anxieties (with appropriate support as required) and not take them out on others (as happens in occurrences of bullying). It is quite possible, and sadly more common than should be the case, for managers to respond to their own high level of pressure by relating to other people in an I-it way – for example, by simply issuing instructions to them and not having any meaningful I-Thou type of interaction with them.

This concept of connectedness, the way in which human beings actually relate to one another, is therefore very important in terms of authentic leadership. If a leader relies on I-it interactions, and is not able to develop the skills, confidence and commitment to engage with people in I-Thou ways, then their ability to bring about positive change will be severely limited. Cooper (2012) captures well the link between connectedness and authenticity:

> in order to live authentically – in full awareness, that is, of my freedom – I must honor the freedom of others and work with them to foster a communion of human beings living in recognition of their reciprocal freedom. To be authentic, as Marcel remarks, is not only to 'apprehend' the other as free, but to 'collaborate with his freedom,' [Marcel, 1949] while, in Heidegger's words, people are 'authentically bound together' only when each 'frees the other in his freedom for himself.' [Heidegger, 1962] (p. 46)

PRACTICE FOCUS 4.2

Siân, a receptionist in a technology company, had always seen her job as a way of earning a living. She enjoyed meeting lots of people and was very skilful at making them feel welcome, but that didn't alter the fact that to her it was just a job. When a new managing director was appointed and he invited all the staff to a meeting to hear his 'vision' for the company, she wasn't sure what it was all about and what it had to do with her. However, her view changed during the meeting when the new MD spelled out very effectively what the company was trying to achieve and what good the company's products could do in making people's lives easier. For the first time she started to feel that she was part of an important enterprise. The previous MD hadn't made anyone feel they were doing something important, but now Siân could see that the new MD was much more inclusive and that felt good. Her priority would remain earning a living, of course, but she could see her job and its importance in a new light.

THE DIALECTIC OF SUBJECTIVITY AND OBJECTIVITY

Throughout the history of western thought there have been various approaches that have emphasized subjectivity, the importance of understanding situations from the point of view of the individual concerned. There have also been schools of thought that have emphasized the importance of objectivity and the need to get past subjective experiences, seeing them as unreliable and biased, and trying to establish some sort of scientific truth. From an existentialist point of view, both of these approaches are doomed to failure. This is because they both oversimplify a complex human reality. The idea behind the dialectic of subjectivity and objectivity is the need to take account of the fact that subjective and objective elements will be constantly interacting. That is, how a person perceives the world will be very important in how they relate to the world, but that perception will not exist in a vacuum. Once again, we are back to recognizing the significance of the wider context, and that can be a wider context of facticity and objective constraints. It would be therefore naïve for us to posit the idea of an individual's subjectivity that is totally uninfluenced by wider objective factors.

On the other hand, however, it can be seen as naïve to assume that we can achieve total objectivity without consideration of subjective factors (and this brings us back to the critique of positivism discussed earlier). A leadership approach that denies or marginalizes the subjective element (as sadly much of the leadership literature tends to do) therefore fails to achieve authenticity. Authentic leaders need to be able to recognize the subjective elements and the significance of perception and emotions, for example, in shaping how events unfold within the workplace (this is a key element of the existentialist idea that we need to take account of what it means to be human, including the subjective and emotional dimensions).

Because this dialectic is a dynamic process, it is a driving force for change. Change management is, of course, part of what leaders are expected to deal with. However, given that, from an existentialist perspective, change is seen as constant, this makes the notion of change management more complex than it is usually thought. It can be helpful to understand two types of change:

- *Everyday flux* In a sense, all management is the management of change, given that human beings are constantly 'becoming'. This is one of the reasons that leadership is so important, as it involves

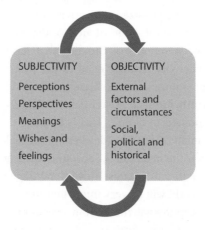

FIGURE 4.1 **The dialectic of subjectivity and objectivity**

guiding that process of becoming in a positive direction. (We will return to this important point in Chapter 5.)

- *Change initiatives* Where organizations deliberately initiate change this intensifies the need for effective leadership in carrying the change through.

Bergson, whose ideas on change we touched on earlier, highlights some problems with common attitudes towards change:

> So change is the essence of process. But our contemporary attitudes to change are an unhealthy mixture of worship and denial. The worship is for novelty, change for the sake of change, and the denial is of the inevitable organic changes in matter, both inanimate and living, and especially of ageing and death. (1934, p. 13)

This represents the two types of change, with change initiatives reflecting the worship element, the constant stream of change initiatives that are rarely successful in achieving what they set out to do, while the denial element relates to the essentialism that underpins the reification of culture, as discussed earlier, with its assumption of fixity. This helps us to appreciate that an existentialist approach to leadership establishes that we need to go beyond a simplistic understanding of change which superficially counterposes change initiatives with the supposed stability. The reality is that what we perceive as stability is a slow process of change, with the autopoiesis of culture acting as a brake to keep that process slow.

Voice of experience 4.2

I have never understood all the emphasis on change management and why people seem semi-obsessed with change. They don't seem to appreciate that change is the normal state – our friends in the East have known that for a long time. We need to be more tuned in to the fact that we should be focusing on managing the change we have got rather than imposing changes on people and alienating them in the process.

Sam, a university lecturer in management studies

MOTIVATION

It is commonly assumed that leaders are expected to motivate their staff, if not actually inspire them. In reality, though, the situation is much more complex than is generally assumed. For one thing, Kouzes and Posner (2007) point out that:

> Researchers in human motivation have long talked about two kinds of motivation – extrinsic and intrinsic. People do things either because of external controls – the possibility of a tangible reward if they succeed or punishment if they don't – or because of an internal desire. People do something because they feel forced, or because they want to. People do something to please others, or because it pleases them. Which condition is more likely to produce extraordinary results?
>
> On this, the research is very clear. External motivation is more likely to create conditions of compliance or defiance; self-motivation produces far superior results. There's even an added bonus. People who are self-motivated will keep working toward a result even if there's no reward. But people who are externally controlled are likely to stop trying once the rewards or punishments are removed. In this case, as psychologist and motivational expert Edward Deci has so aptly put it, 'Stop the pay, and stop the play'. (pp. 115–16)

This passage raises two important issues:

1. Leadership, by shaping meaning within cultures, creates the potential for increasing intrinsic motivation. Kouzes and Posner refer to intrinsic motivation as deriving from an internal desire. However, this is an atomistic assumption, as there is more to intrinsic motivation than internal desire. Intrinsic motivation can be nurtured by authentic leadership in which the individual concerned feels valued, supported, safe and validated and part of an important enterprise (connectedness). There are therefore wider aspects of intrinsic motivation than simply internal desire.
2. They are right to suggest that intrinsic motivation is likely to produce better results. Command and control approaches are much more likely to produce superficial compliance at best and, quite possibly

resentment and even sabotage (Furnham and Taylor, 2004). Intrinsic motivation is based on meaning – doing what needs to be done to move forward constructively happens because the personnel concerned are 'on board' in terms of what the staff group and/or whole organization is trying to achieve.

To motivate someone literally means to 'move' them. This can be done by either pressurizing them (which can range from gentle persuasion to coercion) or by creating the right circumstances for people to motivate themselves. Indeed, there is an argument that only the latter is genuine motivation, as the former has only a short-term effect – that is, once the pressure stops, so does the 'motivation' in most cases. However, where it is possible to create the right circumstances for people to motivate themselves, that motivation can be ongoing. There is a parallel here with empowerment, in the sense that it is rarely, if ever, possible for one person to empower another – what really needs to be involved is a process whereby the circumstances are created in which people can empower themselves (Thompson, 2007a).

It is this notion of creating the right circumstances for people to motivate themselves that links motivation to inspiration. As Zeldin (2004) puts it: 'Inspire others and you will feel inspired yourself' (cited in Gill, 2011, p. 255). This links with the important existential notion of spirituality, as both terms – inspiration and spirituality –have their roots in the notion of 'breath'. To inspire can be understood to mean to breathe life into, while spirit is linked to the Greek word *pneuma*, which means breath.

Motivation is also an important part of what has come to be known as 'transformational leadership'. As Gill (2011) explains:

Transforming or transformational leadership occurs when both leader and followers raise each other's motivation and sense of higher purpose. Transactional leadership on the other hand involves a transaction, or exchange, between leader and followers, such as providing a material or psychological reward in return for followers' compliance with the leader's wishes, with no sense of any higher purpose. Transforming leadership, according to Burns, addresses people's higher-order needs for achievement, self-esteem and self-actualization. It encourages them to look beyond self-interest for the common good. Transforming leadership raises both leaders and followers to 'higher levels of motivation and morality' [Burns, 1978, p. 20] whereas transactional leadership merely reflects what or how people are, appealing to their existing needs, desires and preferences. (pp. 81–2)

There are echoes here of Buber's important distinction between I-Thou and I-it. Leadership is not simply a matter of getting other people to do your bidding. It is the much more complex notion of creating an atmosphere where people are keen to work together to achieve shared goals, empowering themselves and each other in the process. Of course, this is a much more difficult endeavour than it might initially sound, but the efforts required to achieve this end result are more than justified by the rewards that can be gained. Chapter 8 explores some of the challenges involved in this by exploring some case scenarios that present a range of difficulties.

One further aspect of motivation to consider is the role of values. Kouzes and Posner (2007) again make apt comment in arguing that:

Values are empowering. We are much more in control of our own lives, as Radha found, when we're clear about our personal values. When values are clear we don't have to rely on direction from someone in authority. (p. 53)

They go on to argue that:

Values also motivate. They keep us focused on why we're doing what we're doing and on the ends toward which we're striving. Values are the banners that fly as we persist, as we struggle, as we toil. We refer to them when we need to replenish our energy. (p. 53)

Values can be seen as an important part of authenticity, in the sense that integrity involves ensuring that our actions are consistent with our values. If we were to espouse and profess a certain set of values and not act in accordance with them, then we would be indulging in bad faith. If it were apparent to others that we were doing this, then that could have very significant consequences in terms of the level of trust, respect and credibility we enjoy.

PRACTICE FOCUS 4.3

> Mark was head of the claims investigation service in an insurance company. He was actually quite a values-driven person who played things strictly by the book, but he liked to joke about behaving in an unethical way, as if the job was about conning people out of monies they were entitled to. He didn't think it was doing any harm – it was just a bit of fun. However, matters came to a head when Wendy, one of the most experienced members of the team, left and, in her exit interview with one of the HR staff, mentioned that one of the reasons she was leaving was that she was fed up of Mark's lack of integrity and his constant unethical behaviour. It turned out that his joking had backfired on him.

A HOLISTIC APPROACH

I have already argued the case for moving beyond an atomistic approach that focuses simply on individuals in isolation and having a broader, fuller perspective that looks at the overall picture. This can be understood as a 'bio-psychosocial and spiritual' approach (Thompson, 2012a). It is important to break this down into its component parts. 'Bio' refers to biology, the reality of the constraints and opportunities placed on us by our biological nature and the biological processes that underpin our engagement with the physical world. However, it would be an example of bad faith to place too much emphasis on the biological and argue, for example, that certain aspects of human behaviour are purely the result of biology, without considering the influence of wider factors. For example, it has been a common argument over the years to justify discrimination and oppression that difference between ethnic groups, between genders and between other social groups are rooted in a biological determinism (Thompson, 2011a).

There is also a psychological element to be considered, of course. How we think, feel and behave as biological beings will also be significant. Sadly, some managers seem to see psychology as simply a set of ideas to help manipulate others into doing what they want – a sort of behaviour modification programme. However, more realistically, we can see that psychology is a key part of being human (in terms of how we are influenced by a range of factors to establish patterns of thoughts, feelings and actions that become so well established that we come to believe that they are our 'true nature', our 'real self' – our 'essence'). So-called 'common-sense' understandings of psychology can therefore be seen as gross oversimplifications of much more complex existential processes by which we come to define ourselves in response to the wide range of influences that we are exposed to.

The social elements, as we noted in Chapter 3, are also important and if we fail to pay them adequate attention, we present a distorted and distorting picture of human reality. Human beings do not exist in a social vacuum. Our lives are inherently social and if we lose track of the significance of this, we fall foul of atomism and end up with a very one-sided picture of human experience, one that leaves us ill equipped to respond effectively to the human demands of authentic leadership.

Finally, there is the spiritual dimension to consider: how people make sense of the world and their place within it, how they develop the sense of meaning, purpose and direction. These are, of course, not just spiritual concerns relating to religion, but also existential concerns in terms of what it means to be a human being. If we neglect the spiritual dimension, we present a dehumanized picture of the people we seek to lead, and thereby fail to be authentic (and fully effective).

This holistic approach rooted in ideas of bio-psychosocial and spiritual elements can be linked with the leadership concept of vision, in so far as a holistic perspective provides an overview. It addresses the 'big picture', rather than getting bogged down in detail or being partial in its view by emphasizing one element to the neglect of others.

In terms of authenticity, we can link bad faith to each of the four elements. As I have already mentioned, there is a common tendency for biological issues (facticity) to be presented as a whole story with no mention of the potential for transcendence, and this is a common tactic in terms of attempting to justify inequality (Thompson, 2011a). At a psychological level, there can also be bad faith in the form of people trying to argue that their upbringing or their personality or some other determining factor prevents them from acting in good faith. There can also be social aspects of bad faith in the form of people trying to explain their behaviour in terms of their gender, their social class or other aspect of social location, without recognizing that this addresses only the facticity aspect of the equation and not the transcendence – so, again denying authenticity. And then, finally, there can be bad faith in relation to the spiritual elements – for example, through dogmatic adherence to a particular worldview, whether that is religious or secular, which is then used to justify actions, as if there were no individual choice or transcendence involved in them.

> **Voice of experience 4.3**
>
> It never ceases to amaze me how many different ways people seem to be able to find to not take responsibility for their actions. If it isn't one thing it's another. I am constantly having to challenge people and try to get them to take on board that being a leader involves taking ownership. Sometimes they get the point but often they don't.
>
> Sandra, a leadership development trainer

We should also not forget that part of adopting a holistic approach is the acknowledgement of the dynamic nature of human existence, the role of constant change, as discussed earlier. It is not simply a matter of recognizing four dimensions of human experience. We also have to be aware that these four elements will interact with one another and contribute to the constantly evolving nature of life, to the flux that is characteristic of human existence.

CONCLUSION

We have already touched on Tillich's (2000) idea of the 'courage to be', which can be related for our purposes to the 'courage to lead', involving having the courage to risk failure. This helps us to understand that leaders, just like everybody else, are human and therefore vulnerable. The leader is not intended to be someone who is some sort of invulnerable hero, but, rather, a human being with all the fragilities that this implies.

It is therefore to be hoped that an authentic leader can have the courage, impetus and skills to achieve the best in difficult circumstances, while recognizing that, underneath this, are flux and contingency. That is, there is always the potential for things to go wrong and to deteriorate.

The courage to lead is therefore about the courage to be human and vulnerable. Authenticity involves acknowledging that vulnerability and appreciating how this is part of the wider picture of what it means to be a human being. Once we lose sight of that 'humanness' and its central role in leadership, we fail to be authentic.

chapter 5

Understanding human existence: ontology

INTRODUCTION

This is the second of three chapters exploring how understandings based on existentialism can offer us a clearer picture of the complexities involved in human existence in general and leadership in particular. It builds on the ideas about authenticity discussed in Chapter 4 and paves the way for the discussion of the central role of perception and meaning in Chapter 6. It focuses on four particular existentialist concepts that have much to offer by way of explanatory power. I provide an overview of each of these in turn so that we can see how they cast significant light on important aspects of human existence. This knowledge will then be very useful in developing authentic forms of leadership.

To begin with it is important to explain the term 'ontology'. This refers to the study of being and is therefore an important underpinning of existentialism. In fact, Sartre's major work on existentialism, *Being and Nothingness*, has the subtitle of 'An Essay on Phenomenological Ontology' (Sartre, 2003). Phenomenology is the study of perception and is therefore concerned with meaning ('phenomenon' comes from the Greek word for 'that which is perceived' or 'that which appears'). We will focus more closely on this in the following chapter where these issues are to the fore, but for now I simply want to explain that Sartrean existentialism is based on the idea of adopting a phenomenological approach to the study of being – that is, an approach to understanding what it means to be human in terms of the significant roles of perception and meaning.

Our first topic to be explored is the existential project. This is followed by a focus on 'being-for-others', returning to the theme of the importance of considering wider social factors. Next comes a discussion of the dialectic of subjectivity and objectivity and, finally, the progressive-regressive method. The topics covered relate to technical terms that can be quite intimidating if you are not used to them. But please note that each one is explained, both in this chapter as they arise and in the Glossary at the end of the book.

THE EXISTENTIAL PROJECT

'Project' is a term used by Sartre in a specific technical way. It is closely allied to the usage of the term in everyday language, but is more specific. If we go back to the idea that we are radically free – that is, that we cannot choose not to choose – then each day we are making decisions and acting upon them in ways that will not only shape our future in terms of the doors we open and the doors that we subsequently close, but also in terms of how we are, through that process, creating ourselves. We are creating a sense of who we are by making certain choices. In this way, the choices we make now are *projecting* us into the future. If we think of the term project literally, it means to throw forward; 'pro' meaning forward and 'ject' coming from the Latin word for to throw (*iacere*). Just as a missile can also be described as a projectile, it is something that moves forward. So the idea of the existential project is the recognition that we are not fixed entities on a journey through life but, in a sense, our identity relates to being that journey. We are not a fixed individual on a journey, but that journey is what makes us who we are. This is fundamentally the idea of the existential project. We are constantly engaging with what happens in our life which will be a mixture of facticity and transcendence (and the interactions between them). We are faced with a constant stream of choices and how we relate to those choices will then shape our path forward through our lives.

This concept of the existential project is therefore an important way of explaining identity, selfhood and human behaviour at an individual level, but we also have to be aware that we can have shared existential projects. A simple example of this would be a marriage whereby two people make a commitment to moving forward through their lives together. They project themselves forward as a couple, and so this illustrates nicely the idea of a shared project. The conflicts inherent in such a notion of a shared project explain why so many marriages fail, but it is the ability to handle those conflicts that can make for a successful marriage or, indeed, any successful relationship. But it can be more than just couples. As we saw earlier, there can be group projects where teams can come together with shared goals and move beyond being a series to becoming a group-in-fusion and beyond that into a pledged group. These shared projects reflect what Gadamer (2004) referred to as a fusion of horizons. This relates to how individuals have the capacity to work together to manage their projects (their horizons) in a meaningful and mutually supportive way. How successful these efforts are will, of course, depend largely on the quality of leadership.

PRACTICE FOCUS 5.1	Viv was the chief executive of a large charity. She had achieved promotion after promotion to get there at a relatively young age. What had driven her was not so much ambition in the conventional sense of a desire to get to the top, but, rather, great clarity about what she wanted to achieve in each of the roles she had occupied. She had the impressive ability to develop a clear personal vision of what her goals were to be and what steps she would need to follow to achieve them. When it came to trust, respect and credibility, her clarity about her personal vision – her existential project – gave her these in spades. She came across as quite a charismatic character because she had this clear focus and somehow managed to inspire others to be clear about where they were trying to get to and how they were going to get there.

The existential project is a useful concept for understanding self-hood and identity as self-creation – that is, the notion that we are not fixed individuals, but constantly developing, constantly evolving through our lives as a result of the circumstances we find ourselves in and how we react to them, what choices we make, what direction we take ourselves in. This raises the important question of self-leadership (Gilbert, 2005). This refers to how it can be helpful, if we are intending to lead others, to have clarity about how we are leading ourselves. Are we clear about our own vision and our own path for achieving that vision in our life?

The notion of project should not be confused with having a fixed set of expectations about how our life should unfold. The project is generally fluid – that is, it changes and evolves in response to new events, new insights and new experiences in our lives. It fits with the idea in spirituality about the importance of having sense of direction and purpose that helps to give meaning to our lives.

However, it is not merely a plan, in the conventional sense, that we can choose to have or dispense with. The existential projects refers to the necessity to choose how we move forward in our life. This relates back to my earlier comments about the existentialist notion of radical freedom which means that we cannot choose not to choose, as that in itself is a choice. From an existentialist point of view we are constantly projecting ourselves into the future through our choices and actions and thereby creating our present selves in the process. The key issue, from a (self-)leadership point of view, is the degree of awareness we have over the choices we are making and therefore the direction we are heading in (and, to a certain extent, the direction we are taking others in with us).

One (common) option is to refuse to take responsibility for our project and, in bad faith, convince ourselves that 'whatever will be will be' and wait passively to see what the future brings, as if we have no say in what happens to us or how events unfold. Of course, it is quite right that there will be much about the future that we will have no control over (facticity), but there will also always be the question of how we respond to these matters (transcendence). Fatalism can therefore be seen as a form of bad faith which overemphasizes the role of facticity and denies (or minimizes) the role of transcendence, the choices we can and must make in response to the aspects of facticity we are presented with.

The concept of existential project can also help us to understand the role of leadership in bringing people together with a shared and coherent sense of what they are trying to achieve in unison. As we have seen, a key part of a leader's role will be playing a primary role in forging a shared 'narrative' that unites people in their endeavour. This is, in effect, a process of creating a joint existential project, the fusion of horizons I mentioned earlier.

This is a skilled undertaking, involving the need to bring people together and make a commitment to making things work (rather than simply doing as they are told within a command and control frame of reference). As Ladkin (2010) acknowledges:

Without such shared meaning, leadership visions can be hollow pronouncements. Accomplishing shared meaning is a dynamic activity itself which occurs amongst those who engage with it and consequently co-create it. (p. 124)

Voice of experience 5.1

The best manager I have ever worked with was a man called Colin. He was really good at being inclusive and making sure that everybody's voice was heard. He has this great ability to make us feel that what we were doing was important and so it was only right that we have our say in what happened. There was no doubt that he was the boss, but he still made everybody feel that we were working together, that we were all singing from the same hymn sheet. A lovely man.

Andrea, a manager with a housing association

BEING-FOR-OTHERS

This is a term used by Sartre to refer to the idea that we carry on our lives in relation to other people – that is, we react to circumstances that involve other people and do not operate in isolation. It is important to understand, for example, that what are often seen as individual factors could not exist if they were not linked to other people. For example, Sartre has written about the significance of shame and how it is related to the influence of other people's expectations. If there were no other people to have expectations of us, then shame could not exist as a concept (Sartre, 2003). It is, by definition, a social concept and illustrates well the idea of being-for-others. This is another argument against atomism and the tendency to focus narrowly, if not exclusively, on the individual level.

It helps us to recognize that, not only are we operating in a broad social context in terms of cultural and structural factors, but also we are constantly interacting with other people.

This idea of shame as an example of being-for-others was discussed by Sartre in relation to the concept of 'the look'. What he meant by this is the idea that our behaviour will often be influenced by our expectations of how other people are perceiving us. This means that much of what seems like self-directed actions are actually directed towards what others expect of us. For example, we may behave in ways that are considered polite and well-mannered because we are living up to the expectations of our cultural upbringing to do so. This illustrates the inherently social and interpersonal nature of human existence. As Tillich (2000) reminds us:

> Individualism is the self-affirmation of the individual self as individual self without regard to its participation in its world. As such it is the opposite of collectivism, the self-affirmation of the self as part of a larger whole without regard to its character as an individual self. (p.113)

This brings us back to the idea of selfhood and identity. In his earlier work, Sartre argued that we are what we make ourselves (Sartre, 2007). That is, we have choices that fall upon us each day, and the decisions we take in response to those choices will have a major impact on how our life pans out. In effect, our identity will be formed through the constant choices that we are making, the constant choice of direction: whether to continue as we are, to change or whatever. These will all be part of our evolving sense of self which continues throughout our life.

This approach was subsequently criticized for failing to take account of the wider social context. Therefore, in his later work in which he strongly emphasized the significance of the social context, Sartre took the opportunity to extend his original notion so that it was no longer open to this criticism of being atomistic (Sartre, 1973; 1982). He therefore changed his view from 'we are what we make ourselves', into 'we are what we make of what is made of us'. This was a significant change as it took account of the importance of the social context. We do not operate in a vacuum in which we simply make choices which then shape us as if we are totally unrestricted. Sartre needed to extend his conception of facticity to include such things as culture and social structures, the wider sociopolitical factors that can close off certain doors for us and push us towards other doors. However, it is important not to make the mistake of assuming that what Sartre is saying is that we are what our social circumstances make of us. He was very clear that there are two elements to this – his work was certainly not making deterministic assumptions.

We are what we make of what is made of us means that we have to recognize the facticity arising from the constraints and influences of sociopolitical factors, but still hold on to the fundamental notion of agency – that is, of the ability to transcend those social factors. This opens the door to empowerment at individual and collective levels.

It is a matter of avoiding the unhelpful extremes. If we adopt the individualistic end of the spectrum and assume that wider social factors play no significant part in our lives, then we are descending into atomism and relying on a distorted picture of human existence. We can end up with an idealistic picture of what an individual can achieve and/or blame individuals for matters that are largely beyond their control (for example, assuming that someone who is homeless has simply chosen to be so, as if poverty and deprivation, abuse and trauma, family violence and so on play no part in presenting someone with a set of circumstances in which being homeless is preferable to, say, being abused). At the other end of the spectrum we have social determinism, the idea that individuals are passive victims of their social circumstances – for example, the idea that women in a patriarchal society may as well give up any hope of breaking through the glass ceiling.

The reality is far more complex than either of these simplistic extremes. Social factors have a very strong influence on people's lives (facticity), but much depends on how we react, individually and collectively, to these circumstances (transcendence). What it amounts to is that no one has complete control over their lives, but, by the same token, there is no one who has no control over their lives – hence, we are what we make of what is made of us. The idea of control is linked, of course, to power, and this is where empowerment comes into the picture. Recognizing that we always have some degree of control over our circumstances can help fend off defeatism and cynicism (without going to the other extreme of idealism) and help us explore what our options are. We will return to this point below when we explore the dialectic of subjectivity and objectivity.

Leadership is an example par excellence of being-for-others, of being aware of the fact that everything we do is related, in one way or another, to other people. In a sense, the set of habits that form an organizational culture reflect the habitualized ways that people have related to one another up to now. This presents current members of that organization with the choice of reinforcing and sustaining the culture by behaving in accordance with those habits or playing a part in reshaping that culture by behaving in ways that differ from – and thereby challenge – the habits that make the culture what it is in its present form. Leadership, as a process of culture shaping, involves reinforcing those aspects of a culture that are positive and helpful and seeking to change those aspects that are destructive and unhelpful.

In a sense, a culture is a representation of the legacy of past (and present) members of the organization – the frameworks of meaning they constructed. In this way, being-for-others has a cross-temporal dimension – that is, we are, in the present, being influenced by people from the past whose actions and attitudes constructed the culture that is now a strong influence on our present actions and attitudes. For example, if in the past there have been sexist or racist views held in an organization, these may have passed into today's culture in less overt forms. For example, if sexist forms of language developed in response to sexist views held by a previous generation of workers, the sexist language may still persist in the present culture, even if the sexist views no longer do in the present personnel.

PRACTICE FOCUS 5.2

Sylvia was a human resources manager in a large communications company. She was quite concerned when she was informed by the senior union rep that he wanted to meet with her to discuss allegations of racism in the company. She was surprised because she was aware that the company employed quite a few people from minority ethnic groups and she had not been made aware of any difficulties. However, when she met with the union official she soon realized that the situation was more complex than this. She was presented with evidence that strongly suggested there was institutional discrimination going on. She was given statistics covering the previous 12 months about the ethnic origin of job applicants, the people shortlisted for interview and the successful applicants. She could see quite a few applicants from ethnic minorities, relatively few shortlisted and not a single one successful. She had to admit that the statistics looked quite worrying. She knew she would have to look at the situation quite closely and look at it more holistically, not just from the point of view of the existing minority ethnic staff who had not been raising any concerns about racism.

Underpinning the idea of existential authenticity is a commitment to the principle that organizational success comes through people (Thompson, 2013a), in the sense that, if you do not get your people issues right, it is unlikely that other aspects of organizational life will succeed. The definitions of leadership that I mentioned earlier were criticized for being atomistic, for remaining at the level of the individual. It is to be hoped that this discussion of being-for-others has shown why such a definition is not sufficient and why there needs to be a more holistic understanding of leadership. It is not simply a matter of seeking to influence individuals, but, rather, to be more attuned to wider social and interpersonal matters, so that we are better placed to influence them, Trying to influence individuals without taking account of – and trying to shape – the wider context in which they are operating, is likely to be far less effective than a more holistic view that begins to do justice to the complexities involved in human beings working together in the structured environment of the workplace.

THE DIALECTIC OF SUBJECTIVITY AND OBJECTIVITY

We encountered this concept in Chapter 4 and I emphasized there that existentialism offers us a useful understanding of how we need to take account of both subjective and objective factors and how these relate closely to the ideas of transcendence and facticity, respectively. It is therefore a matter of emphasizing that, when it comes to subjectivity and objectivity, we need to talk about both/and rather than either/or. In particular we need to recognize the interaction (the dialectic) of the two. My subjective experiences, for example, will be strongly influenced by the objective circumstances I find myself in, but those objective circumstances will also be influenced, to a certain extent at least, by my subjective reaction to them. For example, if I find myself in an objective situation where I feel uncomfortable or even in danger, then I can use my subjective transcendence to make the decision to leave those circumstances where possible. In a leadership context, this could be in a meeting where I feel I am being pressurized into doing something that I believe to be unethical or otherwise not something I could agree to, then I could use my assertiveness skills to resist the pressure and, ultimately leave the meeting if necessary. So, the fact that someone has chosen to put me under pressure is something I can do nothing about (facticity), it remains the case that I can choose how I respond to it (transcendence). If I were to leave the meeting, I may then be criticized for doing so. This then becomes a new incidence of facticity and I am now faced with the challenge of how I use my transcendence in terms of how I choose to respond to that criticism (ignore it, justify my actions, criticize the person who put me under pressure in the first place, and so on).

The notion of 'dialectic' is important, because it refers to not only the dynamic, constantly changing, evolving nature of social circumstances, but also the fact that that change owes much to conflict. Change will come about very often through the interaction of conflicting or opposing forces. It is not simply that things change because events happen at random, but rather because there are patterns of interacting forces which come into conflict and bring about change. As Coleman and Ferguson (2014) comment:

> Conflict is not an inherently bad thing. It is natural, fundamental, and pervasive part of life. It is what happens when things are opposed – when different interests, claims, preferences, beliefs, feelings, values, ideas, or truths collide. (p. 1)

For example, at a political level, change will often take place because of competing ideologies about what constitutes a strong and appropriate platform for society.

The dialectic of subjectivity and objectivity helps us, then, to appreciate the dynamic nature of not only existence in general, but also of the workplace in particular. It therefore has implications for leadership. One of the criticisms that is often levelled at management is that there is too much change, that there is often what appears to be change for change's sake. For example, much cynicism has developed over the years about the way in which organizations have a habit of undertaking significant major reorganizations from time to time, even though the evidence suggests that these major change initiatives are rarely successful (Hames, 2007). The dialectic of subjectivity and objectivity is not therefore a vote in favour of change for change's sake, but rather a plea to recognize the dangers associated with trying to understand the workplace in fixed, static terms. As we noted in Chapter 4, very often change is what is deliberately brought about through various initiatives – for example, as a result of a change in law or policy. However, what existentialism helps us to understand is that things are constantly changing and evolving by their very nature. This is the concept of *flux*.

Voice of experience 5.2

I realized when I became a manager that different people can have very different perspectives on the same situation. Even though, objectively, everyone is in the same boat, as it were, you will get such a range of variation about how people see that boat: what direction it is going in, whether it is sinking or floating just fine, whether it is too big or too small, and so on. It's amazing really how we can all see the same world, but through such different eyes.

Keith, a practice manager at a health centre

In our earlier discussion of stability we noted that it is something that is created by conservative forces (autopoiesis), rather than simply reflecting a natural state of stability. That is, if things stay the same, it is because we are doing certain things to make them stay the same (or it could be that they are changing at such a slow pace that we assume that they are remaining stable). The concept of 'negentropy' is an important one here. To understand it we first need to make sense of its opposite, 'entropy'. This refers to a process of decline into disorder, the tendency for order to break down over time. Like autopoiesis, it is a term used in the natural sciences which also has application in the human sciences. It reflects that fact that things will gradually change unless we stop them from doing so, order will become disorder unless we maintain that order. The process of maintaining that order is then known as 'negentropy'.

The reason negentropy is important is that it teaches us that we cannot assume that what is working well now and needs to be retained will automatically remain in place – it may well 'decline into disorder'. This brings us back to the dialectic. What often appears to be a stable situation is in fact where two or more conflicting forces are in balance, in effect cancelling each other out. For example, strong conflict between two members of staff may be pushing them in the direction of being antagonistic towards each other, but the strong sense of teamwork may be pushing against that, producing a situation of polite tolerance of one another. However, what appears superficially to be stable situation may change at any moment if, for example, something happens to intensify the conflict, the sense of teamwork is reduced somehow, or both. It would then seem as though conflict has suddenly erupted whereas, in reality, it has been there all along.

Consequently, an important part of leadership is being able to not only guard against things going wrong, but also to constantly reinforce those positive forces that are holding some of the negatives in check. Paradoxically, then, a key element of change management is managing stability – making sure the good things stay good, that the inevitable change that characterizes human existence is moving in the direction of maintaining (and, where possible, enhancing) the positives, while guarding against the negatives.

What we can also learn from the dialectic of subjectivity and objectivity is that there are two sides to shaping culture as a key leadership activity. First of all, there is the challenge of influencing objective factors that can have an impact on, for example, morale. This would include making sure that staff have adequate facilities for their work. These 'objective' factors can have a significant impact on subjective feelings – for example, as to whether they feel valued and supported on the one hand or manipulated and exploited on the other. Second, there is a need to address subjective issues directly. As we have noted, it is important to focus on getting the best out of people, rather than just attempting to get the most out of them. Getting the best out of people involves creating and maintaining a culture in which they feel safe and valued and where they are involved in a shared endeavour to do something important. These are largely subjective matters – that is, how people perceive the way they are treated and the meanings they associate with this – but they will have an objective effect in terms of quality and quantity of work, strength of working relationships, degree of commitment, levels of well-being and so on.

Albrecht (2006) echoes the significance of addressing subjective factors (and thereby producing objective results) when he talks about toxic behaviours which he defines as: 'those that cause others to feel devalued, inadequate, intimidated, angry, frustrated, or guilty' (p. xiii). He contrasts these with 'nourishing behaviours' which are those which: 'cause others to feel valued, capable, loved, respected, and appreciated' (*ibid.*). While we may not expect leaders to 'love' their followers, the need to avoid toxic behaviours and engage in nourishing ones is clearly an important implication of appreciating the need to address subjective as well as objective factors and the relationship between the two.

It should be clear, then, that the concept of the dialectic of subjectivity and objectivity should be a potentially very useful one for leaders, as it helps us to appreciate, and begin to make sense of, some of the complexities and challenges involved.

THE PROGRESSIVE-REGRESSIVE METHOD

This is another important concept that can cast considerable light on some of the intricacies of working with people and trying to have a positive influence on those people from a leadership point of view. The basic idea underpinning the progressive-regressive method is that, to understand people, we need to understand their future and their past. We need to understand what their hopes, aspirations and ambitions are, what they are trying to achieve. This is the progressive element. It means looking forward, and so it is about examining and appreciating the motivations of individuals and groups. As Hames (2007) comments: 'Most people think the future is a destination or a goal – somewhere we are headed in time. It is not. It is something we help to create every time we make a decision about what we will do next and then act out that decision. In spite of that, we can never be too sure about the future' (p. 211).

This is clearly significant for leadership. If we are not aware of how the people we are working with and seeking to lead view their futures, then our notion of communicating a vision is meaningless. To have a meaningful conception of vision we need to be appreciative of people's perspectives on their future. However, it is not simply about the future dimension. Sartre also emphasizes that we need to understand where people are coming from – that is, how their past experiences (and how they are currently interpreting those past experiences) are shaping their current thoughts, feelings and actions. Practice focus 5.3 illustrates this nicely.

PRACTICE FOCUS 5.3

Roger was from a public sector background. He lost his job because of council cutbacks, but he would ultimately like to return to the public sector. Now working in the private sector, his heart was clearly not in it; he just didn't feel at home in a commercial setting. He was just doing the bare minimum to get through the day and could eventually have faced burnout if things continued like this. Susheela, his line manager, recognized the problem. She could understand that, for Roger, both his past and his future (in terms of aspirations) were in the public sector and this made for a very unhappy and unproductive present in the private sector. She therefore arranged to meet with him and talk about this. She laid her cards on the table and explained how she could see that things were not working for him and therefore weren't working for her, the team or the organization. Susheela was a very shrewd manager, so this is what she put to him: If things continued to go on like this, there would be a steady

> decline, making Roger a far less attractive proposition for a potential public sector employer in the future. In effect, he was digging himself into a deeper hole. If, however, they acknowledged openly that his future was back in the public sector, then they could look closely at how they might use his current role to enable him to widen his skills base, broaden his perspective on working life and use his experience in his current post to strengthen any future public sector applications. This turned out to be a win–win option, as this made Roger's current situation more meaningful for him – he began to see it as a stepping stone back to where he really wanted to be, rather than as a failure to be doing something he could put his heart into. This made him not only a much happier worker, but also a much more productive one. He also started to relate better to other team members, so the result was positive all round.

The progressive-regressive method is not simply a matter of trying to understand two different dimensions, future and past. It is also about appreciating how the present is constantly being shaped to a large extent by the interactions of the future and the past. For example, what our future aspirations are will depend to a large extent on our past experiences, but how we make sense of our past experiences will also owe a great deal to our future aspirations. These temporal dimensions interact in a subtle but significant dialectic. It is not simply that the past is gone and the future is yet to be, and therefore all we have is a focus on the present. That perception would deny the significance of how both the past and the future influence the present and do so by influencing each other – that is, the past influencing the future and vice versa.

The insights presented by the progressive-regressive method can be of major significance. Too often people are trying to understand individuals simply in terms of the current circumstances, their everyday motivations and concerns. But once again that fails to do justice to the complexities of human existence. It fails to recognize that each day the influence of the past and of the future weighs heavily on the present moment.

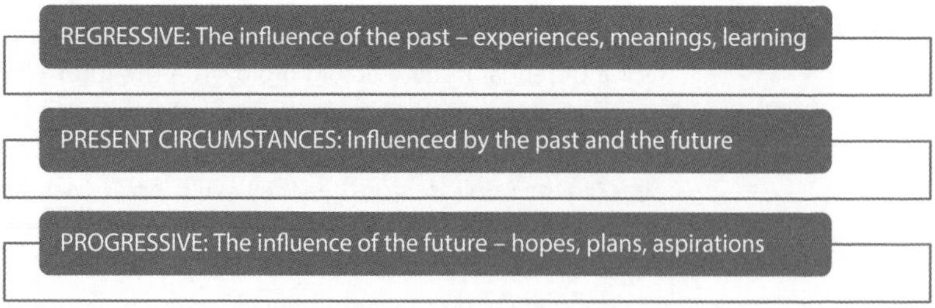

REGRESSIVE: The influence of the past – experiences, meanings, learning

PRESENT CIRCUMSTANCES: Influenced by the past and the future

PROGRESSIVE: The influence of the future – hopes, plans, aspirations

FIGURE 5.1 **The progressive-regressive method**

Voice of experience 5.3

I had always wanted to be involved in delivering training and development, because I just found the whole idea of helping people learn quite exciting. But what caused me a lot of difficulties for a long time was that I had been brought up in a very loving, but very strict family. The result had been that I was quite shy, always timid about speaking out in case it got me into trouble and caused any unnecessary bad feeling. So, I suppose it had taught me that it is wise to keep my views to myself and play it safe. But, the older I got, and the more training courses I attended, the more I realized that I would have to change my ways if ever I wanted to deliver training myself. Public speaking and shyness don't go well together. So, I set about trying to unlearn what my past experiences had taught me, because that was standing in the way of what I wanted my future to be.

Anne, a workforce development officer in a private health care company

CONCLUSION

Ontology, as we have seen, is the study of being, and that relates closely to the idea of what it means to be a human being. Existentialism is a philosophy that has focused very heavily on trying to make sense of what it means to be human, to explore the implications of the human condition. This partly explains why, at one time, it was an extremely popular and fashionable philosophy that appealed to the hearts and minds of a significant number of people. However, despite the fact that its fashionable status has long since passed, it remains a philosophy that offers a number of important theoretical concepts that can cast significant light on the challenges involved in leadership. By reviewing four of them here (the existential project, being-for-others, the dialectic of subjectivity and objectivity, and the progressive-regressive method) I have put together an argument for the importance of taking account of ontological factors, particularly as highlighted by existentialist thought, in making sense of the workplace and the role of leadership within it.

An important part of leadership is the idea that certain human beings have the opportunity to get the best out of other human beings in a spirit of shared endeavour. Existentialism, particularly through the concepts highlighted in this chapter, can very much play an important part in providing a consistent and coherent framework of understanding to fuel the drive towards getting the *best* out of people and not settling for the common, but highly problematic, approach of trying to get the *most* out of them (and thereby risking alienating them in the process).

chapter 6   The role of meaning: phenomenology

INTRODUCTION

We have already come across this important but complex term of phenomenology. In this chapter I examine it in more detail and emphasize its significance. Phenomenology is not so much a specific philosophy as a style of philosophizing, a way of approaching philosophical issues that seeks to make sense of them in terms of key issues around perception and meaning. Given the important leadership role of culture shaping, which in effect involves negotiating sets of meanings and influencing people's perceptions, then phenomenology is clearly something that has relevance to developing a fuller and deeper understanding of leadership.

As mentioned earlier, a common oversimplification of existentialism is that it declares life to be meaningless and therefore does not engage with questions of meaning. The reality is far more complex than this. Existentialism is based on the premise that life has no absolute or ultimate meaning, no 'grand plan' that is unfolding before us. However, this is not to say that life is meaningless. In fact, from an existentialist point of view, meaning is a central feature of human existence. We are constantly creating meanings, developing narratives that help us make sense of life. Indeed, it is the fact that there is no ultimate meaning that drives us to create our own meanings, individually and collectively.

I begin by clarifying in more detail the nature of phenomenology and then highlight a number of important aspects of phenomenology, six in particular, that will help to develop our understanding of how meaning plays such an important role in authentic leadership. These six elements are: meaning; spirituality; identity and interaction;

ontological security; leadership as culture management; and an existentialist approach to the notion of 'realism' as a balance of optimism and pessimism.

WHAT IS PHENOMENOLOGY?

Literally, phenomenology is the study of perception. As we have noted, a phenomenon is 'that which is perceived' or 'that which appears'. The main idea behind phenomenology is that it is essential to appreciate the significance of perception in shaping human thoughts, feelings and actions. Implicit in the idea of phenomenology is that there is no objective reality untouched by human perceptions. What this means is the idea of a purely objective science or a purely objective understanding of any situation is mythical; it is beyond our reach because whatever happens has to be perceived through human lenses and, if we ignore the significance of those lenses, we present a very one-sided picture of reality. This is not to say that there is no such thing as objective reality beyond our perception, but rather that we need to understand how our perception interrelates with that objective reality (taking us back to the dialectic of subjectivity and objectivity, as discussed in Chapter 5). This is where the role of meaning comes in, because it is through attaching meaning to objective circumstances that they matter to us, that they become part of how we understand the world, and therefore how we engage with that world in terms of our responses to the situations we encounter. For example, two people may lose their jobs because of financial pressures on their employers. This is the same objective event (loss of a job) for both of them. But it may be that, for one of them it means a catastrophic loss of earnings at a time when they are already finding it difficult to cope, plus considerable anxiety about the potential for finding another job, while for the other it means the opportunity to pursue the change of career direction they have been thinking about for quite some time now. Phenomenology therefore teaches us that it would be a significant mistake to view the same objective reality (loss of job) as having the same meaning for the individuals concerned. Such a mistake could cause considerable ill feeling and make a bad situation much worse.

Ladkin (2010) explains that:

phenomenology recognizes the subjective nature of knowledge and pays close attention to lived experience as a valid source of knowing. Many of the more traditional ways of exploring leadership attempt to describe it 'from the outside' in accordance with accepted social science methods and assumptions about validity and objectivity. In contrast, phenomenology embraces the significance of meaning within human sense-making processes. (p.6)

What we need to bear in mind is that, while objective facts are clearly important, it is the subjective meanings that will shape how we think, feel and act. For example, if someone makes a joke at my expense, with no malice or ill will intended, but I misread it as a personal attack on me, my response will be governed by my perceptions and the meaning I attach to them (I am being attacked and need to defend myself) and not to the objective event (this is humour that I can share and enjoy without any need to be defensive). An important lesson here is that, as leaders, we need to be able to empathize with the people we lead, to be able to see the situation from their point of view and 'walk a mile in their moccasins', as the saying goes. This is an important part of developing the trust, respect and credibility that we keep coming back to as core foundations for effective leadership.

Ladkin (2010) again makes apt comment when she points out that:

Although meaning is not an objective, scientifically verifiable thing, phenomenology recognizes its central role in the day-to-day way in which humans live their lives and interact with one another. Shared meanings allow human beings to collaborate and live together in productive and potentially harmonious ways. (p. 19)

To understand more fully why phenomenology is important, we have to take account of Nietzsche's notion of 'perspectivism' (Wicks, 2002). Nietzsche argued that there is no single Truth (with a capital, definitive T), but only truths, multiple truths in multiple situations. This reflects his notion of perspectivism: everything has to be seen from a perspective. Unless we posit the idea of a God who is able to see the world from a position detached from that world, then we are faced with the recognition that all facts are contextual – that is, they are facts that only make sense to us within a particular framework of meaning. For example, it is a fact that 25 December is designated as Christmas Day. However, what that fact means will depend upon the context. Consider the following examples, which are far from forming a comprehensive list:

- To a devout Christian it is a sacred day to celebrate the birth of Jesus.
- To a Jewish person it is another religious festival that falls close to the time of their own sacred time of celebration, Hannukah.
- To a Muslim it may well be just another ordinary day.
- To one business owner it may be a time of high turnover, whereas to another it may be a very quiet time.
- To someone who lives away from their family, it may be a time of great happiness to be able to return home for a while and spend time with loved ones, while for someone who has lost their family or is alienated from them, it may be a time of great sadness and loneliness.

This links closely with the dialectic of subjectivity and objectivity and the need to take account of the central role of subjectivity in human experience. This is not only something that relates to life in general of course, but also specifically to workplace challenges and the role of leadership in tackling those challenges.

A focus on phenomenology, then, helps to alert us the need to take account of perceptions and associated meanings, as it is these that will shape organizational life, both directly through current circumstances (that is, how the current situation is being perceived and interpreted by the various stakeholders involved) and indirectly through past perceptions and meanings that have created a culture the influence of which is still perhaps going strong some years later by becoming today's habits, unwritten rules and taken-for-granted assumptions. If we fail to take account of meanings and perceptions, then we are not giving due attention to these aspects of the human dimension of the workplace and thereby failing to be authentic.

The remainder of this chapter focuses on six key elements of phenomenology. Each of these will be explored in turn from an existentialist perspective and with a focus on their implications for leadership practice and development.

PRACTICE FOCUS 6.1 | Jeff was the CEO of a transport company. He was irritated when he received an email from the head of human resources saying that the company would need to pay attention to being flexible in relation to religious and cultural festivals as observed by various members of staff from ethnic minorities. He thought it was just another way of people trying to get extra time off. However, when he got home that evening and mentioned his annoyance to his wife, she provided a more balanced approach by asking him how he would feel if no allowance was made for him to have time off at Christmas. So, by the time he met with the HR Chief to discuss the issue, he had already started to realize that he had been a bit hasty and was now more prepared to accept that different people had different needs when it came to their own culture or religion.

MEANING

Leadership involves helping to make working life meaningful, as Goffee and Jones (2006) explain:

> Great leadership has the potential to excite people to extraordinary levels of achievement. But it is not only about performance; it is also about meaning ... Leaders at all levels make a difference to performance. They do so because they make performance meaningful. (p. 2)

It is therefore important that, as leaders, we are tuned in to the significance of the role meaning plays. First of all, we need to recall our earlier discussion of how meaning is in some respects unique to the individual concerned, but also has one foot in the wider context of cultural frameworks and sociopolitical structures. In other words, if we are talking about meaning, we have to look at the cultural level in terms of discourses and other established frameworks of meaning and the power relations associated with them. These will then connect with the even wider frame of the uneven, unequal structure of society. What this means is that we need to be wary of adopting an atomistic approach to meaning. While meanings are, by their very nature, personal and unique to the individual concerned, they are rooted in our experiences of, and the influences from, the wider cultural and structural context (as we explored in Chapter 3). Meaning is, of course, how we make sense of our lives, how we retain a sense of coherence. Existentialism recognizes that, as human beings, we are, in effect, meaning-making creatures – we are constantly seeking to make sense of the situations we find ourselves in. This is why the term 'narrative' is often used in relation to meaning, because, in a very real sense, what we are doing when we seek to make sense of the world and what is happening to us within it, is that we are integrating new experiences into our own narrative, adding a new chapter to our biography, as it were.

Nelson-Jones (1997) highlights the fact that we are likely to suffer and struggle if we cannot do that integration effectively. Referring to the existentialist authors, May and Yalom, he indicates that they:

> observe that when situations or sets of stimuli defy patterning, humans experience dysphoria, that persists until they fit the situation into some recognizable pattern. The search for meaning is a representation of this need to fit situations into a pattern because 'in an unpatterned world an individual is acutely unsettled and searches for a pattern, an explanation, a meaning for existence' [May and Yalom, 1995, p. 276] (p. 10)

This raises important issues for leadership, in so far as it means that people will inevitably create some sort of meaning, develop their own narrative. If we are not making a contribution to that narrative in terms of helping them feel safe, valued and supported, they may well develop a narrative of alienation and disaffection.

Nelson-Jones also points out that: 'Frankl considers the three main sources of meaning are: doing a deed, for example work; experiencing a value, for example loving another person; and the attitude you take towards suffering' (1997, p. 73). It is worth considering each of these in a little more detail, as they have a bearing on the significance of meaning for leadership:

- *Doing a deed* It has long been recognized that work can be a major source of meaning. It can give a sense of purpose and direction

(Colling and Terry, 2010a; Stein, 2007). If we fail to take account of this we can be: (i) missing out on opportunities to be effective leaders by playing a part in helping to create positive meaning; and (ii) contributing to a negative experience of the workplace.

- *Experiencing a value* Work also enables us to put values into practice – for example, treating people fairly, if justice is one of our values. As we saw in Chapter 4, values are a significant source of motivation.
- *Attitude towards suffering* The inevitability of suffering as a feature of human existence is a well-established existentialist theme. How we relate to experiences of suffering, our own and other people's, will shape, and be shaped by, our 'narrative', our framework of meaning.

Leaders can influence each of these in either a positive or negative direction. The issue of suffering introduces the important theme of well-being, a point to which we will return later.

To develop our understanding of meaning further. It is worth returning to Bourdieu's idea of habitus, which refers, in a sense, to the individual's experience being filtered through social lenses. Grenfell (2012) describes habitus as 'the subjective element of practice' (p. 47), by which he means the way in which we relate to the world, the connection between our perception (the subjective element) and the activities in which we are immersed (practice).

To a certain extent, habitus is to an individual what culture is to a group of people, namely a habitualized set of behaviours, responses and understandings. As such it is an important feature (and source) of meaning.

Grenfell goes on to state that: 'We cannot understand the practices of actors in terms of their habituses alone – habitus represents but one part of the equation; the nature of the fields they are active within is equally crucial' (2012, p. 51). (He is here using the term 'actors' in the sociological sense to refer to *people* – that is, those who carry out actions, rather than to actors in the everyday dramatical sense.) Field is another technical term used by Bourdieu. As we noted earlier, it refers to the various contexts in which habitus plays out. This means that habitus adapts to the different contexts in which it is placed, reflecting the existentialist concept of the dialectic of subjectivity and objectivity – the interplay, in a sense, between the inner meanings and the outer context.

This concept of habitus once again helps us to recognize the dangers of atomism and encourages us to appreciate the social aspects of how we relate to other people, to our work and to our lives more broadly. Habitus is generally not presented as a spiritual concept, but it is relatively easy to draw significant links between this sociological concept and the spiritual notion of connectedness, meaning, purpose and direction. In particular, habitus helps us to get our bearings in terms of the worldview that we adopt in relation to our life.

Having a good understanding of habitus in particular and meaning in general can help leaders understand what is required in terms of shaping culture in a positive direction and creating a sense of security. This discussion of the significance of meaning is far from comprehensive, but it should be enough to establish that this is an area of human experience that we would be foolish to neglect.

SPIRITUALITY

As we noted in Chapter 4, for many people, spirituality is automatically associated with religion, with the mistaken assumption that, if there is no religion in place, spirituality is not an issue. However, this fails to recognize that there are many millions of people on this planet who are not religious, but who none the less have spiritual needs and strivings. Spirituality is therefore a much broader concept than religion. Spirituality involves trying to make sense of who we are and how we fit into the world, how we connect with things that are important to us. This therefore builds on our discussion of the significant role of meaning, particularly as it relates to notions of purpose and direction (note the link here with the progressive-regressive method and the importance of the temporal dimensions of past and future). The Dalai Lama (2013) adopts an approach that might surprise many religious people when he argues that:

> any religion-based answer to the problem of our neglect of inner values can never be universal, and so will be inadequate. What we need today is an approach to ethics which makes no recourse to religion and can be equally acceptable to those with faith and those without: a secular ethics. (pp. xiii–xiv)

Of course, this is not to reject religion or its role in so many people's lives, but, rather to say that spirituality and associated matters of ethics and values do not have to be seen purely within a religious context.

Voice of experience 6.1

I had worked in general nursing for many years without thinking much about spirituality other than the basic idea of respecting people's religious needs. But, when I started to work in palliative care and was constantly working with people who were dying or grieving, it hit home to me just how important spirituality is, with or without religion. In fact, some of the most deeply spiritual conversations I have had have been with people who have no particular religious beliefs.

Sandra, a hospice manager

Spirituality is commonly seen as a personal, individual matter, but this again takes us into the realm of atomism. Spirituality operates in a social context and, in particular, within an organizational context. Allcorn (2005) points out that:

William Guillory (2000, 25) directly links organizational success to adaptiveness that is supported by spirituality. He writes,

[S]piritual values are often the source of an organization's ability to adapt effectively to change, particularly during difficulty or crisis. Unfortunately, adaptation is too often motivated by survival; and a survival mentality promotes short-term, adversarial behavior. On the other hand, adaptation based upon enduring spiritual values promotes behavior that is truly beneficial to customers, the organization, and the business system. (p. 161)

Going beyond atomism involves realizing that all these issues about meaning and spirituality apply not only to individuals, but also to teams and, indeed, whole organizations. Spiritual factors relate strongly to the workplace, and there is now a growing literature on the significance of these factors in a variety of work settings (Marques *et al.*, 2009). In trying to make sense of leadership, we are therefore omitting what is potentially a key set of issues if we pay no attention to matters of spirituality. A key message to take on board if we take seriously the idea of existential authenticity is the need to fully acknowledge the *human* dimensions of the workplace. Neglecting issues of spirituality clearly runs counter to this idea.

If we also bear in mind that authenticity is concerned with recognizing the situations we are in and their implications for us in terms of the choices presented to us, then understanding how our spiritual worldview will both shape and be shaped by those choices is an important matter to take into consideration. An authentic leader will therefore be somebody who is tuned into the significance of spirituality, not just their own spiritual needs and strivings, but also those of the people they are seeking to lead. This may involve religious factors for many people, but need not do so. However, it would be a significant mistake to assume that spirituality is not important in the workplace unless there are religious issues to take into account.

IDENTITY AND INTERACTION

We have already explored Sartre's important thesis that identity is a matter of 'we are what we make of what is made of us'. This serves to remind us that selfhood is better understood as a journey characterized by contingency and flux, rather than a fixed entity, some sort of essential self, resting upon an inborn 'essence'. Indeed, this is the mistake made in so much of the literature relating to authentic leadership: to draw on the false assumption that, underneath the flux of human life is a fixed, real self. This fails to recognize, of course, the dynamic nature of identity and the need to understand identity in terms of the wider context of interaction with others.

This emphasis on interaction brings us back to the key concept of being-for-others and the recognition that we do not operate in a vacuum separate from others. In this respect, existentialism shares with social constructionist thinking the understanding that our lives take place within a social context, and that so much of the meaning that we attribute to our lives – and which moves us forward in terms of motivation – has its roots in social factors. These can be interpersonal factors or, returning to our earlier discussion of PCS analysis, cultural or structural factors – or indeed a combination of them all.

This emphasis on identity and interaction helps us to acknowledge that a key aspect of leadership is how we relate to others, how we 'engage' with other people and how we encourage them to engage with us. Once again we come back to Buber's emphasis on the importance of relating to people in a genuine spirit of respect – what he called an I-Thou inter-action or relationship. Much of this will depend on how they perceive us, which, in turn, will depend in part on what messages we give off in terms of our behaviour and nonverbal communication, as well as what we actually say or write. It is important, therefore, to acknowledge that there is a phenomenological aspect to leadership. An authentic leader would need to be able to recognize the significance of perception in general and particularly the ways in which it has a bearing on identity and interaction.

Implicit within this is the role of self-awareness. If, as leaders, we are not attuned to how we are coming across to others, then we are in a weaker position when it comes to influencing them as part of our role of culture shaping. Pressure of work can often lead managers into a pattern of work that involves rushing. This can easily create a vicious circle in which rushing means that there is little scope for self-awareness, which can lead to a failure of leadership. This then means that staff are not performing to their best and there may be dissatisfaction and disaffec-tion creeping in, all of which can add to the pressures which then, in turn make it more likely that people will be rushing. The 'antidote' to this is reflective practice, a key topic that we will explore in Chapter 7.

The existentialist conception of selfhood as an emergent process rooted in the choices we make and the circumstances in which we make them differs significantly from the essentialist notion that people have fixed or 'true' selves. The existentialist approach places great emphasis on interactions (being-for-others), as these can have a significant bearing on our perception of ourselves. For example, if someone is condescend-ing towards us, we may interpret this as a sign that we are somehow not worthy, and our self-esteem can suffer as a result of this. Alternatively, if someone praises our efforts and/or achievements, we are likely to feel more, rather than less, confident. The dialectic of subjectivity and objectivity is operating here.

This has particular implications for leaders in terms of empowerment. How we relate to people can play a part in encouraging empowering self-perceptions or disempowering ones. Of course, individuals are free to reject the 'messages' we give them through our interactions, but it would be unwise to ignore the potential for making a significant difference as to whether people are empowered (have greater control) or disempowered (have less control) through our interactions with them – especially as leaders are generally in positions of power and therefore relatively well placed to influence the perceptions of others.

What this means is that every time a leader interacts with one or more followers (or, indeed other leaders) the interaction can either help or hinder, make a positive contribution or a negative one. The reason for this is that everything that happens relies on perception – that is, all interactions pass through the lens of interpretation and are integrated into the narrative of that individual, the team or the wider work group. Perceptions and meaning, phenomenology teaches us, are inescapable. This echoes the discussion in the Introduction of the common misunderstanding of existentialism as a philosophy that is based on the idea that life is meaningless. On the contrary, the phenomenological roots of existentialism show us that, while life may have no ultimate, absolute meaning, the process of creating and sustaining meanings is a core element of human existence. So, at all times, it is essential that authentic leaders are aware of what meanings they are contributing to, what messages they are delivering to the people they interact with. The essentialist notion that 'you are who you are' can therefore be seen as a recipe for complacency, in so far as it fails to recognize that identities are largely shaped through interaction, through the dialectic of subjectivity and objectivity.

What is particularly important about this, from an authentic leadership point of view, is that our interactions can either reinforce or challenge bad faith. Where people are trying to avoid taking ownership of their actions, we can either collude with this and thereby reinforce their 'narrative' or we can (gently, constructively, tactfully) challenge that narrative by highlighting the key role of ownership as a basis for authenticity. So, an important question to ask ourselves is: might we (perhaps unwittingly) be reinforcing bad faith or are we encouraging a narrative of ownership and authenticity?

PRACTICE FOCUS 6.2	Paula was a manager in the headquarters of a restaurant chain. She was getting frustrated about the fact that, whenever anything went wrong, no one was prepared to take responsibility. There were always excuses, some of them quite laughable at times. She remembered her leadership training about culture shaping which helped her to stop focusing on the individual actions of particular staff members and focus on the culture. It soon dawned on her that she had inherited a blame culture. There was little sense of openness or honesty, no recognition that, of course, mistakes would happen from time to time. It was a defensive 'cover your back' culture, which, ironically, made it more likely that people would make mistakes because of the negative impact on confidence and the raised levels of tension this brought about. Paula now realized that she would have to look carefully at how she could get people to move away from this negative culture towards a more open one based on ownership not blame or defensiveness. She was already getting some ideas about how she could do this and was identifying some key people to get on board to start the process off.

ONTOLOGICAL SECURITY

As we noted in Chapter 5, ontological security relates to the feeling of safety we have or the sense of rootedness we strive for in terms of our identity and our location in the world. In this respect, it can be seen as a spiritual concept. It is important to achieve a degree of balance in terms of ontological security (Thompson, 2011a). This is because a shortage of ontological security can leave us feeling anxious and ill-equipped to deal with the challenges that we face, while, by contrast, too much ontological security can lead to complacency and inauthenticity because it means that we fail to take account of the risks and vulnerabilities that we all face as human beings.

Ontological security is important in terms of leadership, because a key factor when it comes to shaping a culture in a positive direction is the ability to create a sense of security to enable people within a particular culture to be able to say, first of all: 'I am safe'; second: 'I will be treated fairly'; and third: 'I will be valued'. These are all important aspects of the leader's challenge of being able to shape or create a culture characterized by a sense of security. This security needs to be not just specific, in the sense of feeling safe from physical attack, for example, but taking this broader existentialist concept of ontological security that people need to feel secure 'in themselves'. They need to feel 'at home'. Heidegger used the term *Unheimlichkeit* (not feeling at home) to describe the absence of this sort of security (Heidegger, 1962).

Clearly, a key element of this will be trust. Without trust there will be insecurity, and this can create a vicious circle of mistrust. For example, if there is an absence of trust, then people will not feel secure. If they do not feel secure, they are more likely to mistrust. If they are mistrustful, then they are likely to create greater insecurity, and so it goes on, round and round in a destructive cycle. This is one of the reasons why an emphasis on trust, respect and credibility is a recurring theme in this book.

An important role for a leader, therefore, is to have the authenticity to be able to recognize that a sense of security is a key factor in effective leadership and not deny ownership of the need to generate such security. This, of course, is a phenomenological concept, because the security involved is a matter of perception – it is a matter of how those people involved in the organization perceive their position. There is no such thing, of course, as a totally risk-free environment, but much will depend on what amount of risk people associate with that environment and particularly what extent of ontological risk – that is, the risk posed to their very being, to their sense of who they are and how they fit into not just the world in general, but also specifically to their organization, their profession, their role and their aspirations.

Ontological security is not a matter of trying to create some sort of mythical risk-free situation. Rather, it is a matter of creating an empowering atmosphere in which people can feel confident in taking (sensible) risks. This highlights a significant paradox, in so far as 'playing it safe' (that is, being risk averse and thereby creating unnecessary tensions and a distorted, unduly negative picture of the situation) is in itself a highly dangerous strategy. A balanced, undistorted view of risk is a far safer enterprise. Where security is lacking (perhaps because leadership is lacking), such a balanced approach is far less likely to arise.

LEADERSHIP AS CULTURE MANAGEMENT

There has already been a strong emphasis in the earlier chapters on the significance of leadership as a form of culture shaping to produce positive results for all concerned. The atomistic definitions of leadership mentioned and criticized in the Introduction fail to acknowledge or address this role and can therefore be seen not to do justice to the wider factors. It also has to be recognized, as was mentioned in Chapter 2, that it is a significant mistake for a leader to try and fight a culture, rather than seek to shape that culture. Now here we are back again on firm phenomenological territory, in the sense that a culture is largely a set of perceptions and the meanings that have developed from those perceptions. Cultures do not exist in their own right in any objective sense. They are, in a sense, made objective to a certain extent through shared subjectivities, by people contributing to the maintenance of a set of habits, taken-for-granted assumptions and unwritten rules. Cultures are therefore social or human constructions. They were created through human interaction and activity and can therefore be changed through human interaction and activity, and this will depend, of course, on how key aspects of the situation will be perceived. The role of culture manager therefore involves influencing perceptions. This means that influencing skills are an important part of the authentic leader's repertoire of skills. This then brings us back to one of our key themes, that of of trust, respect and credibility. This is because, without these three key elements, our ability to influence people will be severely restricted.

PRACTICE FOCUS 6.3

Ben was a diversity manager in a large local authority. When he was appointed it didn't take him long to become aware that he would have to do something to change the culture if he was going to get anywhere. What concerned him was that issues relating to equality and diversity appeared to have been handled in a very confrontational way in the past and this had developed a culture of fear, a 'walking on eggshells' mentality. He was one of the few black staff in his office and he could see that many of the white staff seemed reluctant to engage with him. He had come across this problem before and knew it was likely to be down to this culture of fear – driven by a powerful belief that the less that is said, the lower the chance of being accused of being racist. Ben decided that he would write an article for the departmental newsletter about his experiences of a culture of fear in a previous post and how much unnecessary tension and bad feeling that had caused. He envisaged being able to use that to get diversity issues on the agenda and start to break down this destructive culture.

REALISM, BEYOND OPTIMISM AND PESSIMISM

There is a large and growing literature on positive psychology which emphasizes the importance of optimism (see, for example, Seligman, 2003). There is, however, also a literature base and school of thought that criticizes positive psychology for overemphasising the significance of optimism and failing to recognize that, at times, pessimism is actually a wise and helpful approach to take (Chang, 2002; Dienstag, 2006). From an existentialist perspective, what we have is a situation that is, in effect, grossly oversimplified, in so far as it replaces the complex reality of human existence as a mixture of positives and negatives with a superficial choice between a positive outlook or a negative one (see also Ehrenreich, 2009).

To reduce our approach to life as either positive (optimism) or negative (pessimism) is to do violence to the immense complexities of human existence. Existentialism offers what can be described as a *realistic* perception – that is, one that affirms that there are both positives and negatives in life and that it is important to take account of both. This brings us back to the idea of existentialism as a holistic and dynamic philosophy of 'emergence'. This is because, at times, the positive, hopeful, optimistic approach will be appropriate and helpful, but not at all times, and those times can shift and change, of course. In addition, one person's positive approach can be nullified by another person's pessimistic approach and vice versa, so these things have to be understood in interaction and not, once again, as simply static categories to which we can assign people. Therefore the whole debate about optimism versus pessimism can be understood as a gross oversimplification of an important aspect of human experience. How we perceive the world (and again it is very much a matter of perception) in terms of optimism or pessimism is far more complex than simply opting for one approach over the other.

Unfortunately, this oversimplified approach has become dominant thinking in some places and has led to a process of 'commodification' – that is, a form of marketing device in which the benefits of positive psychology, as they are often put forward, are presented as some sort of magic potion to make our lives better. The sophisticated philosophy of existentialism will, of course, not accept such a simplistic and potentially destructive approach.

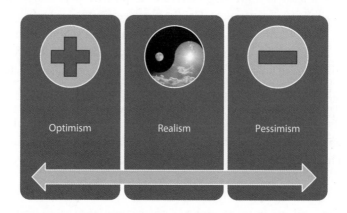

FIGURE 6.1 **Realism: balancing optimism and pessimism**

Voice of experience 6.2

I just don't buy all this positive psychology stuff; it's way too simplistic. In my job I see people going through great suffering and finding life extremely challenging, but I also see a lot of people overcoming their suffering in one way or another. There are times when it pays to be positive and optimistic, but there are also times when we have to be down to earth and recognize that things are just not going to get better. It's all down to getting the balance right, I suppose.

Pat, an emergency response team manager

CONCLUSION

Phenomenology is a complex topic, particularly when we use phenomenology to try and make sense of what in itself is a complex topic, namely leadership. However, what I hope this chapter has done is to show that there are certain phenomenological concepts within a framework of existentialism that can be drawn upon to make sense of the many challenges that leaders face. It is to be hoped that the philosophical complexities will not put you off wanting to know more about how these ideas can be brought to bear to cast light on leadership challenges in the modern workplace.

This now completes Part II where we have explored the significance of (existential) authenticity and then broadened and deepened our understanding of it by looking at the two major theoretical components of existentialism: ontology (in Chapter 5) and phenomenology (in this chapter). The main focus has been on the theoretical insights existentialism offers, while also making links to practice issues. In Part III the emphasis switches so that practice becomes our primary concern and we then look at how existentialist ideas can cast light on the leadership challenges involved.

part III

Authentic leadership in practice

CHAPTERS

INTRODUCTION TO PART III

In planning this book I was clear that, although it would draw on some very complex and multi-level philosophical ideas, there would also be a clear and explicit emphasis on how these ideas make sense in everyday experience and how they can provide a sound platform for high-quality leadership practice informed by an understanding of the complexities of what it means to be human. So far we have discussed a range of theoretical issues and related them to practice at various junctures. Now, in Part III, to complement the theoretical emphasis up to this point, we switch the focus to a more specific consideration of practice, while not losing sight of the importance of the underpinning theory base. So, in effect, while each of the chapters up to this point has made links with practice where appropriate, the three chapters in Part III can be seen as an attempt to consolidate the understanding of how existentialist ideas in general and the central notion of authenticity in particular can offer powerful and extremely useful insights to guide leadership practice.

First we have Chapter 7, which is entitled 'Leadership praxis'. This chapter explores the relationship between theory and practice and highlights the importance of 'theorizing practice' – that is, of beginning with real-life practice situations and concerns and drawing on theoretical insights to make sense of them (as opposed to the traditional, but flawed, notion of 'applying theory to practice'). This fundamental idea will also be considered in relation to critically reflective practice and the need for leadership practice to be underpinned by sound foundations of theoretical understanding.

Next comes Chapter 8 with its focus on 'Existentialism in practice'. This chapter explores a number of the key existentialist ideas discussed in Part II and relates them to real-life leadership practice situations, providing readers with a clear picture of how existentialism can be an invaluable foundation of understanding for facing the complexities of leadership practice. The bulk of the chapter is taken up by five scenarios that represent situations leaders may well encounter in their own workplace setting. Each chapter is considered in terms of how an authentic approach is likely to differ from methods of working that are not informed by existentialist insights.

The final chapter is Chapter 9, 'Authentic leadership', which sums up the various ways in which existentialist thought can lay the foundations for authentic leadership practice. While giving prescriptive practice guidance would run counter to the very idea of authentic leadership, there is much educational value to be gained by outlining a set of practice principles that flow from the notion of (existentially) authentic leadership. This chapter is structured around six principles of existentialist thought. Each is explained and its implications outlined. This should extend and complement the learning to be gained from the practice scenarios discussed in Chapter 8.

Of course, it is fair to say that authentic leadership is ultimately about practice, in the sense that all professional practice exists to make a positive difference at a pragmatic level. That is, while theoretical understandings are vitally important in shedding light on the complexities and subtleties involved, it is what happens 'on the ground' that will make all the difference to leaders and the impact – positive or otherwise – that they have on their followers, their organizations and, in some ways, on wider society. Part III should therefore be seen as the culmination of the book and what it represents. It is followed by a short conclusion which sums up the key messages the book has sought to convey.

chapter 7   Leadership praxis

INTRODUCTION

Praxis is a philosophical term which refers to the fusion of theory and practice. Theory is an attempt to explain, to develop a set of related ideas (a conceptual framework) that help us to understand whatever that particular theory focuses on. Practice refers to actually carrying out a set of work tasks in a particular context, in this case the exercise of leadership. Leadership praxis therefore refers to how we can bring together theory and practice in ways in which they support one another to develop.

Praxis is an important concept, because, as Langan and Lee (1989) have shown, theory without practice is useless and practice without theory is dangerous. So, in this chapter we are going to be exploring the relationship between theory and practice and, in particular, the importance of fusing the two together in meaningful and pragmatic ways. This is important because it is essential that leaders understand what they are dealing with as leaders, otherwise they run the risk of making situations worse and/or being overwhelmed and feeling the need to 'fake it' to get through the challenges they face, thereby abandoning authenticity in the process.

There has long been a tendency to separate out theory and practice, as if they are two distinct domains, as if theory is something that belongs in the academic world and is unconnected with the 'real world', while practice is about day-to-day concrete reality. This is a dangerous oversimplification, because what we need to be aware of is that day-to-day practice needs to be informed by an understanding of the complexities involved. If we are putting ourselves into situations where we have little or no understanding of the factors that are influencing that situation, then we leave ourselves vulnerable to all sorts of difficulties. This is partly why Langan and Lee (1989) say that practice without theory is dangerous.

While some have argued for the importance of a scientific approach to the theoretical understandings underpinning leadership, an existentialist perspective does not deny the importance and the potentially significant role of science, but it does emphasize the limitations of an approach that focuses on the objective elements without taking full consideration of the highly significant subjective elements. This brings us back to the important concept of the dialectic of subjectivity and objectivity. So, when we are facing real-life situations as leaders, there is much to be gained from having a consistent and insightful theory base to draw upon. Existentialism, as we have already seen, offers some important contributions to that theory base. In this chapter, though, the emphasis is not on the theory *per se*, but on how the theory can be used in practice, hence the term 'praxis'.

We begin by questioning the traditional notion of 'applying theory to practice'. This leads into a discussion of reflective practice and then critically reflective practice. Finally we explore what is involved in using praxis to make a difference.

APPLYING THEORY TO PRACTICE?

The traditional approach to the relationship between theory and practice is encapsulated in the notion of 'applying theory to practice'. However, there are two difficulties with this approach. First of all, it implies that theory is in some way superior to practice; that theory is on some sort of pedestal compared to the more lowly world of practice. Many practitioners have objected to this assumption and consequently it has not been uncommon for there to be a rejection of theory, which then can prove to be highly problematic because they then find themselves wrestling with complex situations without an adequate understanding of the issues involved. The second problem with the notion of applying theory to practice is that it implies that it is a one-way street, that theory should inform practice, but there is no notion of practice informing theory. For this reason, my own work on this topic has tended to use the term *integrating* theory and practice, because this gets past the idea that it is a one-way process or relationship. The notion of integrating theory and practice reflects the idea that the two elements can and should influence each other, that theory can inform practice, but practice can also inform and, indeed, test theory. These are necessary considerations because they highlight the importance of being able to connect theory and practice in meaningful ways, rather than falling into the trap of having them as separate boxes as it were – one box for theoretical ideas and another box for practice, and ne'er the twain shall meet.

PRACTICE FOCUS 7.1

> Jan's role as a sales manager in a shoe company brought her into regular contact with a wide range of sales staff. As with most businesses, she thought, you are bound to get a range of levels of competence. What she was interested in was what makes for the highest level of competence: what is it that makes some people excel? Over time she looked closely at what her sales staff were doing. Some, she could see, had good interpersonal skills but were not putting into practice what they had been taught on their training in terms of sales techniques based on the psychology of selling. They were doing a reasonable job but could have been doing better. There were others who were using the lessons they had learned as part of their training, but didn't have strong people skills and showed no sign of developing them any time soon. They did just about OK, but also could have been doing better. The ones who did really well were the ones who had good interpersonal skills *and* used what they had been taught on their training. They were getting the best of both worlds and getting the best results for their efforts.

However, my work has also gone beyond the idea of integrating theory and practice by introducing the notion of *theorizing* practice (Thompson, 2010). The idea of theorizing practice is based on the precept that we should begin with concrete situations (what Sartre refers to as *le vécu* – or 'lived experience'). Practice is the starting point, and we then draw on our theoretical knowledge to make sense of that practice. We draw upon key concepts to cast light on the situations that we are dealing with. In this way we are not starting with theory and then trying to fit the square peg of theory into the round hole of practice. Rather, we are beginning with practice and then trying to understand that practice, being able to develop a fuller picture of the issues involved, so that we are engaging with such situations in a more informed way.

This approach is consistent with existentialism, with the idea that we are faced with day-to-day situations (being-in-the-world, as Heidegger, 1962, called it) and our challenge is then to create meaning from such situations, to make sense of what we are doing. In a way this is what theoretical knowledge can help us to do. We combine our own practice wisdom, gained over however long we have been practising in our current career, with the insights from other theoretical analyses, research and so on. Of course, we need to engage with these critically and not just take other people's ideas (or indeed our own ideas) at face value, but in this way, we end up with a significant body of knowledge that we can draw upon as we see fit in each fresh situation that we encounter.

This approach is also consistent with reflective practice, and so it is worth exploring the links more fully, which we shall do in a moment. However, for now I want to emphasize the importance of theorizing practice. Instead of risking rejecting the value of theoretical knowledge by falling into the trap of trying to 'apply theory to practice' as a one-way street, with theory privileged over practice, theorizing practice enables us to recognize the importance of practice in the real-world situations we are dealing with, but also fully to recognize that it is dangerous to try and engage with these without a significant knowledge base. Fortunately we have such a significant knowledge base available to us, if only we take the trouble to draw upon it and use it critically. This is where reflective practice comes into the picture.

REFLECTIVE PRACTICE

This is a concept that has become very influential in many forms of professional practice – for example, nursing, social work and teacher education – and is increasingly playing a part in shaping management thinking and practice (Golding and Currie, 2000). Unfortunately, though, it is often oversimplified and reduced to a simplistic notion of just taking time out from time to time to reflect on our practice. In reality there is far more to reflective practice than this basic idea of 'having a little think every now and again' (Thompson and Thompson, 2008b).

Voice of experience 7.1

At university there was a lot of talk about reflective practice, but nobody actually explained what it was. It was only when I went on a training course about it that I realized that there was a lot more to it than just the idea of finding time and space from time to time to think over what I was doing. I wished that had been explained to me when I was at university, so that I could have been getting better at it over the years.

Noel, a social work team manager

Reflective practice can be understood as intelligent and informed practice that does justice to the complexities involved. It is thoughtful practice – that is, practice which involves engaging our brain, our intellectual faculties and our analytical skills to be able to make sense of the intricacies of the situations we find ourselves in. Schön (1983) used the term 'a reflective conversation with the situation', and I find this a useful way of characterizing reflective practice. It is about being able to ask ourselves such questions as: what is happening in this situation? What do I need to do? What risks are involved that I need to be aware of? What knowledge can I draw on to help me understand this situation? And so on. I am not suggesting that these should be the precise questions asked in every situation, but, rather, simply using these as an example of the types of question that can help us to make sense of whatever it is we are trying to address or resolve.

Reflective practice can therefore be understood as alert and 'mindful' practice, as opposed to relying on habit, routine or simply copying others (Thompson and Pascal, 2011).

Pressure of work can easily produce situations in which people are not being reflective – that is, they are not drawing on their professional knowledge and values or using their thinking skills to analyse and make sense of their work challenges. Once again a vicious circle can easily develop in which, first of all, work pressures increase and evoke a hurried, non-reflective approach. This makes the person concerned less effective, gives them less of a sense of control (potentially contributing to stress, as control – or the lack of it – is a key factor when it comes to occupational stress – Thompson, 2009a). This then adds to the pressures, which can result in more rushing, less reflection and, with it, less creativity little or no learning and potentially a significant lowering of morale. This sort of downward spiral can be very dangerous and, if we are not careful, this type of unthinking, hamster-wheel practice can become the basis of a team culture – that is, it becomes the norm to rush about and give little thought to what you are doing. This scenario indicates a lack of reflective practice, but, ironically, reflective practice can be the answer to it. Part of reflective practice is the ability to step back from time to time to review what we are doing, examine whether there are better ways of operating and change our approach accordingly.

Reflective practice is an important underpinning of praxis, of the ability to integrate theory and practice and, indeed, to theorize practice, as I have already mentioned. This can be doubly important for leaders. This is because it relates to our own practice as leaders and, secondly, to the practice of those we manage. First of all, we need to consider our own practice as leaders to make sure that it is indeed (informed and intelligent) reflective practice and not non-reflective practice which just draws on habit, routine or copying others unthinkingly. The second dimension to this is that part of the role of a leader is to empower those who are being led, and this in itself can be seen to be an important place where reflective practice can come into its own. It is therefore not just a matter of, as leaders, making sure that our own practice is reflective, but also encouraging, supporting and initiating reflective practice in others.

This is particularly relevant in terms of trying to make sure that a pledged group does not become an institutionalized group as discussed in Chapter 3. For example, if members of a group are continuing to think, plan, analyse and learn from their experience, then they are far less likely to become a rigid institutionalized group where practice is based largely on habit and the influence of the dead weight of habit that is culture. So we can see that this has important implications for leaders, given that I have already explained that making sure that a pledged group does not solidify into an institutionalized group is a key aspect of the handling group dynamics element of effective leadership.

There is also another important aspect of leadership to consider in terms of the role of security, as already highlighted. A key part of leadership to note again is the role of maintaining safe boundaries where people can achieve their best. Reflective practice can again be doubly helpful here. First of all, if the leader is being alert and mindful and is engaging in intelligent and informed practice, then they are going to be in a much stronger position to help to create and sustain a culture that involves safe boundaries, whereas a leader who is simply reacting to situations in a non-reflective way, is likely to generate anxiety and be counterproductive in terms of creating a sense of safety and security in which people can thrive. Secondly, if a leader is able to promote and reinforce reflective practice in the personnel they manage, then this is also likely to help in terms of generating a sense of safety and security – for example, by boosting confidence and enabling practitioners to operate on the basis of a stronger foundation of knowledge and understanding. These can be important factors in terms of keeping insecurity and anxiety at bay.

CRITICALLY REFLECTIVE PRACTICE

Critically reflective practice is not an alternative to reflective practice, but rather an extension of the core idea. In a previous work (Thompson and Thompson, 2008b), I have discussed the significance of making sure that our reflective practice is also *critical* practice. This can be understood in terms of two key factors, critical breadth and critical depth. It is worth exploring each of these in a little more detail.

Critical breadth means being prepared to go beyond atomism, to not rely simply on looking at individual factors in a situation, but to adopt a more holistic perspective which takes account of wider sociopolitical factors, such as the strong and far-reaching influences of cultural and structural factors. The idea of critical breadth, therefore, is that we need to adopt a sociological as well as a psychological approach to making sense of the situations we are involved in. This takes us back to the discussion in Part II of existentialism as a holistic approach involving biopsychosocial and spiritual concerns. Critical breadth, then, is about going beyond atomism and adopting this more holistic perspective, so that we have a fuller and more meaningful understanding of the situation with a view to not relying on a partial, limited perspective that could distort our understanding.

Critical breadth is important in terms of fulfilling a commitment to equality and diversity. It involves considering how sociopolitical factors like class, race and gender can affect individuals, interpersonal interactions, group dynamics and organizational cultures. This takes us back to the discussions in Chapter 3 about the importance of understanding the social context. This is precisely what critical breadth is all about.

Voice of experience 7.2

The make up of the staff group continues to be male dominated, although not as much as when I first came. But what has changed most is that the very strongly masculine culture that tended to put women in a secondary role has been softened considerably. People are more aware now that that sort of thing won't be tolerated. It was holding the women staff back because there was a lot of insensitivity around, with people not realizing women were being assigned typically feminine roles and not being allowed to explore their capabilities across the board. Things are much better on that front, although we still have some way to go.

Karima, the head of a university department

Complementary to this is critical depth, which is basically a matter of not taking things at face value. Critical depth entails being prepared to question and look beneath the surface at what is presented to us. This prevents us from being seduced by ideologies or by other people's attempts to present a distorted picture that may suit their interests, but which may cause difficulties for what we are trying to do. It is also important for critical depth to be employed in questioning cultural assumptions. If leaders are to be effective in shaping culture in a positive direction, then it is important to be aware of what the strongly influential cultural assumptions are that are part and parcel of a particular team, staff group or organizational context. In this way, the critical depth aspect of critically reflective practice can help us to make sure that we are not simply passive victims of culture and that we are actively engaging with the thoughts, feelings and actions that are such an important part of the workplace.

Clearly leaders need to be reasonably well versed in both critical breadth and critical depth if they are to achieve optimal results. However, these are not the only elements of critically reflective practice to take into consideration. We can identify three types of critically reflective practice, immanent, transitive and transformational. Immanent reflection is when people think about an issue and try to develop an understanding but this leads to no outlet, no change in the situation. Immanence is a philosophical term that refers to entities which are, in a sense, self-contained. They have no impact on anything outside of themselves. Mahon (1997), writing about the work of existentialist author, Simone de Beauvoir, describes immanence as:

> a sphere or mode of existence characterized by passivity, submission to biological fate, and confinement or restriction to a narrow round of uncreative and repetitive chores. Thus defined, immanence is to be contrasted with *transcendence,* which refers to a sphere or mode of existence characterized by activity, by freedom from biological fate, by the freedom to burst out of the present and into the future, by a capacity to transform the world so that it accommodates itself to one's intentions. (p. 108)

This brings us back to the common misunderstanding of reflective practice as simply finding space in a busy working life to think from time to time, with that thinking having no actual bearing on their practice in terms of bringing about any significant change. Clearly, this form of reflection is of little value, except possibly as a minor benefit in terms of relief from pressure. That is not enough, of course, to recommend it.

Transitive reflection is where our thinking processes produce results, where they actually change the situation in some form. They may solve or alleviate a problem; they may bring about a positive change; they may change our focus in a helpful way – in fact, there are various ways in which transitive reflection can be helpful. Clearly, this is an important and positive step forward compared with immanent reflection. It fits well with the existentialist concept of transcendence, which relates to how we respond to the situations we find ourselves in, how we go beyond those circumstances through our choices and actions. Transitive reflection therefore involves some degree of praxis, the fusion of theory and practice, thought and action. Our reflection should enable us to develop our understanding of the situation we find ourselves in and identify constructive ways of taking the situation forward.

Once again, there are two aspects to this from a leadership point of view. First there is the need to ensure that our own thought processes rise above immanence and reach a level of being transitive, focused on bringing about positive change, rather than just reflecting in a way that serves no useful purpose. Second, leaders need to develop a culture in which transitive reflection is expected, supported and encouraged. Our own transitive reflection can act as a worthwhile role model, but that on its own is not enough – we need to do whatever we can to promote critically reflective practice in general, and transitive reflection in particular.

However, transformational reflection can be better still. This refers to where we not only bring about a positive change because of our reflective activities, but actually go beyond this to transform the situation. For example, if we are regularly encountering a certain problem, transitive reflection may come up with a way of dealing with that problem whenever it arises. Transformational reflection, by contrast, could potentially radically transform the situation so that the problem concerned no longer arises. For example, if a group of staff find they are wasting a great deal of time because the information they receive from another department does not tell them what they need to know (and they therefore have to spend a lot of time finding out that information for themselves), they may respond, as a result of transitive reflection, by determining to go back on each occasion to the other department and ask them to provide the missing information. This solution will be helpful compared with finding it out for themselves, and so this represents progress. The reflection on the matter has therefore been transitive rather than immanent. However, if reflecting on the problem were to produce the proposal that, instead of going back to the other department each time, they should provide a guide to what core information is needed (and their departmental head could be asked to meet with the other departmental head to ask for the guidance to be used), this would amount to potentially transforming the situation – not just alleviating the problem, but removing it altogether.

This is therefore a step further in the direction of the positive use of reflective practice. We have to be realistic, though, and recognize that transformational reflection is not always possible. Being able to transform a situation will often be beyond our reach because of particular constraints (facticity) that prevent us from transcending that situation in a transformational way. However, the potential for transformation in any situation is something we should not lose sight of. When it comes to trust, respect and credibility, using transformational reflection to bring about positive change can have a major payoff.

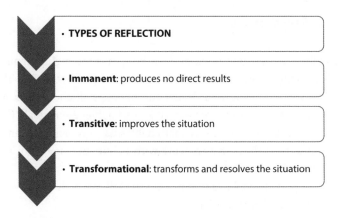

FIGURE 7.1 **Types of reflection**

PRACTICE FOCUS 7.2 | Michael was the chair of a committee involving representatives of four organizations involved in community development initiatives. Each of the four organizations was happy to offer its facilities for committee meetings, but each venue had some sort of problem or drawback (limitations on parking, security, catering and so on) and efforts to address the problems caused more problems because of the ill feeling created when it was felt that a particular venue (and thus the organization who owned it) was being criticised. Some people saw this as just a minor niggle, but Michael decided that he needed to resolve the problem, as the irritation caused over venues was undermining the spirit of partnership that the committee needed to be successful. After giving the matter a lot of thought Michael came up with a solution that would transform the situation and remove the venue problem altogether. He had a good contact at the local college and, because the committee was doing what was seen as worthwhile work for the community, it was arranged for them to have the use of a room at the college free of charge. There was plenty of parking, security staff on duty and the college canteen on the doorstep. For once everyone was happy.

MAKING A DIFFERENCE

Peter Gilbert's important book on leadership has the highly significant subtitle of *Being Effective and Remaining Human* (Gilbert, 2005). This is a good way of capturing what leadership praxis is all about. It is about making sure that positive steps are taken to achieve our goals (being effective), but doing so in a way that enables us to remain human ourselves and to treat those that we work with as human beings too. This is back to Buber's idea of I-Thou rather than I-it.

This can be achieved in a number of ways, all of which can be seen as key aspects of authentic leadership:

- *Listening* It is interesting how often people mention the importance of listening, but do not necessarily carry it out in practice. Listening is not just simply hearing; it is actually being able to be responsive to what we are hearing, to respond in a fully human way. An important concept here is the Australian Aboriginal notion of 'Dadirri listening' (Tehan, 2007). This refers to listening not just with our ears, but with our heart, of actually connecting in a meaningful way with the person(s) we are interacting with (reflecting the I-Thou vs. I-it distinction once again). One of the main reasons that this is so important is that it gives a powerful message of valuing. We are affirming and validating someone as a human being when we do them the honour of listening properly. What is also vitally important to recognize is that the opposite also applies. If we do not listen to somebody, then we are devaluing them. We are giving them a message that invalidates them and can create problems in terms of motivation and engagement – but, most of all, it is potentially highly detrimental in terms of our trust, respect and credibility.

Being prepared to listen does not mean that we have to do what we are being asked to do. We may well find ourselves in a situation where we have listened carefully and appropriately to someone's request, but we still have to turn them down. This may disappoint the person concerned, but nowhere near as much as not listening to them would have. In fact, the more effective we are at listening, and the stronger our reputation as a good listener, the more willing people are likely to be to accept our decision when other circumstances dictate that we cannot accede to their request.

- *Security* An important role of a leader is to help keep anguish, anxiety and stress at bay, and a fundamental part of this is creating and sustaining a culture or an ethos of security where people feel safe and valued. This security helps to ensure that they are prepared to make a commitment to the shared endeavour of their team, work group or indeed whole organization. There are various things that a leader can do to promote security, but an essential part of this, of course, is the authenticity involved in taking ownership for their own actions and supporting the personnel they lead in taking ownership of their actions too – in other words, not indulging in bad faith and not allowing others to do so. As we noted earlier, security does not mean being risk free, as that is not possible, but it does mean having the confidence (provided by feeling part of a supportive group of people who have a strong sense of 'we are in it together' and being led by someone who earns trust, respect and credibility) to respond to risks in a balanced way governed by reflective practice, rather than in a defensive way governed by anxiety and knee-jerk responses.

- *Honesty and integrity* Honesty involves encouraging open communication, so that there is a commitment to shared endeavour, but integrity is also important. In a sense, integrity is about making sure that our actions are consistent with our values. Sadly, it is not uncommon for people to profess certain values, but then behave in ways that contradict those values. This will be seen as a sign of inauthenticity in a leader and will undermine trust, respect and credibility. Making a firm and significant commitment to honesty and integrity can therefore be seen as a major part of leadership praxis.

Voice of experience 7.3

I suppose I have been lucky, but I've never worked with a manager I thought of as being dishonest or lacking in integrity. It's a good job, I suppose. I'm not sure I could put my heart into a job if I felt I couldn't trust my manager.

Charlie, a manager in a catering company

- *Vision* I have already emphasized the importance of having a clear, but flexible vision that is shared – a joint existential project in a sense. It is essential that leaders are able to create the trust that will enable people to commit to a shared vision of where they, as a group of individuals, are trying to get to, so that there can be clarity about how they are going to do that and therefore motivation and commitment towards following that path. Where there is no vision, or the vision is not clear, or it is too rigid, or it is a top-down vision that does not have people 'on board', then it is likely to be not only ineffective, but actually counterproductive, in the sense that it can generate cynicism, low morale and defeatism. In other words, it can alienate people.
- *Conflict management* Being an effective conflict manager is part and parcel of effective leadership, in the sense that existentialism helps us

to understand that the very nature of human existence means that people's paths will get in one another's way. There will inevitably be conflicts, and, rather than try and sweep these under the carpet in a bad faith type of way, it is important that we are authentic and honest about conflict by recognizing its existence, its prevalence, its potential dangers (if the conflict is not addressed) and the challenges involved in making sure that, as far as possible, we are effective conflict managers. Coleman and Ferguson (2014) emphasize the importance of being effective conflict managers when they highlight the harm that conflict can do:

> Conflict is a lot like fire. When it sparks, it can intensify, spread, and lead to pain, loss, and irreparable damage. It can distract, distance, derail, and occasionally destroy opportunities and relationships. It makes most people anxious, and as a result it is often mishandled and made worse. It can waste and lessen productivity, impair teamwork and morale, increase counterproductive behaviours like stealing and sabotage, and poison the physical and mental health of employees. So conflict can burn. (p. xii)

Our understanding of conflict as a central feature of human interactions is therefore an element of praxis we need to pay attention to. If we fail to take heed of the significance of conflict and its dangers, we place ourselves in quite a vulnerable position. We also miss the positive potential of conflict and the way, at times, in which can help us move forward by identifying conflicting issues and seeking to resolve them (potentially earning trust, respect and credibility in the process).

- *Avoiding bad faith* Not succumbing to bad faith or allowing others to do so involves taking ownership seriously. As I have emphasized, this is not a matter of blame, but rather, of accountability, of recognizing that individuals in the workplace are, or at least should be, trusted to carry out their duties to the best of their ability. If they feel that they are not being trusted, if they feel that they are not being valued, then there is a danger that they will indulge in bad faith and not take ownership of their actions. This can take the form of finding various excuses for why certain things were not done or were not done to a good enough standard. It involves a degree of game playing, and this can be quite destructive, not only in terms of the individual concerned, but also how it has an impact in turn on the overall morale of the staff group concerned. Ownership, then, should be seen as a positive phenomenon, something to be valued, because it means that we are being trusted.

In a sense avoiding bad faith is at the heart of authentic leadership. It means not just taking ownership of our choices and actions (and encouraging others to take ownership of their choices and actions), but also being aware of the various other ways in which we can lose sight of the fact that leading people effectively is premised on being true not to our 'real self', but to what it really means to be human, with all the complexity that entails: flux, contingency and emergence; the dialectic of subjectivity and objectivity; the influence of the past and future on the present and so on. As we noted in the Introduction, scientific approaches to the study of leadership do not do justice to these complexities and, if anything, paint a less than human picture of leadership, rather than one that fully acknowledges our humanity (Ladkin, 2010).

CONCLUSION

This chapter has given an overview of some key issues that relate to how theory and practice relating to leadership can come together in meaningful ways to produce high-quality leadership praxis. I have drawn on existentialist concepts and related these to some other established ideas about aspects of good leadership. What now needs to be considered is what existentialism in particular has to say about leadership practice. The remaining two chapters will therefore have a focus on this. Chapter 8 will present and analyse a number of practice scenarios and highlight how existentialist concepts can be used to understand what is involved. Chapter 9 will then complement that by highlighting eight principles of existentialist thought and showing how these can be useful in making sense of the complex world of leadership in the modern workplace. In this way it is to be hoped that Part III will have offered you a helpful picture of how existentialist ideas can be used to inform authentic leadership.

chapter 8　Existentialism in practice

INTRODUCTION

In this chapter I present six practice scenarios and offer analysis for each from the point of view of existentialist thought specifically relating to the key concept of authenticity. In each one I will be addressing the question of what is an authentic way forward for a leader in facing the challenges involved. The use of scenarios in this chapter reflects the importance of the point I was emphasizing in Chapter 7 of the need to start with concrete situations, to begin with practice and then seek to theorize it by drawing on relevant theoretical understandings, rather than trying to apply theory to practice in an artificial way (as discussed in Chapter 7).

Each of the scenarios presented reflects either a direct situation that I have encountered in my work, or is a composite of various situations I have encountered which have the same themes running through them. But, in all instances, these reflect real situations, and not fictional ones that may be dismissed as having little relevance to actual real-life contexts.

Each scenario is presented in three parts. First, there is a brief overview of the scenario itself to set the scene. Next comes 'The leadership challenges' in which the issues the leader would need to be aware of are outlined. The final section presents 'An authentic response' in which I explain how existentialist ideas around authenticity could be applied to the scenario and the leadership challenges contained within it. No easy answers are offered, as that would not be consistent with one of the core messages of this book, namely the need for leadership thinking to be aware of the complexity of human experience.

The range of issues covered by the scenarios and the discussion of them is far from comprehensive. The aim is not to give an exhaustive account of any particular practice scenario, but, rather, to provide food for thought for further consideration of what is involved in developing an (existentially) authentic approach to leadership.

POOR PERFORMANCE

The scenario

John is doing less work than the other team members and his work is generally of a lower quality. The team are resentful and have started to demonize him by moaning about him behind his back and talking about him in very uncomplimentary terms. They are resentful not only of the poor quality of his work compared with the work of other team members, but also of the fact that he does not seem to be bothered by his lower quantity and quality of work compared with the others who seem to work harder and produce better quality results. They are therefore annoyed by what they perceive to be his lack of commitment to any sense of shared endeavour. They feel that it is unfair that he is allowed to get away with putting less in but getting the same salary as people who are far more committed and hard-working.

The leadership challenges

Managing performance can be difficult and challenging at times (Thompson, 2013a). As Clutterbuck (2007) acknowledges: 'teams are highly complex social entities, ... the influences on their performance are even more complex, and ... there are no simple answers or approaches when working with teams. Improving individual performance does not necessarily improve team performance' (p. 74).

Pedler *et al.* (2010) also comment on the problems associated with performance management:

> The downsides of performance management are as well understood as the benefits. How can we manage performance without making people target-obsessed, risk-averse, closed and defensive? In this context,

leadership must create the processes, structures, cultures and relationships that balance performance with development to protect the precious capacity for learning. (p. 19)

One of the main dangers with this scenario is that the ill feeling towards John could contribute to increased tensions and a possible vicious circle in which morale is reduced, leading to further tensions and so on. A further danger is that the leader's credibility could be lost. That is, if team members are aware that the leader knows about John's perceived 'swinging the lead', but is not doing anything about it, he or she will lose the faith of the team and therefore be in a much weaker situation when it comes to influencing them as part of a process of shaping and sustaining a positive workplace culture. Sadly, this is a common occurrence whereby leaders either lack the courage to tackle certain issues, allow themselves to become too busy to notice important issues or, for whatever other reason, do not address issues that are of concern to the staff group. The price to be paid for this tends to be quite high, as it can undermine the sense of security and being valued and supported that are important foundations for enabling people to achieve their best.

So, in this particular scenario, the irony is that concerns about one person's performance not being addressed could result in problems in terms of other people's performance. Their good will and commitment could well be replaced by a growing resentment and a feeling of disappointment in their leader. On the other hand, however, tackling the problem directly with John, if not well handled, could potentially alienate him and lead to further tensions within the team. It could easily come across to John that he is being 'got at' and that the leader is 'firing the bullets' that members of the team have provided. It could even result in a claim of bullying being made. The stakes, then, are potentially quite high.

An authentic response

We now need to consider how existentialist ideas could help cast some light on this situation. Perhaps the first one to consider is phenomenology, with its emphasis on perception and meaning. Is John actually working less than the others or does it just appear that he is? Perhaps he works quietly without making any fuss in a culture where others tend to talk more openly about what they are doing. If he is perceived as a 'slacker', perhaps the other team members are then more critical of his work and perceive that there is a problem with the quality of his work as well as the quantity. Of course, it cannot be assumed that this is the case, and so these issues would have to be checked out carefully.

Assuming that it is not a matter of perception, and that there really is a problem with the quality and quantity of work, another important consideration would be to what extent (and in what ways) this may be a reflection of the culture. For example, if John is the only male in the team (or the only black person), does he feel that he does not belong as part of the team? Has he been sensing that he is perceived as an outsider? If so, is this demotivating him? This could be the dialectic of subjectivity and objectivity in operation, in the sense that his (objective) status as a person from a minority could be experienced subjectively by him as a degree of rejection. His behaviour in response to his (subjective) perceptions could have been a lower level of motivation and commitment, which then manifests itself as an (objective) example of low levels of quality and quantity of work which is then (subjectively) perceived as laziness or a lack of team spirit.

This is, of course, just one example of how it might be a cultural matter. There are many more possibilities. The main point is that we need to consider cultural factors before jumping to conclusions that the fault lies with the individual worker. We need to think holistically and not fall foul of atomism and simply assume that it is a matter of laziness on John's part.

We should also not rule out that the issues may actually rest with John and not the culture. There may be factors unconnected with the culture that are leading him to produce lower levels of work than the others. These would include:

- *Lack of knowledge and/or skills* John may lack some of the knowledge or skills needed to carry out the work to a standard or at a pace that other staff are able to do. This means that a learning need is being identified that may require a training or coaching input. This is not simply a matter of identifying some sort of flaw or inadequacy on

John in an essentialist way. Rather, it involves being aware that knowledge and skills can be learned – reflecting the existentialist idea of 'becoming'; people can change by developing new knowledge and understanding and by practising and steadily developing new patterns of behaviour (skill development).

- *Lack of confidence* Perhaps John does have the knowledge and skills he needs, but lacks the confidence to put them into practice. Confidence is generally understood in essentialist terms – that is, as a 'quality' that individuals possess to a greater or lesser degree. However, from an essentialist point of view, confidence can be understood as the attitude we adopt (in other words, a choice or series of choices) towards the task in hand. 'Confidence' means faith or trust. To lack confidence therefore means that we do not trust ourselves to be able to achieve the task; we do not have faith in ourselves. For example, if we approach a task telling ourselves that we cannot do it, then that amounts to not trusting ourselves to be able to do it. In this way, we disempower ourselves. If, however, we approach a task with the attitude that we are prepared to try and see whether we can do it, we have some degree of faith in ourselves – we have chosen to trust ourselves to at least give it a try. This is tentative confidence which can develop over time into consolidated confidence where we reach the point that we feel fully confident about what we are doing.

- *Personal problems* There may be factors outside the workplace that are interfering with John's ability or willingness to work more effectively. This can raise issues of workplace well-being and, in the process, highlight the importance of authentic leadership as a *human* endeavour that treats people as people (with all the complexity that entails). Human resources are first and foremost human, and will therefore face difficulties and challenges in their lives, including their working lives. Leaders who fail to take account of this are out of touch with the reality of the workplace and are therefore being far from authentic.

There is much more that could be said about this scenario, the challenges it presents and the ways in which existentialism could cast light on it, but it is to be hoped that this brief overview will be sufficient to show how existentialist ideas can be used in practice.

ANXIETY AND LOW MORALE

The scenario

The staff team are highly anxious. A vicious circle has developed. They work in a context where risk is a key factor, but a culture has developed where they have become risk averse – that is, they have become defensive and tend to overestimate degrees of risk. They are so anxious about things going drastically wrong that they adopt a very rigid and almost paranoid approach to risk situations. This then proves to be difficult to implement in a professional and effective way because they are not recognizing the need to balance risks. They are ignoring the fact that trying to remove one set of risks is likely to have the effect of introducing new (and possibly more serious) risks. What should be a professional, carefully thought-through well-informed approach to risk issues has become reduced to a simplistic and misguided attempt to minimize, if not actually eradicate, risk. So, what has evolved is a vicious circle in which their risk-averse approach makes it harder for them to deal with the risk issues effectively, and then recognizing that they are not dealing with the risk issues effectively makes them more anxious and, in turn, more risk averse. The manager is trying to 'play it safe' by being ultra-cautious about risk (thereby both reflecting and reinforcing a risk-averse culture), and is therefore actually reinforcing the problem, rather than taking steps to rectify the difficulties being encountered. The net result is a dangerously low level of morale.

The leadership challenges

There are (at least) two main challenges in this scenario. One relates to the misguided approach to risk and the other to the consequences of that, low morale. The existentialist focus on flux and contingency enables us to see that risk issues are around us all the time – there is no such thing as a risk-free zone. I have already made the point that a 'playing it safe' approach is, paradoxically, a dangerous one to adopt, in so far as it oversimplifies a complex picture and leaves us in a situation whereby our distorted approach can actually make matters worse.

For example, an anxiety-driven approach on the part of child protection professionals can lead to an unduly restrictive or heavy-handed approach to families, resulting in lower levels of cooperation and therefore less chance of being able to safeguard the child(ren) concerned from abuse.

This can apply to how managers approach their leadership duties too, in so far as anxiety about staff making mistakes or behaving inappropriately can lead them to indulge in micro management and rely on command and control methods, rather than empower their staff to achieve their best. I have emphasized at various points the central role of trust, respect and credibility. We are less likely to be trusted, respected or seen as credible, if we are not prepared, to a certain extent at least, to show trust, respect and credibility to those who are relying upon as for leadership.

The morale problem is also one that can have disastrous results. This is because low morale can lead to a vicious circle of self-disempowerment. It works like this:

- There is dissatisfaction which lowers morale.
- Moaning and 'ventilating' become common means of expressing that dissatisfaction.
- These activities give temporary relief, but make no difference to the problems and the underlying causes. People start to feel helpless and trapped. This can lead them into becoming negative and defeatist, cynical even.
- After the temporary relief subsides, people revert to moaning.
- The moaning reinforces the dissatisfaction and sense of negativity.
- A culture of hopelessness and helplessness develops.

The net result is that low morale has produced a situation in which people are disempowering themselves, placing obstacles to progress in their own way.

These two sets of concerns can then reinforce one another: anxiety-driven risk aversion and defensiveness contributes to low morale. The negativity and defeatism associated with low morale can then fuel the anxiety that in turn leads to risk-averse practices.

An authentic response

Phenomenology once again offers helpful insights here, as perception is a key factor in anxiety and risk assessment. This is because: (i) anxiety is a response to a perceived threat; and (ii) there is no definitive scientific way of determining risk and so much depends on professional judgement, which of course will depend on perception. A clear challenge for the leader here is to create a culture in which anxiety is better managed and morale is not so destructively low – the former is likely to make a significant positive contribution to the latter.

A key part of this will be ontological security. Can the leader make staff feel more secure and confident in how they respond to the challenges of their work, especially the risk elements? Developing a clear, shared vision that is communicated to staff in a way that is meaningful to them will be a positive step in that direction. That vision would need to incorporate an understanding of the importance of not allowing anxiety to distort the task of assessing and managing risk so that it becomes unbalanced, unfair and potentially counterproductive. There would be scope for using the progressive-regressive method to clarify how fears about getting criticized in the future (progressive) are combining with past experiences of threatening situations (regressive) to produce the current level of anxiety and consequent risk aversion, defensiveness and low morale. This could give some clues as to how best to change the negative aspects of the culture.

An authentic leader would also need to guard against bad faith (on their own and their staff's part) – for example, the culture of anxiety being based on the view that staff 'can't help' being anxious and risk averse, as if they have no control over their behaviour or their reactions to the circumstances they find themselves in (thereby disempowering themselves). Cultures are powerful, but they are not all powerful. They can be discontinued if the habits that sustain them can be broken, if the unwritten rules and shared meanings that keep them alive are renegotiated. Bad faith will serve only to make any such change less likely. Members of the team need to take ownership – with the guidance and example of their leader – for the anxiety in particular and emotional tenor in general of their working environment.

CONFLICT

The scenario

This particular team works in a multidisciplinary context, so there are people from different professional backgrounds. Although, as a team, they should be pulling together towards common goals, poor communication means that they are pulling in different directions in accordance with their professional differences, without realizing that they are doing so. This creates tension that is not being recognized or addressed, and so factions have started to develop within the team. This has led to a process of 'pathologizing' in which each group within the team is seeing the other groups as 'being awkward'. There is little or no awareness that conflict is a key factor here. There is an oversimplification of some complex issues and this is what needs to be addressed through authentic leadership.

The leadership challenges

I have already argued that effective conflict management is an important part of authentic leadership. This is because to assume that there will be no conflict in a group of people is to deny the reality of social life, to deceive ourselves about the challenges involved. If we accept that a key part of leadership is to get the best out of people – that is, to be the best workers they can so that everyone benefits – then we need to recognize that it is unlikely that anyone will be achieving their best if unresolved conflicts are causing unnecessary tensions or distractions (and thereby undermining a sense of security).

As we have noted, there is no point aiming for a conflict-free workplace, as that is unachievable. However, what we can do is to: (i) at the very least ensure that conflicts do not escalate and become a source of ill feeling or hostility that can be highly problematic; and (ii) where possible, seek to turn the conflict into a positive – for example, by encouraging people to appreciate differences of perspective and thereby encourage creativity and learning.

Leadership involves the responsible use of power and, as Coleman and Ferguson (2014) point out: 'Conflict puts power differences into focus' (p. xii). They go on to explain that: 'Understanding how conflict and power affect each other is vital to effective conflict management, but talking about power differences openly is still taboo in most places in society' (p. xiii). These are helpful insights, as there is a danger that conflict issues will be allowed to worsen if they are not identified and openly discussed in suitably sensitive and supportive ways. When people are in serious conflict they are likely to be using their power to get their way at the expense of the other party, each trying to do the other down (and thereby wrecking any hope of effective teamwork). A key challenge for leaders, therefore, is to use their power (as authority) to address the conflict effectively before it inflicts significant damage (not only for the warring factions, but also potentially for everyone concerned).

An authentic response

As we have seen, existentialism regards conflict as an inevitable aspect of human existence. This means that we need to understand it not as something pathological or abnormal, but as a basic feature of human interaction. People's interactions will be in part harmonious and in part conflictual. Indeed, it would be naive to expect anything other than this. Recognizing this helps us to realize that it would be far from authentic to delude ourselves into thinking that managing conflict is not part of a leader's role.

Given the inevitability of some degree of conflict, open dialogue about the issues relating to conflict can be helpful. As Coleman and Ferguson (2014) point out: 'Generally the more transparent or explicit a conflict, the easier it is to address constructively through discussion, negotiation, and mediation' (p. 4). Effective leadership therefore needs to include a willingness to acknowledge conflict and not see its existence as in any way a failure or deficit. This needs to be accompanied by the courage to address conflict issues, rather than make the not uncommon mistake of trying to pretend conflict does not exist in the hope that it will go away (the ostrich approach).

Two existentialist concepts that can be helpful when it comes to conflict are phenomenology and the progressive-regressive method. Phenomenology, as we have seen, emphasizes the significance of perception. What underpins conflict is difference in perspective – that is, conflict arises when people have differing perspectives on a situation or issue. Addressing conflict, from an existentialist point of view, can therefore be seen to revolve around identifying differences of perspective that are creating problems. These differences could relate to the meanings attached to particular events or processes; to values, plans or aspirations; or to various other things. Understanding these differences gives us an important basis for moving forward constructively.

The progressive-regressive method also casts light on conflict. This is because differences in perspective can arise from: (i) differences between people in terms of their past experiences (and how the meanings they attach to those experiences are influencing their present thoughts and feelings); (ii) differences relating to future plans and aspirations (and how these too will be influencing the current perspective in the present); and (iii) how the past and future influences are interacting with each other to shape present perspectives.

FIGURE 8.1 **Six areas of challenge**

STRESS

The scenario

A situation of some concern has been reached because of high levels of sickness absence in a voluntary sector project. The small staff group has become smaller and smaller because of sickness absence and the situation has now reached crisis point because there are now two people trying to do the work of six, and their manager is struggling to cope with the situation and is becoming stressed himself.

The leadership challenges

Sadly, stress is not uncommon in the modern workplace, as Hames (2007) acknowledges: 'Stress is becoming palpable as individuals try to achieve impossible targets with fewer resources' (p. 82). This presents a number of challenges for leaders. However, leadership itself can be an important buffer against stress by helping people to feel safe, valued and supported, to be motivated and achieving their best. Good leadership should also create an open atmosphere where staff feel comfortable in discussing their pressures and helping each other deal with them.

In this particular scenario the danger is that the whole situation could collapse because: (i) the leader is becoming stressed and will therefore be in a weak position to lead the under pressure staff group; and (ii) two people attempting to do the work of six is likely to amount to trying to do the impossible, but there appears to be no strategy in place to deal with the situation in any other way.

Clutterbuck (2007) highlights the dangers of people working flat out without any opportunity for respite, reflection or review:

> It's not practical or reasonable to expect the team to work at full throttle all the time: variation in pace is important in maintaining interest and concentration. It's rather like working muscles. Athletes learn to pace exercise so that heavy exertion is followed by a period of lighter activity that breaks down and disperses the by-products of muscle use that cause cramp. Similarly, teams need to intersperse concentrated effort with periods of light-heartedness; action with reflection; doing

with reviewing. A high-performing team and its members develop a rhythm of work that builds what we might call performance stamina. (pp. 220–1)

There is clearly, then, a need for significant change in this scenario if things are not to go from bad to worse to disastrous.

An authentic response

It is often claimed that 'stress is good for you', but this is to confuse stress with pressure. Pressure can be positive (energizing and stimulating) or negative (overstretching and undermining), while stress refers to levels of pressure that are harming us in some way – for example, harming our health, well-being, relationships or quality of work. As the Health and Safety Executive explain, stress is experienced when levels of pressure exceed our ability to cope with them. To assume that 'stress is good for you' is, at best, a misunderstanding of stress and, at worst, an example of bad faith – an unwillingness for leaders to take ownership of the all-too-common problem of stress in the workplace.

So, in terms of an authentic response to this scenario, perhaps the first step needs to be to move beyond a pathologizing atomism ('stress is the sign of a weak individual') to a more holistic approach that acknowledges stress to have individual, social and organizational dimensions and not simply be a matter of individual failing (Thompson, 2009a). This recognition in itself can make a very positive difference – for example, by having a significant impact on morale and encouraging teamwork and mutual support.

As we noted earlier, control has been recognized as a key factor in relation to stress, in so far as a lack of it can undermine coping and encourage a sense of helplessness. The existentialist concepts of facticity and transcendence can be applied to this. As we have noted, there are many aspects of life that we have no control over (facticity), but we can control how we respond to these circumstances (transcendence). This can be a useful way of approaching potentially stressful situations (see the discussion of the CIA Framework in Thompson, 2012d). This recognition of transcendence can be empowering by removing any sense of helplessness. An authentic leader could therefore move away from the bad faith of assuming 'there is nothing we can do about the situation' by beginning to develop strategies for addressing the difficulties involved – that is, by exploring what steps can be taken to reduce the pressures and increase the level of resources for dealing with them.

DISCRIMINATION

The scenario

This staff group are of a diverse ethnic background. Approximately forty per cent of the group are from a minority ethnic background. This situation has not been handled very well and tensions have developed. This is largely because the white workers in the group are anxious about the need to avoid being perceived as racist. The black workers in the group are picking up the tensions and interpreting these as a reluctance to work with them, and are therefore beginning to perceive their white colleagues as actually racist – in a way it is becoming a self-fulfilling prophecy. The white manager of the team is feeling extremely challenged by this situation and, to begin with, is unsure of where to turn.

The leadership challenges

Diversity needs to be understood as an asset to benefit from, not a problem to be solved (Kirton and Greene, 2010), although many organizations fail to capitalize on this. As Clutterbuck (2007) explains:

> Several studies have found that top management teams that have diverse backgrounds and capabilities make more innovative, higher-quality decisions than those that are relatively homogeneous.
>
> Being diverse isn't enough, however. Using diversity effectively in decision making demands that the team has processes that allow its members to have open and positively critical dialogue, to investigate issues with an open mind and to be willing to learn from the situation and from each other. They also need to be able to identify and understand others' perspectives and synthesize these into a decision that is better than that which might have emerged through the horse-trading

and compromise that so often characterize management decision making. (pp. 55–6)

In addition, diversity in the workplace can be a focal point for problems when discrimination is allowed to feature. If leaders are to get the best out of people, then clearly they need to ensure that discrimination is not happening within their sphere of influence, However, discrimination is a complex matter and not simply a matter of (atomistic) personal prejudice (Thompson, 2011a). Leaders need to have a more sophisticated understanding of the subtleties of discriminatory process if they are to succeed in this endeavour.

An authentic response

One way in which bad faith can manifest itself is through not taking ownership of discrimination – for example, by assuming that certain groups are 'by nature' worthy of less consideration or respect than others. Authenticity therefor entails taking (individual and collective) ownership of creating and sustaining cultures based on equality not discrimination. PCS analysis, as discussed earlier, can help us to understand the complexities involved in this by recognizing that discrimination operates at all three levels, personal (prejudicial attitudes, for example), cultural (discriminatory assumptions and stereotypes embedded within cultural frameworks of meaning) and structural (society is not a level playing field, with more privileged groups having more power and life chances). This framework can give us a helpful basis for making sense of the complex processes and interactions that contribute to discrimination.

Phenomenology is also helpful in relation to this specific scenario, as a key factor in this situation appears to be misguided perceptions – white workers perceiving black colleagues as potential sources of complaint about them and black workers understandably interpreting their distance and defensiveness as reflections of racist attitudes towards them. In particular, we can see the dialectic of subjectivity and objectivity in operation. Subjective perceptions produce objective tensions which in turn shape subjective perceptions. Tackling the problems involved will therefore require leadership intervention to change the dynamics of this dialectic to prevent the situation from deteriorating further.

Once again a culture of openness where people feel safe, valued and supported will be necessary to allow these difficult issues to be addressed in a way that will not add to the difficulties. The fact that this situation has developed in the way it has strongly suggests that such a culture of openness has not existed to date. The manager will therefore face a significant, but not impossible, challenge to turn the situation round.

IMPOSED CHANGE

The scenario

The company had been taken over by a major competitor. Fears of wide-scale job losses had proven unfounded, but there were still major changes brought about by the new owners. People felt disorientated and concerned that their previous ways of working were being devalued. The result was a significant drop in morale, with all the attendant problems of lower quality and quantity of work, increased tensions and a greater risk of stress.

The leadership challenges

Ballat and Campling (2011) make the point that:

> Any change, especially imposed from 'outside', is emotionally disruptive and can affect the way people think about their work, their colleagues, their patients and themselves. Most staff are attached to their job and particular ways of working. They invest valued parts of themselves, often at personal cost, and take pride in what their particular service offers. They have found ways of managing their difficult feelings, ways that have become intimately entwined with the way things have been done. A culture where the focus is always on newness leaves people feeling inse-cure, undervalued and sometimes abandoned. If their service is cut or redesigned, they will feel bereaved, even if they can understand the reasons for the change. (p. 134)

As Ballat and Campling imply, significant changes can provoke a strong grief reaction, although it is often the case that this is not recognized (Thompson, 2009b). If leaders are to be authentic, then they need to be attuned to what it means to be human, and this includes understanding, and being able to respond to, human reactions to loss in the form of grief. Failing to recognize the significance of grief in the workplace can create a number of problems – not least the undermining of any sense of security. The result can then be the undermining of trust, respect and credibility.

A further challenge in this scenario is that major changes present opportunities as well as problems. These opportunities could be missed if the negative effects of the change are allowed to predominate.

An authentic response

This scenario describes one significant change due to a takeover. However, as Hames (2007) points out, a culture characterized by constant change initiatives can do a great deal of harm. As he puts it: 'One might even argue that the cost of inaction would be far less than the constant merry-go-round of re-structuring and other so-called "change" activities that have become routine for lazy managers attempting to hide their distinct lack of imagination and ability' (p. 65). The existentialist concepts of flux and contingency help us to understand that change is part of the fabric of human existence and that any stability that exists is as a result of actions that reproduce existing arrangements (autopoiesis) and is not simply a natural state. This means that how change is managed needs a more sophisticated understanding of what is involved than the simplistic process of imposing change without taking into consideration the human costs of doing so.

As Lear (2009) puts it: 'If People are the center of the driving force for high levels of performance in an organization, then it is creating an emotional connection between those people and the organization that is the key to unleashing that force' (pp. 85–6). Alienating people by imposing change after change is likely to be counterproductive, while creating an atmosphere where people are confident and responsive to a constantly evolving situation is likely to be far more effective. This takes us back to the key point of the importance of aiming to get the best out of people by engaging them in mutually beneficial projects that allow them to grow and develop.

Without such engagement, the result can be cynicism, which in many ways is the antithesis of what authentic leadership is intended to achieve. Cynicism will prevent opportunities arising from change to be capitalized upon and will therefore contribute to an unduly negative, unbalanced approach to the situation.

The existentialist concepts of flux and contingency help us to understand why grief is more common a phenomenon than people generally realize (Thompson, 2012c). Grief is a reaction to loss, and loss is a product of change. Change is a reflection of flux and contingency. Grief is an important existential challenge, as it can undermine our sense of self (what is often referred to as 'biographical disruption') and affect how we relate to others and, indeed, to our work.

As we noted earlier, Doka (2002) uses the concept of 'disenfranchised grief' to refer to grief that is not recognized or socially sanctioned – for example, the grief that can arise when one's secret lover dies and open mourning is restricted. In an earlier work (Thompson, 2009b), I put forward the argument that grief in the workplace is often disenfranchised because of the common tendency for workplaces to sweep grief (and, often, emotional matters in general) under the carpet. Leaders who reinforce this tendency by not recognizing – or by recognizing but not addressing – the grief associated with imposed change will fail to take adequate account of the human dimensions of working life and will therefore fall short of being authentic. Being attuned to grief as a feature of human existence will, by contrast, make an important contribution to authentic leadership.

CONCLUSION

It is to be hoped that these six scenarios will have given you a picture of how authentic leadership, informed by existentialist thought, can be not a magic answer or panacea, but none the less an important foundation of good practice in rising to some very significant management challenges. Each scenario has presented a set of circumstances that can be challenging for any leader and, if not handled properly, potentially disastrous. Existential authenticity can be seen as a firm foundation for rising to these challenges, but not a source of easy answers – indeed the idea that there are no easy answers, that each situation represents an existential struggle in terms of the choices we are called upon to make and the consequences of those choices is fundamental to existentialism. These practice examples, then, should not be seen as a protocol to follow, but as food for thought to encourage reflection and analysis of these complex issues.

In the next and final chapter we will complement these discussions by looking at how eight important principles of existentialist practice can help to inform the way we carry out our leadership duties.

chapter 9　Authentic leadership

INTRODUCTION

Some years ago I was invited to write a chapter for a book on social work about how existentialist thought can inform social work practice (Thompson, 2012e). That chapter was built around eight principles of existentialist thought and how each of these can cast light on practice. I am now going to carry out a similar operation in this chapter by revisiting those eight principles and showing how they can equally well cast light on leadership practice, and thereby make a contribution to the development of authentic leadership. I will therefore explore each of the eight principles in turn, give an overview of the significance of the principles, and then offer some ideas about how these can be useful in practice.

As this is the final chapter, the discussions here can be seen as a form of conclusion, a restatement in summary form of some of the key theoretical issues as they relate to practice situations, reflecting the Part III theme of integrating theory and practice. This leads into the Conclusion proper where I will briefly review what I see as the key 'messages' of the book.

FREEDOM AND RESPONSIBILITY ARE BASIC BUILDING BLOCKS OF HUMAN EXPERIENCE

This takes us back to our earlier discussion of the importance of recognizing authentic leadership, in the sense I am using it here, as not relating to being true to our 'real self', when there is no fixed underlying self. Existential authenticity is premised on the idea that selfhood is not fixed; it is, in a sense, the journey of our life as we live it, the pathway we follow as we become 'what we make of what is made of us'. This is a core feature of existentialism, as it is based on the idea that freedom – the ability, and indeed necessity, to continually make choices – is what shapes the direction our life takes. It is what shapes who we are. There is therefore no underlying fixed identity, but, rather, an ongoing process of interaction of personal, cultural and structural factors inter-relating and shaping our lives (and therefore our sense of who we are).

With that freedom comes responsibility, in the sense that every choice a person makes will close certain doors and open other doors. This means that we are building our future each and every day. We are moving towards certain things and away from others by making choices. Many of these choices will, of course, have become habitual and unthinking, but that does not alter the fact that they are our choices and that we could act differently if we chose to do so. Continuing to act in a habitual way without reflecting on what we are doing is in itself a choice, and we continue to have the potential to make different choices.

This is not to say that there are no constraints on our choices. Sartre, for example, was keen to emphasize the role of facticity which involves the recognition that there are many things that we have no control or influence over, but we do have control over how we respond to them and the facticity they represent.

The implications of this for leadership are far-reaching and profound. This is because it helps us to recognize that, as leaders, we have to take account of our own radical freedom and responsibility – the ownership for our actions that comes with being a free human being, in the existentialist sense. But, in addition, we have to be aware that the people we lead are also free in this sense and need to take ownership of their actions, attitudes and overall responses. Helping people to take ownership of their actions as part of a sheared endeavour of achieving collective goals is a central part of leadership.

This has significant implications in terms of how we relate to the personnel we lead. For example, if we adopt the traditional command and control method by simply issuing instructions, then that may be effective up to a point, but it is certainly not going to be sufficient to enable people to maximize their potential. If we are to aim for maximizing potential (thriving), rather than simply achieving the bare minimum needed (surviving), then we need to move beyond the command and control approach and focus on empowerment. People often interpret empowerment in a literal sense of giving power to people, whereas, in reality it is far more complex than this (Thompson, 2007a). This is because, if people are indeed free individuals, then they already have the power. It is about helping them to use that power in a responsible – and indeed authentic – way. In a very real sense this can be seen as being at the very heart of authentic leadership. It also involves helping them not to disempower themselves through bad faith rooted in a reluctance to take ownership of the power they have.

PRACTICE FOCUS 9.1

Eryl was asked to take over an events management subsidiary of the media company he had been employed by for many years. The previous events manager had left after being criticized for poor results in takings. Eryl had no experience of events management, but he was very adept at managing people. He quickly realized that there was a culture of blaming others for what hadn't worked out. It soon became apparent that a defensive culture had developed in which people were prone to look for someone to blame if anything didn't go according to plan. He became aware that his predecessor was quite harsh on anyone who made a mistake and this had contributed significantly to defensive working practices that left no room for honesty and openness. Eryl appreciated that he would need to look carefully at how to dispel this culture and shape a culture based on honesty and ownership. He felt it would be wise to start by trying to get across to the staff group that mistakes are inevitable in any work setting and make it clear that he wanted them to be open and transparent about anything that went wrong, rather than play cover up games and try and wriggle out of ownership.

FREEDOM IS BOTH LIBERATION AND HEAVY BURDEN

The fact that we can choose how we relate to situations, we can choose what direction we want to take our lives in, is an example of liberation. It frees us from so many of the restricting 'common-sense' ideas that we have a fixed personality or a fixed nature and that we are simply who we are, and there is nothing we can do about that. The existentialist notion of radical freedom opens up a wide range of opportunities to us and gives us considerable hope and positivity about how we can make changes in our life. Of course, once again, facticity needs to be considered, recognizing that there will be certain options closed off to us. But the fact that certain options are closed off does not alter the fact that we face a huge array of options that we can explore if we choose to. The existence of facticity as a factor to be considered does not eradicate radical freedom, it just presents the context in which that radical freedom can take place. Going back to the point I made earlier, existentialism presents freedom as absolute, in the sense that we have to choose, we have to adopt an attitude towards the circumstances we find ourselves in; we cannot simply allow them to dictate to us, because we, at each stage in our thinking, will react to the external factors. The tendency not to recognize this radical freedom and to focus rather on facticity can be seen as a form of self-disempowerment. Authentic leadership can therefore be understood as having two sides. First of all, we need to make sure that we do not disempower ourselves and, second, we are active in challenging the self-disempowerment of those we lead.

Freedom therefore offers considerable opportunity in terms of liberation, but, because of this, there is also the heavy burden it brings to consider. We are, as Sartre said, condemned to be free. What he meant by this is: not only can we choose, but we *must* choose. At each point we face options and alternatives. If we decide not to adopt any of those options or alternatives, that in itself is a choice. There is therefore no way of escaping choice and freedom. This means that the direction we take today, tomorrow, next week, next month and indeed throughout our lives is largely down to us – there may well be powerful influences acting upon us, but it is the individual who makes the choice, not the influences. This is where the notion of anguish comes in, because this is the tension that we can feel when we become aware of the profound implications of the choices we make – based on the recognition that an unwise choice could have profound and far-reaching detrimental consequences.

Of course, some choices will have much more of a bearing on our lives than others. Deciding whether to have tea or coffee will generally pale into insignificance compared with deciding whether to apply for a job or not, but even minor choices which may often seem trivial can at times have profound and far-reaching consequences. This recognition of the extent of our freedom can, for some people at some times, be quite frightening. It may be overwhelming, and it is therefore understandable, although highly problematic, that many people will seek refuge from this freedom and its heavy burden by denying that it exists and thereby be in bad faith.

This, then, presents challenges for authentic leadership. First of all, we need to make sure that we ourselves are not denying that freedom and the responsibility that comes with it. We have to make sure that we are taking full ownership of our actions and not playing self-deluding games (for example, by acting as if the workplace culture we are part of is something that we can have no part in shaping – an attitude that many people have brought to leadership courses I have run, but which they have abandoned by the end of the event). But, echoing the point I made earlier, we also have to make sure, as far as reasonably possible, that we are supporting our followers in not going down the road of denying ownership of their actions.

Voice of experience 9.1

For years I had been telling myself there were things I couldn't do, things that I thought were beyond me, and no one had ever challenged me on that. But that all changed when Rae became our manager. It came as quite a shock to a few of us when Rae made it crystal clear that each of us would be helped to fulfil our potential, and that meant not accepting any defeatism on our part. Saying we couldn't do something before we had even tried was now a no-go area. It was a little

AUTHENTICITY IS THE KEY TO LIBERATION, WHILE ITS OPPOSITE – BAD FAITH – IS THE COMMON (UNSUCCESSFUL) STRATEGY FOR COPING WITH THE BURDEN

Here we are getting to the heart of what this book is all about. Authenticity is indeed the key to liberation: recognizing that it is not a matter of being true to our fixed, real, underlying self, but actually acknowledging that our life is, in effect, our self, that we are that journey, rather than a fixed self on a journey. This is a key part of existentialist thinking, as we have seen, but it is also an essential underpinning of authentic leadership, in the sense of drawing on existential authenticity, of not denying ownership for our actions, of not trying to seek refuge in fictions such as: 'It's my nature, I can't help it'; 'It's the way I was brought up, I can't help it'; or 'That's the sort of person I am, I can't help it'. These are all examples of bad faith – the attempt to deny that we have responsibility for our choices, trying to place the locus of control outside ourselves by extending the notion of facticity (that is, those things we cannot control) into the realm of freedom, of therefore presenting to ourselves and to others our choices and the consequences of those choices as if they were matters separate from ourselves, beyond our control. This is clearly not a recipe for authentic practice on the part of staff or for authentic leadership in relation to staff. In effect, what this means is that authentic leadership is the antidote to bad faith, our own potential bad faith and that of others.

An authentic leader needs to be well attuned to bad faith to ensure that, whenever it rears its head, it is dispatched and not allowed to get a foothold. It can do a lot of harm by undermining a leader's trust respect and credibility when it is apparent in leaders' behaviour and by allowing employees to disempower themselves and thereby place significant obstacles in the way of achieving the best work they are capable of (and obtain maximum job satisfaction and potential for learning in the process).

DESPITE FREEDOM, EXISTENCE IS CHARACTERISTICALLY EXPERIENCED AS POWERLESSNESS AND HELPLESSNESS

This brings us back to this important dyad of facticity and transcendence. Of course there will be limitations and constraints in terms of what we can do, but there will also be, at every moment, opportunities for us to determine how we react to those circumstances. At every point, as we have seen, there is an element of choice. However, the way human existence is presented through the media, through dominant ideologies and discourses, can mean that the way people experience their lives is rooted in bad faith, because wider influences have convinced them that there is little that they can do about their circumstances. For example, capitalist ideology creates forms of thinking that gives a very strong message that economic inequalities are an inevitable and even desirable consequence of having a successful economy. Patriarchal ideology will put forward very strongly, very powerfully and very pervasively the idea that gender inequalities are natural and rooted in our biological make up. These are examples of how the tremendous opportunity for change is pushed to one side by dominant ideas that are, in effect, rooted in bad faith, because that bad faith protects the vested interests of powerful groups. Bad faith is a very powerful conservative force and therefore a major obstacle to progress.

This has very important implications for social and political life more broadly, but in particular it has significant implications for authentic leadership. This is because it helps us to appreciate that the message of freedom and ownership may fall on stony ground if we are not able to get past a sense of powerlessness and helplessness that may well have been inculcated in the people we are leading through the media, the education system and the wider socializing influences of ideology. What this means is that authentic leadership can very often be quite challenging because we may be having to go against ideas that people have been embracing throughout their lives. We are in a sense swimming against the tide.

PRACTICE FOCUS 9.2   Ian was a manager in a pharmaceutical company. He had been in post for almost a year when he decided he couldn't continue any more. He felt he had been getting nowhere and the staff he managed all seemed so unmotivated. He just couldn't break through. After one particularly frustrating week he went to see his boss to tell her he was going to be leaving as soon as he could get another job as he had just had enough. For a variety of reasons, a culture of hopelessness and helplessness had developed. As Ian had had no leadership training he was not aware of the dangers of becoming a passive victim of such a negative culture, rather than being the catalyst to shape a more positive and confident culture that would challenge the bad faith of the staff who had been allowing themselves to wallow in negativity. When this was explained to him, Ian realized he faced a huge challenge to make any impact on such a stolidly helpless, self-defeating culture, but the fact that he had something to work on made him feel more hopeful that he just might be able to make a difference. His own sense of hopelessness had started to crack and he was prepared to put in the effort to develop a more positive approach – first of all for himself and then for the staff team.

EXISTENTIALISM PROPOSES A SHARED SUBJECTIVE JOURNEY, A PARTNERSHIP IN ACHIEVING ORGANIZATIONAL GOALS AND MAXIMIZING PERSONAL AND PROFESSIONAL DEVELOPMENT

This is a matter of authentic leadership trying to create a sense of shared endeavour, a sense of partnership in which it is recognized that everyone benefits if they work together towards shared goals. Of course, there will be the facticity of organizational requirements in any work setting, but, within that context, it is possible for people to work together to maximize their effectiveness, to optimize their learning and development and basically get the best results possible for their working lives.

This notion of shared subjective journey or partnership is therefore a very important one. Leaders need to be able to create a culture, and indeed sustain that culture, with a strong message that there are shared goals and a shared acceptance of the path that needs to be followed to achieve these goals. This takes us back to the important concept of vision, not the oversimplified and unhelpful notion that is often adopted in many organizations and has the effect of generating cynicism, but a more sophisticated notion of vision as something that connects with the progressive-regressive method. This involves recognizing once again that the present will be influenced not just by our past experiences, but also by our future aspirations and, indeed, by how the past and the future then influence and shape each other as a result of how we interpret them from our present standpoint. So, what this means is that there needs to be the clear and flexible vision that was discussed earlier if we are to be able to achieve the best results.

Voice of experience 9.2

There's a lot of simplistic nonsense been written and said about teamwork, as if it is just some sort of straightforward process of holding each other's hands and being nice to each other. In reality, developing a team that is a real partnership, with people properly on board and committed to supporting one another, and with a strong focus on what the team is supposed to be all about is really hard work. It takes a lot of skill and a lot of persistence. It won't happen overnight and it won't happen at all unless you have a good understanding of what makes people tick, not just as individuals, but as groups at all levels.

Li, a team development trainer and consultant

THE DYNAMIC TENSION BETWEEN ORGANIZATIONAL AND PROFESSIONAL REQUIREMENTS, ON THE ONE HAND, AND CREATIVE EMPOWERING WORK ON THE OTHER IS ONE TO BE TAKEN INTO CONSIDERATION

It is a conflict that has to be managed on an everyday basis, rather than resolved once and for all. This is a longstanding feature of working life: the tension between what the people who own or run the organization want and their interests, on the one hand, and what the paid staff and managers want and what their interests are, on the other. It has to be understood that there is no simple answer to this tension. It is indeed one that needs to be managed on an everyday basis, but what needs to be recognized is that this fits very well with the existentialist concepts of facticity and transcendence. There will, of course, be aspects of organizational life that may cause us problems, and we may have limited control of those problems, but we can always transcend those limitations in terms of how we react to the circumstances involved. Unfortunately, where there is poor or non-existent leadership, the reaction to that facticity can be a vicious circle of cynicism, defeatism and low morale. I call this a vicious circle because basically it locks people in to cycles of negativity, where people are resentful of aspects of their organization that they can do little or nothing about. They can become negative and defeatist, which then makes it harder for them to get any satisfaction from their work, or indeed to be effective or to learn from their experience. This can then dampen morale even further, which can then add to the negativity, which in turn then makes it even more difficult to achieve job satisfaction or learning, and so round and round it goes, locking people into a cycle of negativity and self-disempowerment.

This, though, refers to situations where there is poor or non-existent leadership. Where there is effective leadership there is the potential for changing that cycle of negativity into a virtuous circle of empowerment. This involves being realistic and accepting that there will always be aspects of working life that we are not happy with, but then, rather than allowing ourselves to enter a cycle of disempowerment, what can be done is in effect to, at the very least, make the best of a bad job and gain as many positives as we can from it.

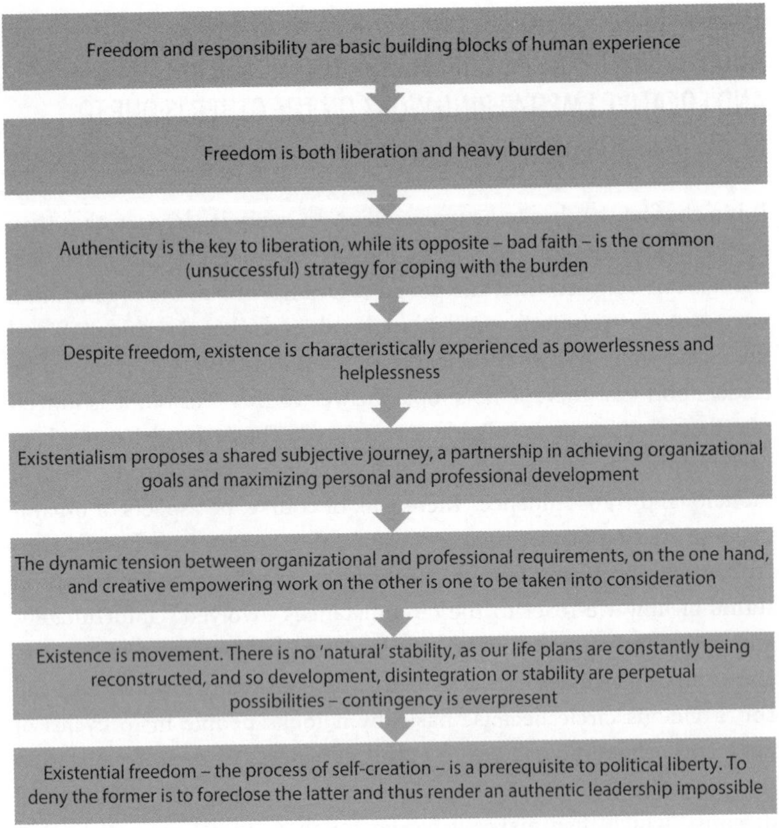

FIGURE 9.1 **Principles of existentialist practice**

This again relates to the idea of authenticity, because what is happening in these situations is that where such a cycle of self-disempowerment has developed, this is characterized by bad faith, by denying that there are steps that can be taken to change the situation in some ways at least. In other words, there is a failure to recognize that, where there is facticity, there will also always be the potential for transcendence. What is happening, then, in circumstances of a vicious circle of self-disempowerment is that the boundary between facticity and transcendence is not being recognized, the role of freedom and transcendence is being excluded and seen as simply an extension of the realm of facticity.

EXISTENCE IS MOVEMENT. THERE IS NO 'NATURAL' STABILITY, AS OUR LIFE PLANS ARE CONSTANTLY BEING RECONSTRUCTED, AND SO DEVELOPMENT, DISINTEGRATION OR STABILITY ARE PERPETUAL POSSIBILITIES – CONTINGENCY IS EVER PRESENT

Some change processes are rapid and visible, while others are at a slower pace and less obvious, often leading people to assume that there is no change taking place, that what we are seeing is something fixed and unchanging. Existentialism helps us to understand that this illusion of fixity, when applied to people and human affairs, is highly problematic, in so far as it presents a distorted picture of human potential that has the effect of disempowering people. Assuming fixity (essentialism) creates artificial barriers, placing obstacles to making progress in certain directions.

Failing to recognize this dynamic nature of human existence can make people resistant to learning, growing and developing. They may limit themselves by assuming that changes in their behaviour, understanding, knowledge, skills and values are either not possible or of limited scope. Being aware that 'existence is movement' therefore creates opportunities for optimizing learning and quality of practice; it opens doors to new avenues of growth and development that otherwise would not have been considered.

This principle also warns us that we cannot assume that situations will remain stable. For example, positive aspects of a situation, such as high morale, could be lost if occurrences take place that undermine that level of morale – perhaps a leader acts in a way that reduces or removes altogether, trust, respect and credibility. This should help leaders to guard against complacency and the dangerous assumption that good things will necessarily remain good.

One final implication of recognizing contingency as a basic feature of human existence is that meaning needs to be understood as a key issue in making sense of, and responding to, the uncertain 'shifting sands' of life in general and the workplace in particular. In seeking to develop an adequate understanding of each situation leaders encounter, attention therefore needs to be given to the specific meanings attached to events or circumstances. This emphasizes the important role of phenomenology, with its focus on perception and perspectives. If we simply see the world through our own eyes and fail to recognize that other people are likely to have different perspectives, we will fail to grasp the complexity of the human situations we are trying to influence. As with all things, meanings and perspectives change over time, and we need to be alert to any such changes.

PRACTICE FOCUS 9.3 | Linda was a manager in a retail setting. She relied heavily on the two supervisors, Dave and Stella, she had working alongside her. By sheer coincidence, both Dave and Stella went through a divorce at about the same time. However, they responded to their respective family changes in vastly different ways. Dave became quite anxious and nervous and could be volatile, losing his temper quite easily. People had to walk on eggshells around him if they were to avoid any unpleasantness. Stella, by contrast, tried to put a brave face on it and attempted to be as normal as possible and she seemed to be coping quite well most of the time. However, from time to time, it all got too much for her and she would burst into tears. This made Linda realize just how quickly things could change. One minute she had two excellent supervisors she could rely on and the next she had two people who were really struggling. What made it even more challenging for Linda was that Dave and Stella were responding to the same objective situation (a divorce) in vastly different subjective ways. Clearly divorce meant different things to each of them.

EXISTENTIAL FREEDOM – THE PROCESS OF SELF-CREATION – IS A PREREQUISITE TO POLITICAL LIBERTY. TO DENY THE FORMER IS TO FORECLOSE THE LATTER AND THUS RENDER AN AUTHENTIC LEADERSHIP IMPOSSIBLE

If we adopt a deterministic approach to human experience by assuming that matters that are actually within our control are things we have to accept as inevitable, then not only are we indulging in bad faith and distorting our reality, we are also creating unnecessary barriers to social and organizational progress. This is because, if we deny ourselves the agency to make choices relating to our individual circumstances, if we fatalistically assume that the way things are is the way they have to be, then not only are we blocking our own individual avenues to progress in our lives, but also denying the possibility for collective progress in terms of improving society in general and workplace experiences in particular. For example, if we make the mistake of assuming that, because there are differences between men and women at a biological level, it is 'natural' for men to be in positions of power and dominance, then we create artificial barriers to developing gender equality and allowing both women and men to fulfil their potential without being held back by gender stereotypes or other arbitrary restrictions.

The recognition of such freedom at a personal level (transcendence) does not deny the importance of wider cultural and structural factors (elements of facticity), but, rather, serves as an acknowledgement that the three levels (personal, cultural and structural) are intertwined and interdependent.

If we rely on an essentialist conception of human existence that portrays individuals as fixed entities, rather than as self-creating processes who exercise choice and agency, we reduce them to pawns pushed here and there by forces beyond their control. We then rule out the possibility of changing or influencing the broader circumstances which can be a source of pressure and difficulties. Recognizing that we have a degree of control over our actions (and responsibility for their consequences) enables us to work towards a collective approach to social problems and, specifically in terms of leadership, to workplace problems. This provides a much more solid foundation for developing workplace well-being as part of our commitment to a fully human approach to leadership (Thompson, 2013a; Thompson and Bates, 2009).

Voice of experience 9.3

So many organizations now seem to think that confidential counselling is the answer to all workplace problems. Counselling can be really helpful in the right circumstances, but there's more to well-being at work than this. There has to be a collective response to problems like stress, bullying and conflict. Just leaving it to individuals to seek counselling amounts to turning organizational problems into just individual ones – and that's not a positive message to people who are already facing difficulties. There needs to be a much stronger sense of collective responsibility for workplace problems.

Les, a workplace well-being development officer in the hospitality industry

CONCLUSION

It is to be hoped that the exploration of these eight principles of existentialist thought will have proved helpful in deepening and extending your understanding of the significance of what this philosophical outlook has to offer in developing authentic leadership. Of course, existentialism is a philosophy which, by its very nature, is complex and operates at multiple levels. It can therefore be quite confusing if you are not used to philosophical thought to 'get your head round' the subtleties involved. However, it is important to recognize that this book is not about trying to make you into an expert in philosophical thought, but, rather, to provide a foundation of understanding about how existentialism in particular can provide for us the basis for effective leadership by making sure that it is authentic leadership.

These eight principles do not offer a comprehensive picture, but they should be sufficient to provide a platform of understanding that can be built upon over time. They should offer, in a sense, a gateway to further understanding, in so far as each of these principles can be explored in much greater depth through further study and practice. The *Guide to further learning* section at the end of the book has been developed with just such a process of further study and learning in mind.

Conclusion

This has been a wide-ranging book, covering a number of philosophical concepts and their implications for aspects of leadership practice. Part I laid the foundations by exploring various aspects of leadership and a range of problems associated with current understandings of them. Part I also emphasized that leadership issues need to be considered within a wider social context. Part II examined authenticity from an existentialist perspective and introduced a number of key concepts designed to cast light on how existential authenticity (as opposed to the simplistic essentialist authenticity commonly found in much of the leadership literature) can be of value. Part III sought to extend our understanding of those concepts and their usefulness in practice by, first of all, discussing the relationship between theory and practice, then highlighting a number of practice scenarios and exploring how existentialist thought could be drawn upon to make sense of them and, finally, focusing on eight principles of existentialism that can be useful in forming a useful theoretical base for developing authentic leadership practice.

Running through the three parts have been a number of key 'messages'. By way of conclusion I will now restate in summary form those key messages to help digest the complex material covered in the nine chapters.

CHANGE IS CONSTANT

Leadership is often described in terms of change management, but this mainly refers to imposed change initiatives. Authentic leadership involves a more sophisticated understanding of change, recognizing that change is a constant feature of human existence. Stability is something that has to be constantly maintained. This incorporates such key concepts as: contingency, flux, emergence, autopoiesis, entropy and negentropy.

LEADERSHIP NEEDS TO BE HOLISTIC RATHER THAN ATOMISTIC

There is a strong tendency in the leadership literature to focus narrowly on individual factors (atomism), rather than to see the wider picture (holism) that also takes into account wider cultural and structural factors that have a significant influence on the individual, on groups of people and on organizations. We must not lose sight of the individual, as that would be dehumanizing and counterproductive, but we must also appreciate that individuals do not operate in isolation – each of us is part of a wider social whole, and so we need to take sociological factors into consideration as well as psychological ones. As Bauman and May (2001) put it: 'Sociology thus stands in praise of the individual, but not individualism' (p. 11).

CONFLICT IS INEVITABLE

It would be naive to assume that so many people can be employed in the same work setting without, at times, some people getting in the way of others. It is important for leaders to recognize this, as a failure to do so is a failure to address a key aspect of human experience and is therefore inauthentic. In particular, leaders need to take ownership of this aspect of working life, in the sense that, while they may not be directly respon-sible for the conflict, they have an important role in shaping a culture in which people feel safe, valued and supported. Cultures characterized by unresolved conflicts are unlikely to offer optimal circumstances for peo-ple achieving their best.

Leaders need to be able to: (i) ensure that conflicts are not allowed to escalate and cause unnecessary tensions and ill feeling; and (ii) seek opportunities to use the conflict constructively (for example, to see whether the conflicting perspectives can give us fresh insights that will fuel innovation and/or learning).

OWNERSHIP IS ESSENTIAL

Trying to deny the choices we have available to us and seeking refuge in essentialism can be doubly problematic. For one thing it distorts our picture of the situations we are dealing with and limits the control we can exercise over them – in a sense, it is a form of self-disempowerment. For another, it is giving a misleading message to staff, in the sense that we can be conveying that it is acceptable to deny ownership of factors we can control or at least influence and, in the process, running the risk that we will be undermining our level of trust, respect and credibility. We need to take ownership of the choices we make (and become confident and skilled in doing so) and ensure that staff do so too.

Guignon (1993b) makes the important point that:

> The authentic stance toward life makes us face up to the fact that to the extent that we are building our own lives in all we do, we are 'answerable' for the choices we make. Heidegger tries to capture this by saying that the authentic person 'chooses to choose.' At the same time, however, to be authentic is to recognize that circumstances may arise that force us to take back our basic decisions. Thus, authentic Dasein [existence] 'resolves to keep repeating itself' [1962, p. 355]; that is, it keeps renewing its commitments knowing that it might have to change its course. (pp. 232–3)

This speaks directly to leadership if we interpret 'change its course' as change the vision and/or change the path chosen to achieve the vision.

EMPOWERMENT IS MORE EFFECTIVE THAN COMMAND AND CONTROL

As I have acknowledged, there will be times when issuing commands is entirely appropriate. However, to rely on this as a first port of call will not help people achieve their best. Giving people more control over their work patterns is far more likely to encourage commitment and help people maximize their effectiveness and their job satisfaction (Sayer, 2007). This helps both leaders and staff to be authentic, in the leadg

sense that it raises awareness of the choices being made and thus the ownership of them.

However, as Pollard (2005) highlights, there is a certain irony in this, in so far as there is much to be gained from authentic selfhood and empowerment, but people must come to this decision for themselves. Someone attempting to be authentic because they have been instructed to be so is likely to struggle to achieve authenticity. People have to be helped to realize the value of authenticity for themselves, to embrace it voluntarily rather than under orders.

MEANING PLAYS A CENTRAL ROLE

As we have seen, the idea that existentialism presents life as 'meaning-less' is misleading. While there may well be no ultimate or absolute meaning, we are constantly engaging in meaning making, adding new pages and chapters to our biography, as it were.

This has implications for leadership, in so far as leaders are called upon to develop shared narratives that are meaningful to the individuals concerned. As Potter (2011) indicates, we have reason to be highly critical of simplistic approaches to authenticity:

> this is the authenticity hoax in full throat: a dopey nostalgia for a non-existent past, a one-sided suspicion of the modern world, and stagnant and reactionary politics masquerading as something personally meaningful and socially progressive. (p. 270)

He is basically saying that superficial approaches to authenticity encourage superficial meanings and thereby fail to do justice to the complexities involved. By contrast, leaders need to be attuned to the central role of meaning.

TRANSCENDENCE IS ALWAYS POSSIBLE

As the proverb puts it, you cannot stop the birds of sorrow from flying overhead, but you can stop them building a nest in your hair. In other words, while there is much that we cannot do anything about (facticity), we can control how we react to what befalls us (transcendence). This is an important message for leaders, as it is a significant counterbalance to the defeatism, negativity and even cynicism that can characterize low-morale cultures. Too many people assume that because certain things that have gone badly, the only realistic response is a negative one.

Effective leaders can help to create a more positive culture, rooted in the idea of transcendence, which seeks to make the best of a bad situation, rather than to make a bad situation worse – in effect, a culture that asks the question: So, what are you going to do about it?

AUTHENTICITY BRINGS TRUST, RESPECT AND CREDIBILITY

Staff who do not trust or respect their leaders or do not ascribe any credibility to them will be reluctant followers who are highly unlikely to achieve their best (or, if they do, it will be despite their leaders, rather than because of them). Without authenticity, such trust, respect and credibility will be hard, if not impossible, to achieve.

Much of this comes back to the core idea that authentic leadership is a *fully human* approach to managing and guiding people, one that takes account of the leader's own humanity and that of their followers – recognizing the full emotional and spiritual richness of that humanity, rather than relying on positivist approaches that focus on what can be counted rather than on what counts. As Adorno (2003) reminds us: 'Existentialism has been described by Paul Tillich as "an over one hundred year old movement of rebellion against the dehumanization of man [*sic*] in industrial society"' (p. vii).

For people to work effectively together, there needs to be at least a bare minimum of trust, respect and credibility. Existential authenticity is a key factor in developing these positive personal resources.

These eight messages are, of course, not the only points put forward in the book, but they do encapsulate some of the key learning points. They provide a platform for further learning and practice development. If they have convinced you of the value of investing time and energy into cultivating existential authenticity, then they will have served my purpose well. So many of the problems to be found in our workplaces and, beyond that, in wider society, can be traced back to poor or non-existent leadership. Despite the plethora of literature and other resources peddling simplistic approaches to leadership development, the reality is that it is a very complex and demanding undertaking. It requires certain knowledge, skills and values, but most of all it requires an ability to develop a full understanding of what it means to be human. It requires authenticity.

Glossary

In the Introduction I explained that existentialism is a complex philosophy. Add to this the fact that leadership is a complex topic and we get a mix of considerable complexity that relies on a number of key concepts. Some of these key concepts can be very difficult to grasp if you are not already familiar with them (and especially if you are not familiar with philosophical concepts generally). In recognition of this I have put together a glossary of some of the key terms used in the book. I hope it will help you wrestle with the complexities involved. I could, of course, have bypassed these complex concepts and simply explained everything in simple terms, but that would have risked oversimplifying the subject matter and therefore falling into the trap that I criticize others for doing in Chapter 1 by presenting a distorted picture of what is involved in authentic leadership.

Agency This refers to a person's ability to act, to make a difference. It is the opposite of determinism, the belief that everything we do is predetermined (by genes, upbringing, social influences or whatever). Existentialism emphasizes the importance of agency as, without agency, there would be no freedom, no ability to choose. Agency is often contrasted with structure (especially in the work of Giddens, 1984 – see also Archer, 2000). Agency represents our ability to choose and structure refers to the wider social context that constrains and influences those choices. This has similarities with the dialectic of subjectivity and objectivity (see below). Agency is an important concept for leaders, as Jenkins and Delbridge (2007) indicate:

We would stress that human agency is rich, multi-faceted and complex and workers should be conceived as knowledgeable, capable and inventive and creative. The challenge for managers is to develop organisational contexts and employment relationships that encourage workers to display these qualities to the benefit of the organisation. (p. 216)

Atomism An atomistic approach is one which focuses narrowly on individual factors and fails to take account of the influences and constraints of wider factors like culture and social structure. While individual factors are important and should not be disregarded, it would be a significant mistake to focus solely on individual issues without recognizing the significant role of wider contextual factors.

Authenticity Literally this refers to being genuine. In much of the existing leadership literature it refers to the idea of acting in accordance with your 'true self'. However, existentialist thought rejects the idea that there is an underlying 'true self' (see **Essentialism** below). Existential authenticity means taking ownership for our actions, the choices we make and their consequences, and thereby avoiding bad faith (see below). It also involves appreciating the significance of the situations we find ourselves in and especially the human dimensions of them (for emotional and spiritual aspects). If we neglect such aspects we are behaving inauthentically, as we are not being true to what it means to be human.

Autopoiesis This is a biological term that has been adapted for use in the social sciences. It refers to the process by which biological regeneration occurs (for example, how skin cells die off and are replaced by new versions). By analogy, the term is used to refer to how cultures reproduce themselves. For example, a group of staff coming together to form a team for the first time will quickly form a culture, but that culture may still be going strong some twenty years later when all the original members have moved on, because each new member who has joined the team in the meantime has been socialized into that culture (a process often referred to as 'cultural transmission').

Bad faith To act in bad faith is to behave as if matters we have control over are not within our control. For example, we may present choices on our part as if they were matters beyond our control: someone who chooses to behave in a cowardly way saying: 'I couldn't help it; it's just the way I am'. People can try to justify bad faith by reference to various forms of determinism (personality, genes, upbringing, social circumstances and so on). Bad faith is harmful because it distorts the reality of the situations we find ourselves in and leads to a denial of ownership – that is, people failing to take responsibility for their choices and the actions that flow from those choices.

Being-for-others This echoes the point made above about atomism. Being-for-others is a philosophical term that refers to the fact that individuals do not operate within a social vacuum. We are constantly relating to other people, being influenced by social rules and conventions and so on. Language is a good example of this. We could not have language-based communication if there were not others who spoke the same language. This concept therefore helps to remind us of the need to think holistically about the situations we encounter as leaders.

Contingency Fundamentally, consistency means that things do not need to be as they are; they could be otherwise. In this sense it is the opposite of necessity. It is closely linked to the idea of **flux** (the inevitability of change – see below). The idea of contingency is captured by the idea of 'no guarantees' – that is, human experience contains very many elements that are contingent or variable. Contingency is therefore a major source of uncertainty and can be linked with the idea of **ontological security** (see below). Authentic leaders need to be attuned to contingency and not be complacent about it.

The dialectic of subjectivity and objectivity Existentialist thought includes the idea that there can be no purely objective reality without a subjective experience on the part of individuals to make sense of it, and there could not be a (human) subjectivity if there were no objectivity ('out there') for subjective experiences to take place in. Dialectic refers to the interaction of opposing forces, so the dialectic of subjectivity and objectivity refers to the process whereby, for example, a change in the external environment (objectivity) is interpreted from the point of view of the individuals concerned (subjectivity) and they then act accordingly

189

(which can then affect the external environment). The subsequent effect of their actions on the environment (objectivity) will then have a knock-on effect in terms of how the changed circumstances are interpreted (subjectivity). And so it goes on, a constant interaction of subjective and objective factors.

Emergence An 'emergent' phenomenon is one that evolves over time; in a sense it is a product of its history. An organizational culture is an example of this. It does not appear fully formed; it emerges gradually over time and is likely to continue to evolve over time. Emergent phenomena are therefore subject to flux and contingency. From an existentialist perspective, identity is also an emergent phenomenon. As discussed earlier, life is not a process whereby someone with a relatively fixed personality travels through it over time. Rather, we are that journey – our identity or sense of self 'emerges' across the life course and will continue to evolve as we move forward through our lives.

Essentialism This refers to the assumption that there are underlying 'essences' that are the core of what we perceive. Plato, for instance, thought that, while we may see different shapes and sizes of table, for example, there is an underlying 'essence' that each actual table is a representation of. This approach has now largely been abandoned, but the same type of thinking is still applied to various aspects of human existence. For example, it is often assumed that individuals have a 'real self' beneath the surface of how they come across to others. Essentialism is therefore the opposite in some ways of emergence and is strongly rejected by existentialist thought.

Entropy Literally entropy means 'in transformation'. In physics it is used in a narrow sense to refer to an aspect of thermodynamics, but in philosophy it is used more broadly to refer to the process of decline – that is, the process by which order gradually breaks down into disorder. For example, a set of rules may be established that people respect to begin with when they are new. However, over time, more and more people may ignore those rules and so the order the rules were intended to establish gradually declines. This can be a common phenomenon in many organizations. It fits well with the concept of **flux** (continuous change – see below) and is based on the premise that things will change unless steps are taken to retain stability (see **negentropy**, below) – an important consideration for leaders.

The existential project Each time we make a choice we play a part in shaping our future (and, indeed, shaping who we are – as Camus famously put it, life is the sum total of the choices we make). This means that we are, in effect, 'throwing ourselves forward' into our lives, and that is what the existential project refers to (project meaning literally 'to throw forward'). So, this is an important concept because it captures well the idea that we are not static, fixed entities (**essentialism**), but, rather constantly evolving beings, evolving in whatever direction our choices (and the wider context in which those choices are made) will take us.

Facticity In life there are things we can do something about and things we can do nothing about. Facticity refers to the latter. It is those things that, in the short term at least, we have to accept. Some aspects of facticity will never change (death, for example). Others could change in the future and no longer therefore be counted as facticity. For example, cultural and structural factors can deny certain people opportunities at the moment, but that may no longer be the case in the future: in the apartheid era in South Africa black people were denied basic rights, but that is no longer the case. Facticity needs to be understood in relation to **transcendence** (see below).

Field Bourdieu used this term to refer to aspects of the social context. It helps us to understand how our behaviour and responses will change in different contexts. A field is a social arena in which power dynamics operate and in which rules for how to behave become established – for example, local politics could be one field, while company management might be another. Leaders need to be aware of this because they will generally need to operate across different fields.

Flux This refers to the fact that everything is changing. Some things change rapidly and visibly, while others change far more slowly and therefore appear to be fixed and stable. This concept teaches us that we need to become skilled in change management in more sophisticated ways than simply imposing change initiatives form time to time.

Group-in-fusion Unlike a series (see below), a group-in-fusion refers to people who are in the process of coming together with a shared purpose, prepared to support one another in achieving shared goals.

Habitus This concept derives from the work of Bourdieu. Lovell (2000) describes it in the following terms:

> By *habitus* Bourdieu understands ways of doing and being which social subjects acquire during their socialization. Their *habitus* is not a matter of conscious learning, or of ideological imposition, but is acquired through practice ... 'knowing how' rather than 'knowing that'. *Habitus* names the characteristic dispositions of the social subject. It is indicated in the bearing of the body ... and in deeply ingrained habits of behaviour, feeling, thought. (p. 27)

Negentropy This is the process of countering **entropy**. It is a process of maintaining stability by halting or counterbalancing processes of change. For example, house maintenance activities slow down the process of the condition of the house deteriorating. In a leadership context negentropy is the process of maintaining the positive aspects of a culture and seeking to ensure that they do not die out over time. In this way it is a form of **autopoiesis**, as discussed above.

Ontological security Security is about feeling safe and can be used to refer to specific circumstances – for example, feeling safe in a boat when you are wearing a life vest. Ontological security is a more general sense of security and relates to feeling secure with who we are and where our life seems to be going. In a sense it is a spiritual concept – indeed, spiritual security could be an alternative way of expressing it. Ontological security can be temporarily lost following a significant loss, trauma or crisis (Thompson, 2012c) and it can take time to re-establish it.

Ontology This refers to the study of being and is therefore concerned with such questions as: What does it mean to exist? For the most part we tend to take such matters for granted and give them little thought, but we can generally be prompted to consider the issues involved when something happens to unsettle us or make us feel insecure (see **ontological security**, above). Ontology is one of the two major building blocks of existentialism (see **phenomenology**, below).

Organizational culture When people work together they quickly develop a culture – a set of unwritten rules, taken-for-granted assumptions and shared meanings. These become the norm and have a powerful effect on the people involved, as they are generally unaware of the influence. Cultures can contain positive, helpful elements, but also negative, unhelpful ones. A key part of the leader's role is to shape the culture with a view to reducing or eliminating the negative elements and maximizing the positive ones.

PCS analysis An approach to understanding the complexities of social phenomena, such as discrimination. PCS stands for personal, cultural and structural. Personal factors, such as prejudice, need to be understood as part of the wider context of cultural factors, such as stereotypes, which, in turn, need to be understood in the wider context of structural factors, such as class, race and gender.

Phenomenology This is the study of perception, and is therefore concerned with how we develop different perspectives on life in general and specific aspects of it. It helps us to understand that there is no 'pure' objectivity – all aspects of the objective world need to be interpreted. Phenomenology is therefore concerned with meanings, how the perspectives we develop shape, and are shaped by, frameworks of meaning. Phenomenology and **ontology** (see above) are the two main building blocks of existentialism.

Pledged group This refers to a group of people who have passed through the **group-in-fusion** stage (see above) to become established as a highly effective set of people supporting each other towards shared goals.

The progressive-regressive method This way of thinking helps us to make sense of present circumstances by considering how future aspects, such as hopes, plans and aspirations (the progressive element) and past aspects, such as memories, experiences and learning (the regressive element) have a strong bearing on the current situation. Future elements will colour how we make sense of the past and the present, while past elements will colour how we make sense of the present and the future.

Series Sartre uses this term to refer to people who are brought together in some way (a queue, for example), but who have no sense of connection or shared identity. A team that is not functioning well can be series rather than a genuine group.

Transcendence Literally to transcend means to 'go beyond', and is used in slightly different senses in different contexts (as is often the case with philosophical terms). In this context it refers to the fact that, whatever may happen, we have some degree of control over how we respond to it. So, while there may be many things we cannot control (**facticity**), we can control how we respond to them (transcendence).

Guide to further learning

This book has covered a wide range of issues in a relatively short space, and many of those issues are very complex indeed. But, despite its breadth of coverage, inevitably this book will not have addressed all the various aspects of authentic leadership. This *Guide to further learning* has therefore been compiled to give you some guidance on where you may want to go next to take your learning to the next level. It is, of course, not comprehensive, but it should give you a firm foundation on which to build.

The Guide is divided into three parts. In the first the focus is on leadership in general, including the literature on authentic leadership that adopts an essentialist approach to authenticity. The reason for including items relating to this latter topic is that, although I may disagree with the essentialist assumptions so often adopted, this is not to say that these works have nothing to teach us about high-quality leadership. I have no intention of throwing the baby out with the bathwater.

The second part focuses on existentialism in its various forms, including its roots in such important thinkers as Kierkegaard and Nietzsche. The final, shorter part encompasses works that are at least indirectly relevant to the ideas covered in this book and potentially useful for you to take your understanding further.

LEADERSHIP

Important texts

There is a huge literature relating to leadership, and so the suggestions here are very selective. Books I have found helpful include:

Gilbert, P., *Leadership: Being Effective and Remaining Human*, 2005.
Gill, R., *Theory and Practice of Leadership*, 2nd edn, 2011.
Grint, K., *Leadership: Limits and Possibilities*, 2005.
Hall and Janman, *The Leadership Illusion: The Importance of Context and Connections*, 2010.
Kouzes and Posner, *The Leadership Challenge*, 2007.
Ladkin, D., *Rethinking Leadership: A New Look At Old Leadership Questions*, 2010.
Northouse, P.G. *Leadership: Theory and Practice*, 5th edn, 2010.
Pedler, Burgoyne and Boydell, *A Manager's Guide to Leadership: An Action Learning Approach*, 2nd edn, 2010.

Authentic leadership texts

These books adopt an essentialist conception of authenticity, which should be borne in mind. However, this does not mean that they are without value.

George, B. *Authentic Leadership: Rediscovering the Secrets to Creating Lasting Value*, 2003.
George, with Sims, *True North: Discover your Authentic Leadership*, 2007.
Goffee and Jones, *Why Should Anyone Be Led By You?: What it Takes to be an Authentic Leader*, 2006.
Irvine and Reger, *The Authentic Leader: It's About Presence, Not Position*, 2006.

One book that has a much more sophisticated understanding of authentic leadership is R. D. Hames, *The Five Literacies of Leadership: What Authentic Leaders Know and You Need to Find Out*, 2007.

The following articles are also helpful:

Lawler, J., 'The Essence of Leadership? Existentialism and Leadership', *Leadership* 1:215, 2005.
Lawler and Ashman, 'Theorizing Leadership Authenticity: A Sartrean Perspective', *Leadership*, 8(4), 2012.

EXISTENTIALISM

General introductions

A good starting point is Panza and Gale, *Existentialism for Dummies*, 2008. I was a bit wary at first of the idea of a *For Dummies* book on such a complex topic as existentialism, but the authors do a very impressive job.

Another very basic introduction is Appignanesi and Zarate, *Introducing Existentialism*, 2006. It is part of a series of books that present complex ideas in graphic form.

The following also have much to offer:

Kaufmann, W., *Existentialism: From Dostoevsky to Sartre*, 1986.
Macquarrie, J., *Existentialism: An Introduction, Guide and Assessment*, 1974.
Sartre, J-P., *Existentialism is a Humanism*, 2007.
Wartenberg, T. E., *Existentialism: A Beginner's Guide*, 2008.

A more intellectual overview is provided by S. Crowell, *The Cambridge Companion to Existentialism*, 2012.

Helpful works relating to Sartre include:

Fox, N. F., *The New Sartre: Explorations in Postmodernism*, 2003.
Priest, S., *Jean-Paul Sartre: Basic Writings*, 2001.

Classic texts

These are just some of the classic texts of existentialism:

de Beauvoir, S., *The Ethics of Ambiguity*, 1976.
de Unamuno, M., *Tragic Sense of Life*, 1954.

Heidegger, M., *Being and Time*, 1962.

Kierkegaard, S., *Fear and Trembling*, 2014.

Nietzsche, F., *Thus Spoke Zarathustra: A Book for Everybody and Nobody*, 2008.

Sartre, J-P., *Being and Nothingness*, 2003.

Tillich, P., *The Courage to Be*, 2000.

OTHER WORKS OF RELEVANCE

Authenticity

Berman, M., *The Politics of Authenticity: Radical Individualism and the Emergence of Modern Society*, 2009.

Boyle, D., *Authenticity: Brands, Fakes, Spin and the Lustre for Real Life*, 2004.

Golomb, J., *In Search of Authenticity: From Kierkegaard to Camus*, 1995.

Guignon, C., *On Being Authentic*, 2004.

Potter, A., *The Authenticity Hoax: Why the 'Real' Things We Seek Don't Make us Happy*, 2011.

Taylor, C., *The Ethics of Authenticity*, 1991.

Trilling, L., *Sincerity and Authenticity*, 1972.

Conflict

Coleman and Ferguson, *Making Conflict Work*, 2014.

De Bono, E., *Conflicts: A Better Way to Resolve Them*, 1991.

Lewis, C., *The Definitive Guide to Workplace Mediation and Managing Conflict at Work*, 2009.

Existentialist thought

Armstrong, J., *Life Lessons from Nietzsche*, 2013.

Card, C. (ed.), *The Cambridge Companion to Simone de Beauvoir*, 2003.

Gordon, L. R. (ed.), *Existence in Black: An Anthology of Black Existential Philosophy*, 1997.

Kaufmann, W. (ed.), *Basic Writings of Nietzsche*, 2000.

Van Deurzen and Arnold-Baker, *Existential Perspectives on Human Issues: A Handbook for Therapeutic Practice*, 2005.

Workplace well-being

Fevre *et al.*, *Trouble at Work*, 2013.
Haworth and Hart, *Well-being: Individual, Community and Social Perspectives*, 2012.
Robertson and Cooper, *Well-being: Productivity and Happiness at Work*, 2011.
Schnall *et al.*, *Unhealthy Work: Causes, Consequences, Cures*, 2009.
Thompson and Bates, *Promoting Workplace Well-being*, 2009.

References

Adorno, T. (2003) *The Jargon of Authenticity*, London, Routledge.

Albrecht, K. (2006) *Social Intelligence: The New Science of Success*, San Francisco, CA, Jossey-Bass.

Allcorn, S. (2005) *Organizational Dynamics and Intervention: Tools for Changing the Workplace*, London, M. E. Sharpe.

Appignanesi, R. and Zarate, O. (2006) *Introducing Existentialism*, Cambridge, Icon Books.

Archer, M. S. (2000) *Being Human: The Problem of Agency*, Cambridge, Cambridge University Press.

Armstrong, J. (2013) *Life Lessons from Nietzsche*, London, Macmillan.

Armstrong, K. (2011) *Twelve Steps to a Compassionate Life*, London, Bodley Head.

Ashman, I. and Lawler, D. (2008) 'Existential Communication and Leadership', *Leadership* 4(3).

Back, L. and Solomos, J. (eds) (2009) *Theories of Race and Racism: A Reader*, 2nd edn, London, Routledge.

Ballat, J. and Campling, P. (2011) *Intelligent Kindness: Reforming the Culture of Healthcare*, London, Royal College of Psychiatrists.

Bauman, Z. and May, T. (2001) *Thinking Sociologically*, Oxford, Blackwell.

Beauvoir, S. de (1976) *The Ethics of Ambiguity*, New York, Citadel Press (originally published in 1948).

Bergson, H. (1934) *La Pensée et le Mouvant*, Paris, Flammarion.

Berman, M. (2009) *The Politics of Authenticity: Radical Individualism and the Emergence of Modern Society*, 2nd edn, London, Verso.

Billington, R. (1990) *East of Existentialism*, London, Unwin Hyman.

Bolton, S. C. (2005) *Emotion Management in the Workplace*, Basingstoke, Palgrave Macmillan.

Bolton, S. C. (ed.) (2007) *Dimensions of Dignity at Work*, Oxford, Butterworth-Heinemann.

Bolton, S.C. and Houlihan, M. (eds) (2007) *Searching for the Human in Human Resource Management*, Basingstoke, Palgrave Macmillan.

Bono, E. de (1991) *Conflicts: A Better Way to Resolve Them*, London, Penguin.

Bourdieu, P. (1997b) *Outline of a Theory of Practice*, Cambridge, Cambridge University Press.

Bourdieu, P. (2005b) *The Social Structure of the Economy*, Cambridge, Polity.

Bourdieu, P. and Wacquant, L. (1992) *An Invitation to Reflexive Sociology*, Cambridge, Polity Press.

Boyle, D. (2004) *Authenticity: Brands, Fakes, Spin and the Lustre for Real Life*, London, Harper Perennial.

Buber, M. (2013) *I and Thou*, London, Bloomsbury.

Burns, J. M. (1978) *Leadership*, New York, Harper & Row.

Card, C. (ed.) (2003) *The Cambridge Companion to Simone de Beauvoir*, Cambridge, Cambridge University Press.

Carson, J. B., Tesluk, P. E. and Marrone, J. A. (2007) 'Shared Leadership in Teams: An Investigation of Antecedent Conditions and Performance', *Academy of Management Journal*, 50(5).

Chang, E. C. (ed.) (2002) *Optimism and Pessimism: Implications for Theory, Research and Practice*, London, American Psychological Association.

Churchill, S. and Reynolds, J. (ed.) (2013) *Jean-Paul Sartre: Key Concepts* Durham, Acumen.

CIPD (2013) *Real-life Leaders: Closing the Knowing-Doing Gap*, London, Chartered Institute of Personnel and Development.

Clutterbuck, D. (2007) *Coaching the Team at Work*, London, Nicholas Brealey.

Coleman, P. T. and Ferguson, R. (2014) *Making Conflict Work*, London, Piatkus.

Colling, T. and Terry, M. (2010a) 'Work, the Employment Relationship and the Field of Industrial Relations', in Colling and Terry (2010b).

Colling, T. and Terry, M. (2010b) *Industrial Relations: Theory and Practice*, 3rd edn, Chichester, Wiley.

Cooper, D. E. (2012) 'Existentialism as a Philosophical Movement', in Crowell (2012a).

Corporate Leadership Council and Corporate Executive Board (2004) 'Driving Performance and Retention through Employee Engagement: A Quantitative Analysis of Effective Engagement Srategies', London, Corporate Executive Board.

Corsini, R. J. and Wedding, D. (eds) (1995) *Current Psychotherapies*, Itasca, IL, F. E. Peacock Publishers.

Crowell, S. (ed.) (2012a) *The Cambridge Companion to Existentialism*, New York, Cambridge University Press.

Crowell, S. (2012b) 'Existentialism and its Legacy', in Crowell (2012a).

Dalai Lama, The (2013) *Beyond Religion: Ethics for a Whole World*, London, Rider Books.

Deci, E. L. with Flaste, R. (1995) *Why We Do What We Do: Understanding Self-motivation*, New York, Penguin.

Deurzen, E. van and Arnold-Baker, C. (eds) (2005) *Existential Perspectives on Human Issues: A Handbook for Therapeutic Practice*, Basingstoke, Palgrave Macmillan.

Dienstag, J. F. (2006) *Pessimism: Philosophy, Ethic, Spirit*, Woodstock, Princeton, NJ, Princeton University Press.

Doka, K. J. (ed.) (2002) *Disenfranchised Grief: New Directions, Challenges, and Strategies for Practice*, Champaign, IL, Research Press.

Easterby-Smith, M. and Lyles, M. A. (eds) (2005) *Handbook of Organizational Learning and Knowledge Management*, Oxford, Blackwell.

Ehrenreich, B. (2009) *Smile or Die: How Positive Thinking Fooled America and the World*, London, Granta.

Elkjaer, B. (2005) 'Social Learning Theory: Learning as Participation in Social Processes', in Easterby-Smith and Lyles (2005).

Faubion, J. D. (ed.) (2002) *Power: The Essential Works of Michel Foucault 1954–1984: vol. 3*, Harmondsworth, Penguin.

Fevre, R., Lewis, D., Robinson, A. and Jones, T. (2013) *Trouble at Work*, London, Bloomsbury.

Fisher, B. A. (1974) *Small Group Decision Making: Communication and the Group Process*, New York, McGraw-Hill.

Foley, M. (2013) *Life Lessons from Bergson*, Basingstoke, Palgrave Macmillan.

Follett, M. P. (1924) *Creative Experience*, New York, Longmans, Green & Co.

Ford, J. and Harding, N. (2011) 'The Impossibility of the "True Self" of Authentic Leadership', *Leadership*, 7(4).

Fowler, B. (ed.) (2000) *Reading Bourdieu on Society and Culture*, Oxford, Blackwell.

Fox, N. F. (2003) *The New Sartre: Explorations in Postmodernism*, London, Continuum.

Frankl, V. E. (2004) *Man's Search for Meaning*, London, Rider Books.

Froese, K. (2006) *Nietzsche, Heidegger and Daoist Thought: Crossing Paths In-between*, Albany, NY, State University of New York Press.

Furnham, A. (2004) *Management and Myths: Challenging Business Fads, Fallacies and Fashions*, Basingstoke, Palgrave Macmillan.

Furnham, A. (2006) *Management Mumbo-Jumbo: A Skeptics' Dictionary*, Basingstoke, Palgrave Macmillan.

Furnham, A. and Taylor, J. (2004) *The Dark Side of Behaviour at Work: Understanding and Avoiding Employees Leaving, Thieving and Deceiving*, Basingstoke, Palgrave Macmillan.

Gadamer, H. G. (2004) *Truth and Method*, London, Continuum.

George, B. (2003) *Authentic Leadership: Rediscovering the Secrets to Creating Lasting Value*, San Francisco, CA, Jossey-Bass.

George, B. with Sims, P. (2007) *True North: Discover Your Authentic Leadership*, San Francisco, CA, Jossey-Bass.

Giddens, A. (1984) *The Constitution of Society: Outline of the Theory of Structuration*, Cambridge, Polity Press.

Gilbert, P. (2005) *Leadership: Being Effective and Remaining Human*, Lyme Regis, Russell House Publishing.

Gilbert, P. and Thompson, N. (2010) *Developing Leadership: A Learning and Development Manual*, Lyme Regis, Russell House Publishing.

Gill, R. (2011) *Theory and Practice of Leadership*, 2nd edition, London, Sage.

Goddard, M., Mannion, R. and Smith, P. C. (2000) 'Enhancing Performance in Healthcare: A Theoretical Perspective on Agency and the Role of Information', *Health Economics*, 9.

Goffee, R. and Jones, G. (2006) *Why Should Anyone Be Led By You?: What it Takes to be an Authentic Leader*, Boston, MA, Harvard Business Review Press.

Golding, D. and Currie, D. (eds) (2000) *Thinking about Management: A Reflective Practice Approach*, London, Routledge.

Golomb, J. (1995) *In Search of Authenticity: From Kierkegaard to Camus*, London, Routledge.

Gordon, L. R. (ed.) (1997) *Existence in Black: An Anthology Of Black Existential Philosophy*, New York, Routledge.

Grenfell, M. (ed.) (2012) *Bourdieu: Key Concepts*, 2nd edn, Durham, Acumen.

Grint, K. (2005) *Leadership: Limits and Possibilities*, Basingstoke, Palgrave Macmillan.

Guignon, C. (ed.) (1993a) *The Cambridge Companion to Heidegger*, Cambridge, Cambridge University Press.

Guignon, C. (1993b) 'Authenticity, Moral Values, and Psychotherapy', in Guignon (1993a).

Guignon, C. (2004) *On Being Authentic*, London, Routledge.

Guillory, W. (2000) *Spirituality in the Workplace*, Salt Lake City, UT, Innovation International.

Hall, T. and Janman, K. (2010) *The Leadership Illusion: The Importance of Context and Connections*, Basingstoke, Palgrave Macmillan.

Ham, C. (2009) 'Lessons from the Past Decade for Future Health Reforms', *British Medical Journal*, 339, b4372.

Hames, R. D. (2007) *The Five Literacies of Leadership: What Authentic Leaders Know and You Need to Find Out*, Chichester, John Wiley.

Hardy, C. (2012) 'Hysteresis', in Grenfell (2012).

Haworth, J. and Hart, G. (eds) (2012) *Well-being: Individual, Community and Social Perspectives*, Basingstoke, Palgrave Macmillan.

Heidegger, M. (1962) *Being and Time*, New York, Harper & Row (originally published in 1927).

Henry, P. (1997) 'Rastafarianism and the Reality of Dread', in Gordon (1997).

House, R. (1971) 'A Path-Goal Theory of Leadership Effectiveness', *Administrative Science Quarterly*, 16: 321–38.

Howells, C. (1992a) 'Conclusion: Sartre and the Deconstruction of the Subject', in Howells (1992b).

Howells, C. (1992b) *The Cambridge Companion to Sartre*, Cambridge, Cambridge University Press.

Hyde, B. (2008) *Children and Spirituality: Searching for Meaning and Connectedness*, London, Jessica Kingsley Publishers.

Iliffe, S. (2008) *From General Practice to Primary Care: The Industrialization of Family Medicine*, Oxford, Oxford University Press.

REFERENCES

Illouz, E. (2008) *Saving the Modern Soul: Therapy, Emotions, and the Culture of Self-Help*, Berkeley, University of California Press.

Irvine, D. and Reger, J. (2006) *The Authentic Leader: It's About Presence, Not Position*, Sanford, FL, DC Press.

Jaeggi, R. (2014) *Alienation*, New York, Columbia University Press.

Janis, I. L. (1982) *Groupthink*, 2nd edn, Boston, Houghton Mifflin.

Jenkins, S. and Delbridge, R. (2007) 'Disconnected Workplaces: Interests and Identities in the "High Performance" Factory', in Bolton and Houlihan (2007).

Kaufmann, W. (1986) *Existentialism: From Dostoevsky to Sartre*, Harmondsworth, Penguin.

Kaufmann, W. (ed.) (2000) *Basic Writings of Nietzsche*, New York, Modern Library.

Kaufmann, W. (2013) *Nietzsche: Philosopher, Psychologist, Antichrist*, Princeton, NJ, Princeton University Press.

Kellehear, A. (2007) *A Social History of Dying*, Cambridge, Cambridge University Press.

Kelloway, E. K. and Barling, J. (2010) 'Leadership Development as an Intervention in Occupational Health Psychology', *Work and Stress*, 24(3).

Kierkegaard, S. (2014) *Fear and Trembling*, London, Penguin.

Kinder, A., Hughes, R. and Cooper, C. L. (eds) (2008) *Employee Wellbeing Support: A Workplace Resource*, Chichester, Wiley.

Kirton, G. and Greene, A. (2010) *The Dynamics of Managing Diversity*, 3rd edn, London, Routledge.

Kouzes, J. M. and Posner, B. Z. (1987) *The Leadership Challenge*, San Francisco, CA, Jossey-Bass.

Kouzes, J. M. and Posner, B. Z. (2007) *The Leadership Challenge*, 4th edn, San Francisco, CA, Jossey-Bass.

Ladkin, D. (2010) *Rethinking Leadership: A New Look At Old Leadership Questions*, Cheltenham, Edward Elgar.

Langan, M. and Lee, P. (eds) (1989) *Radical Social Work Today*, London, Unwin Hyman.

Lawler, J. and Ashman, I. (2012) 'Theorizing Leadership Authenticity: A Sartrean Perspective', *Leadership*, 8(4).

Lear, G. (2009) *Leadership Lessons from the Medicine Wheel: The Seven Elements of High Performance*, Charleston, SC, Advantage.

Lewis, C. (2009) *The Definitive Guide to Workplace Mediation and Managing Conflict at Work*, Weybridge, RoperPenberthy Publishing.

Lovell, T. (2000) 'Thinking Feminism With and Against Bourdieu', in Fowler (2000).

MacLeod, D. and Clarke, N. (2009) *Engaging for Success: Enhancing Performance Through Employee Engagement*, London, Department of Business, Innovation and Skills.

Macquarrie, J. (1974) *Existentialism: An Introduction, Guide and Assessment*, 2nd edn, Harmondsworth, Penguin.

Mahon, J. (1997) *Existentialism, Feminism and Simone de Beauvoir*, Basingstoke, Palgrave Macmillan.

Marcel, G. (1949) *Being and Having*, London, Dacre (originally published 1928).

Marques, J., Dhiman, S. and King, R. (2009) *Workplace and Spirituality: New Perspectives on Research and Practice*, Woodstock, VT, Skylight Path Publishing.

Marris, P. (1996) *The Politics of Uncertainty: Attachment in Private and Public Life*, London, Routledge.

Maslach, C. and Leiter, M. P. (2000) *The Truth About Burnout: How Organizations Cause Personal Stress and What to Do About It*, San Francisco, CA, Jossey-Bass.

May, R. and Yalom, I. D. (1995) 'Existential Psychotherapy', in Corsini and Wedding (1995).

McLellan, D. (2000) *Karl Marx: Selected Works*, 2nd edn, Oxford, Oxford University Press.

Moss Kanter, E. (1977) *Men and Women of the Corporation*, New York, Basic Books.

Murphy, K. R. (2006) *A Critique of Emotional Intelligence: What Are the Problems and How Can They Be Fixed?*, London, Psychology Press.

Neimeyer, R. and Sands, D. C. (2011) 'Meaning Reconstruction in Bereavement: From Principles to Practice', in Neimeyer *et al.* (2011).

Neimeyer, R. A., Harris, D. L., Winokuer, H. R. and Thornton, G. F. (eds) (2011) *Grief and Bereavement in Contemporary Society: Bridging Research and Practice*, New York, Routledge.

Nelson-Jones, R. (1997) *Using your Mind: Creative Thinking Skills for Work and Business Success*, London, Cassell.

Nietzsche, F. (2008) *Thus Spoke Zarathustra: A Book for Everybody and Nobody*, Oxford, Oxford University Press.

Northouse, P. G. (2010) *Leadership: Theory and Practice*, 5th edn, London, Sage.

Nussbaum, M. C. (2001) *Upheavals of Thought: The Intelligence of Emotions*, Cambridge, Cambridge University Press.

Oliver, M. and Barnes, C. (2012) *The New Politics of Disability*, 2nd edn, Basingstoke, Palgrave Macmillan.

Panza, C. and Gale, G. (2008) *Existentialism for Dummies*, Hoboken, NJ, Wiley.

Parker, J. and Doel, M. (eds) (2013) *Professional Social Work*, Exeter, Learning Matters.

Parkes, C. M., Laungani, P. and Young B. (1997) *Death and Bereavement Across Cultures*, London, Routledge.

Parkinson, B., Fischer, A. H. and Manstead, A. S. R. (2005) *Emotion in Social Relations*, New York, Psychology Press.

Pedler, M., Burgoyne, J. and Boydell, T. (2010) *A Manager's Guide to Leadership: An Action Learning Approach*, 2nd edn, Maidenhead, McGraw-Hill

Pollard, J (2005) 'Existential Perspectives on Human Issues', in van Deurzen and Arnold-Baker (2005).

Potter, A. (2011) *The Authenticity Hoax: Why the "Real" Things We Seek Don't Make us Happy*, London, Harper Perennial.

Powell, J. L. (2005) *Social Theory and Aging*, Washington, DC, Rowman & Littlefield.

Priest, S. (ed.) (2001) *Jean-Paul Sartre: Basic Writings*, London, Routledge.

Richardson, D. and Robinson, V. (2007) *Introducing Gender Studies*, 3rd edn, Basingstoke, Palgrave Macmillan.

Robertson, I. and Cooper, C. (2011) *Well-being: Productivity and Happiness at Work*, Basingstoke, Palgrave Macmillan.

Sartre, J-P. (1973) *Search for a Method*, New York, Random House.

Sartre, J-P. (1982) *Critique of Dialectical Reason*, London, Verso.

Sartre, J-P. (1989) *No Exit and Three Other Plays*, New York, Vintage.

Sartre, J-P. (1995) *Anti-Semite and Jew*, New York, Schocken Books.

Sartre, J-P. (2003) *Being and Nothingness: An Essay on Phenomenological Ontology*, London, Routledge.

Sartre, J-P. (2007) *Existentialism is a Humanism*, New Haven, CT, Yal University Press.

Sayer, A. (2007) 'What Dignity at Work Means', in Bolton (2007).

Schein, E. H. (2010) *Organizational Culture and Leadership*, Sa Francisco, CA, Jossey-Bass.

Schnall, P. L., Dobson, M. and Rosskam, E. (eds) (2009) *Unhealthy Worl Causes, Consequences, Cures*, Amityville, NY, Baywood.

Schneider, J. (2012) *Finding My Way: From Trauma to Transformatior The Journey through Loss and Grief*, Traverse City, MI, Seasons Pres:

Schön, D. A. (1983) *The Reflective Practitioner*, New York, Basic Books.

Schultz, K. (2005) *When Work Means Meaning: Existentia Dimensions – Organizations and Leadership*, Copenhagen, Forla get Akademia.Dk.

Seligman, M. E. P. (2003) *Authentic Happiness: Using the New Positiv Psychology to Realise Your Potential for Lasting Fulfilment*, Londor Nicholas Brealey.

Sibeon, R. (2004) *Rethinking Social Theory*, London, Sage.

Sprintzen, D. (2009) *Critique of Western Philosophy and Social Theory* New York, Palgrave Macmillan.

Stein, H. F. (2007) *Insight and Imagination: A Study in Knowing an Not-knowing in Organizational Life*, Lanham, MD, University Press c America.

Stepney, P. and Ford, D. (eds) (2012) *Social Work Models, Methods an Theories*, 2nd edn, Lyme Regis, Russell House Publishing.

Taylor, C. (1991) *The Ethics of Authenticity*, Cambridge, MA, Harvar University Press.

Tehan, M. (2007) 'The Compassionate Workplace: Leading with th Heart', *Illness, Crisis & Loss*, 15(3).

Thompson, N. (2007a) *Power and Empowerment*, Lyme Regis, Russel House Publishing.

Thompson, N. (2007b) 'Spirituality: An Existentialist Perspective', *Illness Crisis & Loss*, 15(2).

Thompson, N. (2009a) 'Stress', in Thompson and Bates (2009).

Thompson, N. (2009b) *Loss, Grief and Trauma in the Workplace* Amityville, NY, Baywood.

Thompson, N. (2010) *Theorizing Social Work Practice*, Basingstoke Palgrave Macmillan.

Thompson, N. (2011a) *Promoting Equality: Working with Diversity and Difference*, 3rd edn, Basingstoke, Palgrave Macmillan.

Thompson, N. (2011b) *Effective Communication: A Guide for the People Professions*, 2nd edn, Basingstoke, Palgrave Macmillan.

Thompson, N. (2012a) *Effective Teamwork: How to Develop a Successful Team*, e-book, Avenue Media Solutions.

Thompson, N. (2012b) *Anti-Discriminatory Practice*, 5th edn, Basingstoke, Palgrave Macmillan.

Thompson, N. (2012c) *Grief and its Challenges*, Basingstoke, Palgrave Macmillan.

Thompson, N. (2012d) *The People Solutions Sourcebook*, 2nd edn, Basingstoke, Palgrave Macmillan.

Thompson, N. (2012e) 'Existentialist Practice', in Stepney and Ford (2012).

Thompson, N. (2013a) *People Management*, Basingstoke, Palgrave Macmillan.

Thompson, N. (2013b) 'The Emotionally Competent Professional', in Parker and Doel (2013).

Thompson, N. (2015) *People Skills*, 4th edn, London, Palgrave Macmillan.

Thompson, N. and Bates, J. (eds) (2009) *Promoting Workplace Wellbeing*, Basingstoke, Palgrave Macmillan.

Thompson, N. and Gilbert, P. (2011) *Supervision Skills: A Learning and Development Manual*, Lyme Regis, Russell House Publishing.

Thompson, N. and Pascal, J. (2011) 'Reflective Practice: An Existentialist Perspective', *Reflective Practice*, 12(1).

Thompson, N. and Thompson, S. (2008a) *The Social Work Companion*, Basingstoke, Palgrave Macmillan.

Thompson, S. and Thompson, N. (2008b) *The Critically Reflective Practitioner*, Basingstoke, Palgrave Macmillan.

Tiberius, V. (2008) *The Reflective Life: Living Wisely with Our Limits*, Oxford, Oxford University Press.

Tillich, P. (2000) *The Courage to Be*, New Haven, CT, Yale University Press (originally published 1952).

Trilling, L. (1972) *Sincerity and Authenticity*, Cambridge, MA, Harvard University Press.

Unamuno, M. de (1954) *Tragic Sense of Life*, New York, Dover Publications.

REFERENCES

Warnock, M. (2002) 'Being Intelligent about Love's Uses' (Review of Nussbaum, 2001), *Times Higher Education Supplement*, 2 August.

Wartenberg, T. E. (2008) *Existentialism: A Beginner's Guide*, Oxford, Oneworld.

Watts, M. (2003) *Kierkegaard*, Oxford, Oneworld.

Wicks, R. (2002) *Nietzsche*, Oxford, Oneworld.

Wittgenstein, L. (2009) *Philosophical Investigations*, Hoboken, NJ, Wiley-Blackwell.

Zeldin, T. (2004) 'What is the Good Life? Richer Not Happier: A 21st-century Search for the Good Life', *RSA Journal*, July.

Zimmerman, M. E. (1993) 'Heidegger, Buddhism, and Deep Ecology', in Guignon (1993a).

Zohar, D. and Marshall, I. (2001) *Spiritual Intelligence: The Ultimate Intelligence*, London, Bloomsbury.

Index

INDEX